JESUIT IN THE LEGISLATIVE GALLERY

JESUIT IN THE LEGISLATIVE GALLERY

A LIFE OF FATHER CARL MATTHEWS, S.J.

By
Michael Power

Welland, Ontario
2005

For Kathleen and Theresa

© Michael Power

First Printing: June 2005, 1000 Copies

Second Printing: November 2005, 1000 Copies

Library and Archives Canada Cataloguing in Publication

Power, Michael, 1953-
      Jesuit in the Legislative gallery : a life of Father Carl Matthews, S.J. / by Michael Power.

Includes bibliographical references and index.
ISBN 0-9686107-3-0

      1. Matthews, Carl J., 1932- 2. Jesuits--Ontario--Biography.
3. Catholic schools--Ontario--History. 4. Separate schools--Ontario-History.
5. Teachers--Ontario--Biography. 6. Catholic Church--Clergy--Biography.
7. Priests--Ontario--Biography. I. Title.

BX4705.M446P68 2005   271'.5302   C2005-903184-0

CONTENTS

Acknowledgments

Introduction vii

Glossary of Abbreviations ix

Chapter One: Becoming a Jesuit 1

Chapter Two: Funding Parity for Catholic Elementary Schools 21

Chapter Three: The High School Crisis 35

Chapter Four: Friendship with the Hon. Bill Davis 81

Chapter Five: Trustee and Toronto Board Chairman 93

Chapter Six: Completion at Last! Alleluia! 121

Chapter Seven: Highs and Lows of a Publisher and Editor 139

Chapter Eight: Jesuit Pastor and Builder 161

Bibliography 175

Index 179

ACKNOWLEDGMENTS

My thanks go to Father Carl Matthews, S.J., for loaning me his papers and his memories and for teaching me a great deal about the intricacies of human affairs; to my wife, Kathleen, and to my good friend, John Burtniak, for reading the manuscript and offering their corrections, comments and criticisms; to the Hon. William G. Davis, P.C., C.C., Q.C., for granting me permission to quote from his correspondence; to Marc Lerman and Gillian Osley of the Archives of the Roman Catholic Archdiocese of Toronto, for their timely and generous fact checking; and to my daughter, Theresa, for her patience, understanding and cheerful support.

This book was published with the financial assistance of Father Norbert Gignac of Thornhill, a retired pastor, and Theo Bernard of Victoria Harbour, a Catholic school board chairman in the 1950s.

INTRODUCTION

"Separate Schools and the politics and history of Ontario, of course, are a subject about which much has been said. I see in the gallery tonight Father Carl Matthews, who, if he were on the floor of this Assembly, I am sure could give us a historical oversight that would be most interesting."

Sean Conway, Liberal minister of education, spoke these words in the Legislative Assembly of Ontario, on the evening of 11 July 1985. The occasion was the second reading of Bill 30, the legislation that completed the separate school system. It passed by a vote of 117-1. Father Carl Matthews, S.J. certainly could have given the members of the legislature that evening a thorough lesson in the history of separate schools in Ontario and could have done so without notes of any kind. For a cabinet minister to recognize publicly someone in the gallery during the course of debate is unusual; for Sean Conway to have looked up to the gallery and pay tribute to Father Matthews was not. Robert Nixon, former Liberal leader, did the same on 23 June 1986, when Bill 30 was given third reading.

Father Matthews had lived and breathed Catholic education most of his life, beginning in his childhood home in Kingston, where his father had been a separate school inspector. He had spent many afternoons and evenings in the gallery of the Legislative Assembly at Queen's Park, listening to John Robarts, Bill Davis, Donald C. MacDonald, Robert Nixon, Bob Rae, Sean Conway and a host of others debate school finances and the merits of completing the separate school system. During his most active years in school politics, Father Matthews formed fruitful working relationships with the leaders, education ministers and education critics of Ontario's three major political parties – the Conservative, the Liberal and the NDP – and one would not exaggerate to claim that he and Bill Davis became good friends in the truest sense of that word. He worked not only with politicians but also with bishops, priests, school trustees, teachers and various Catholic education organizations.

In everything that Father Matthews did on behalf of separate school children – and there was much that he accomplished, always in concert with others – he treated his friends as well as his foes with the greatest respect. He never let anger, disappointment or ambition overcome his better self. If there were times when he offended others, or acted as a lone wolf, his behaviour was never intentionally rude or self-centred. He remains a model of charity and a true and hardworking son of St. Ignatius of Loyola, ever faithful to the Pope, the Magisterium of the Church and to the People of God whom he has gladly served in so many capacities.

From 1955 to 1986, Professor Franklin Walker wrote a three-volume history of Ontario's Separate School system. In 1,200 pages, he presents countless thumbnail sketches of the movers and shakers of separate school politics since 1804. In the middle of his sketch of Father Matthews, on page 290 of Volume III, Professor Walker wrote that the energy that he "devoted to promoting the cause of separate schools represented a zeal and a purity of purpose which had no parallel in Canadian history." Could this be true? I asked myself. My initial inclination was not to believe all the superlatives, but I decided to investigate.

Father Carl Matthews has led an interesting and productive life: thirty years in education as a teacher, lobbyist and trustee; nearly three years as a newspaper editor; and ten plus years as a parish priest. The principal aim of this biography is to give the measure of the man, so that his many and various good works will be remembered and be a positive lesson for generations yet to come. This is Carl Matthews' story, as told through forty years of correspondence, his published and unpublished writings and to a lesser degree his recollections. It does not pretend to tell everyone's point of view about the events that make up this book. It is a popular biography and should be read with reference to at least three other works: Franklin Walker's *Catholic Education and Politics in Ontario,* Volume III, Robert Dixon's *Catholic Education and Politics in Ontario, 1964-2001,* Volume IV and my own *A Promise Fulfilled: Highlights in the Political History of Catholic Separate Schools in Ontario,* Chapter 7.

What follows are my findings about an extraordinary Jesuit.

Michael Power
Easter 2005

GLOSSARY OF ABBREVIATIONS

ACEBO	l'Association des commissions des écoles bilingues d'Ontario
ACHSBO	Association of Catholic High School Boards of Ontario (1966-1985)
CCSTA	Canadian Catholic School Trustees' Association
CPTA	Catholic Parent-Teacher Association
COSS	Completion Office, Separate Schools (1984-1989)
C.S.B.	Congregation of St. Basil (Basilian Fathers)
C.S.C.	Congregation of the Holy Cross
C.S.S.P.	Congregation of the Holy Spirit (Spiritans)
ECEAO	English Catholic Education Association of Ontario
FCPTA	Federation of Catholic Parent-Teacher Associations
G.S.I.C.	Grey Sisters of the Immaculate Conception
MPP	Member of Provincial Parliament
MSSB	Metropolitan Separate School Board, Toronto
OCCB	Ontario Conference of Catholic Bishops
OCSF	Ontario Catholic Student Federation
OECTA	Ontario English Catholic Teachers' Association
OFSAA	Ontario Federation of School Athletics Associations
OISE	Ontario Institute for Studies in Education
OPSTA	Ontario Public School Trustees' Association
OSSTA	Ontario Separate School Trustees' Association
O.M.I.	Order of Mary Immaculate (Oblate Fathers)
SERP	Secondary Education Review Project
S.J.	Society of Jesus (Jesuits)

THE MATTHEWS FAMILY
All the children were university graduates. From the top, clockwise:
Sister Theresa, Ottawa; Father Carl, Toronto; Paul, Fordham; Ursula, Toronto;
Victor, Guelph; Michael, Queen's

CHAPTER ONE

BECOMING A JESUIT

Carl Matthews was a child of the golden age of Catholic family life in twentieth-century Ontario, in which home, school and church, the three pillars of local Catholic culture, successfully nurtured and shaped several generations of believers. These generations were known for their joyous commitment to the faith and its public institutions, in particular the separate schools. For Catholics born during the first half of the century, priest and people were close allies in the Church Militant. Religion was so integral to one's private *and* public life that life without religion would have been unimaginable. Catholicism was an all-enveloping reality. It was one's surefast identity and a badge of honour worn not on one's sleeve but on one's heart. The faith kept Catholics whole and set them apart. They saw themselves as different, demonstrably so at special times, for show and for self-renewal. One thinks of the Corpus Christi processions, the Holy Name rallies, the Rosary crusades and the May Day parades in honour of the Blessed Virgin Mary. And the world outside the Church, either hostile or tolerant, often looked upon Catholics as different.

However, that was the not the whole picture. The national call to arms in 1914 challenged Catholics to show that they were just as Canadian and loyal as their Protestant neighbours. As a result, Catholics as individuals and as a group began to integrate themselves, albeit slowly and sometimes hesitantly, into Ontario society in a myriad of ways never imagined by their grandparents and great-grandparents. After several decades of steady integration, the social, economic and political status of the province's Catholics had greatly improved.

It was into this Catholic world of solid religious tradition and evolving integration that Carl Joseph Matthews was born in Kingston, on 23 February 1932, the third year of the Great Depression. He was the second child and oldest son of C.P. (Charles Patrick) Matthews, a teacher and separate school inspector, and Florence Mary Casey, a registered nurse trained at

St. Michael's Hospital in Toronto. Carl was baptized in historic St. Mary's Cathedral on 6 March 1932. Father G.T. Martin performed the baptism, and Mr. and Mrs. Mullin, who acted as the family's insurance agent, were the sponsors. Already elderly, the Mullins did not play a role in Carl's life. He never knew them and only much later in life did he discover, purely by coincidence, that they were buried in St. Mary's Cemetery in Kingston.[1]

Carl's parents were married on 7 August 1929, at St. John's Church in Newmarket, his mother's parish. His father was twenty-nine years old, and his mother would turn the same age three months after the wedding. It was a relatively late marriage for both of them. The priest who officiated had the interestingly appropriate name of Father Matthew J. Wedlock. Florence Casey's home was just west of Aurora, north of Toronto. She was born on 9 October 1900. Her father was Daniel Casey of Thornhill, and her mother was Mary Ann Trainor from King Township. In addition to Casey, the names of Florence's Irish-born ancestors included MacNamara, O'Neill, Craney, O'Brien, Trainor and Daly. They came from Clare, Cork, Limerick and Armagh. Florence, the youngest of three children, was the first in her family to leave rural Ontario to work in a city, in her case Detroit and then Toronto. C.P. Matthews was born on 14 January 1900, in the Irish Block, an established farming enclave about 10 kms east of Owen Sound. When C.P. was a year old, the Matthews moved to a farm near Shelburne, in Melancthon Township, Grey County, a very Protestant locale with a very Protestant name. C.P.'s father was Michael Joseph Mathews – he too had been born in the Irish Block and later added the second 't' to Matthews – and his mother was Bridget Ellen Breen of Melancthon. The Matthews farm was across the road from the Breen farm. Among C.P.'s many Irish immigrant antecedents were people named Mathew, Breen, McCue, Dwyre, Dean, Whyte, Traynor and Daly. They came from Tipperary, Wexford, Mayo and Armagh, the seat of St. Patrick, which was the common county connection between the Matthews and Casey families in the New World. Carl's ancestry was Irish and Catholic to the core, and, by the time of his birth, his family was thoroughly Canadian. Both sets of grandparents were native-born Ontarians.[2]

One of Florence's classmates at St. Michael's Hospital was Theresa Matthews, C.P.'s only sister to survive into adulthood. She was responsible for introducing her brother to Florence, a fact quickly deduced from the lengthy news item detailing the "Matthews-Casey" wedding.[3] The two women remained the closest of friends. Also mentioned in the wedding story were the names of two priests and one religious brother. They were Father John J.

Traynor and Father Tom B. Traynor of the diocese of Hamilton, first cousins to C.P., and Brother Matthew, one of C.P.'s uncles. Subsequently there would be another priest in the family, Father Edgar Trainor. No relation to the Traynors, he was Florence's first cousin. She took Carl on the train from Kingston to Toronto to attend his ordination at St. Michael's Cathedral, on 3 June 1939. A second priest ordained that day was Father (later Monsignor) Art Welsh.[4] As chancellor at St. Mary's Cathedral, Carl's home parish, he would play an important role in Carl's life as a boy and teenager.

Following an automobile tour of parts of Eastern Canada and the United States, the couple settled in Toronto, where C.P. had a position as science teacher in the Junior Vocational School at Jarvis Collegiate. It would last only one year. C.P.'s career as a classroom teacher came to a close with an unlikely but much welcomed promotion to the inspectorate. Educated at Shelburne High School and St. Michael's College School, where he had been taught by the Basilian Fathers, Carl's father attended Toronto Normal School, graduating in 1922. He was now "a full fledged teacher," according to his parents, in a letter of 14 July 1922. The letter continued: teaching is "a great profession, also a great responsibility and requires putting in practice many virtues." It ended with these solemn words: "Your faithfulness to duty in the Home, School, College makes us feel assured you will also be worthy of this trust. And we earnestly pray God may bless you with health, strength & knowledge and direct you to do His Holy Will."[5] C.P., their oldest child, would live up to his parents' expectations.

His first teaching position was at the school in Melancthon.[6] One of his students was his youngest brother, Eugene. In those days, rural teachers were paid three times a year: Christmas, Easter and June. C.P.'s next position was principal of St. Bridget's in Ottawa. However satisfying that must have been, he realized that if he ever wanted to rise in the ranks of the separate school system, he would have to attend university. With that goal in mind, he moved to Toronto, where he taught at St. Michael's Preparatory School (Grade 8), courtesy of the Basilians and, at the same time, took classes at the University of Toronto. He graduated with a Bachelor of Arts and a Bachelor of Pedagogy. There was marriage, Jarvis Collegiate and then the big promotion. In 1930, the Ontario Department of Education appointed C.P. Matthews the first resident separate school inspector in Kingston. The appointment would last thirty-three years.

C.P.'s inspectorate originally covered territory from Belleville, 80 kms west of Kingston, to Cornwall, 176 kms to the east, or, in other words, eleven counties, from Hastings and Prince Edward in the west to Glengarry in the east. Every second Sunday, he would take the train to Belleville or Cornwall or sometimes to Brockville, 80 kms east of Kingston, and not return until Friday evening. Every Wednesday at seven in the evening, during his road trips, he would phone home and talk with Florence and each of the children for a total of three minutes, never longer. Saturday mornings he did the grocery shopping. School talk often dominated meal times, the children becoming adept at discussing and arguing education issues. For the first twenty years, the family home at 320 William Street was C.P.'s office. It took that long for the department of education to give him space at its own office above a food store at the corner of Princess and Division streets and later at the shopping centre in the west end of Kingston.

Needless to say, family life revolved around the father's comings and goings and his heavy workload. As a separate school inspector, C.P. was expected to be a jack-of-all-trades. He opened up new school sections and new schools; he calculated assessment rates and compared them to five decimal points; he marked high school entrance exams (until they were abolished in 1949); he encouraged all the teachers under his supervision to hold first-class teaching certificates; and he had to work with trustees, parents, teachers, parish priests and education officials. C.P. Matthews is credited with opening the first Union Separate School Board in the province, in Read, Hastings County, in 1944.[7] The job demanded an extraordinary degree of diplomacy and tact, boundless energy, unswerving dedication as well as an in-depth knowledge of the Separate School Act and its countless amendments. An old-fashioned civil servant, he always deferred to his superiors, never openly challenged the system and quite correctly stood above the fray of separate school politics.

One particular project stands out in Carl's memory of his father, the school inspector. It was the planning for the construction of Cathedral School:

> There was some question whether there were enough pupils to warrant its construction in the downtown area, and I recall having a map of the City of Kingston spread out on our dining room table at the home on 320 William Street, and you had the listing of all the boys and girls from age one to age twelve, and we children had little pins with different colour heads on them, and we were expected to push them into a block where the pupils were located at that time. In that way one could see the actual concentration of pupils. It showed that actually they were in quite a reasonable circumference around the location of the school adjacent to the Cathedral.[8]

C.P. was the classic Catholic *pater familias*. In the world, he had achieved success and respect within the Catholic community. At home, he took the lead during Lent in reciting the rosary, the Loretto litany and the prayer for a happy death. At church, each year on the feast of the Holy Family, he gathered his wife and children (including the four Mass servers!) around him in the Matthews pew at the cathedral, third from the front, as if to show God that his family was faithfully imitating the life of Jesus, Mary and Joseph. However, for all that, it was Florence, and not C.P., who was the real centre of gravity for Carl and his siblings, all the more so when C.P. was away on those week-long inspections. During those times, she held both power and authority and was directly responsible for every aspect of her children's upbringing. She was famous in the family for being able to fire off questions from six different catechisms and keep straight the answers fired back at her, as she ironed or sewed at the kitchen table. She was in control, undoubtedly, but never controlling. Love was the supreme virtue and gift of her life.

During the first ten years of her marriage, Florence Matthews had given birth to her six children. They were Theresa, Carl, Paul, Ursula, Victor and Michael.[9] Imbued with right ambition and a work ethic to match, each one earned a university education, and all six became teachers in different fields. While Theresa joined the Sisters of Providence of Kingston and Carl became a Jesuit priest, Paul, Ursula, Victor and Michael married and produced twelve grandchildren for C.P. and Florence. Victor died of Parkinson's disease on 30 June 1997.

In 1942, C.P. bought an eighteen-acre farm located at Washburn Lock on the Rideau Canal, bordering Highway 15 and about 24 kms northeast of Kingston. In the parish of Brewer's Mills, it was intended as a summer retreat for the family. The following year, Carl's father planted an orchard of mostly Macintosh apples. Carl milked the Jersey cow; Paul nursed the six-dozen chickens; Theresa and Ursula cared for the hens and boxed the raspberries; and every autumn, the four boys sold the chickens, apples and any other fruit produced by the farm, on Saturday mornings at the Kingston market and afterwards door-to-door in the new subdivisions. The boys also rented the rowboat and sold bait to fishermen from Pennsylvania who visited the locksmith's house next door each year. Victor received the farm as an early inheritance, and he and his wife Barbara built a bigger home and extended the orchard.

Every summer, the family went on a ten-day holiday. In 1947, all eight of them jammed into the car and drove around the Gaspé Peninsula and through New Brunswick, where they encountered some of the worst roads in Canada.

In 1949, they visited Algonquin Park and Martyrs' Shrine, where they witnessed a pageant presented by Father Daniel Lord, S.J., to mark the tercentenary of the deaths of St. Jean de Brébeuf and St. Gabriel Lalemant. The most memorable trip, however, took place in 1948. They decided to go to New York City. On 16 August, as the car crossed the George Washington Bridge and entered the city, the family could hear paper boys bellowing, "Extra! Extra! Read all about it! Babe Ruth dies!" Two days later, Carl and Paul filed by the Babe's open casket in the foyer of Yankee Stadium. The line-up was three blocks long but moved quickly. The boys were surprised that the home run king was not in the familiar Yankee pinstripes but was wearing a navy blue business suit. Entwined around his fingers was a rosary.

In the summer of 1950, Carl nearly drowned in the canal below the Washburn Lock. The edge of the dock was about three feet above the water line, and the canal itself was about ten feet deep where he was swimming off the dock. The water as usual was muddy and weedy. Swimming back to the dock, he felt absolutely exhausted, and reaching up, he missed the dock and sank to the bottom of the canal. When he managed to come up for air, he was completely disoriented and had no idea where the dock was. Luckily for him, Ken Fryer saw what was happening. Fryer was a university student who boarded at the Matthews' home in Kingston and happened to be at the farm that day. He raced along the dock, sat on its very edge and extended his bare feet over the water. Terrified, Carl grabbed Ken's feet, and with enormous strength, Ken was able to resist being pulled into the water by Carl and lift him out to safety. Later, Fryer would have a distinguished career as a professor and dean of the faculty of mathematics at the University of Waterloo.[10]

Carl grew up in a happy, boisterous and stable family. St. Mary's, across the street from the cathedral, was his elementary school. Opened in 1854, it was Kingston's oldest Catholic school. Although built with the same limestone as the cathedral, its appearance was stern and cold and utterly lacking in the kind of beauty and majesty that graced the cathedral. Carl entered St. Mary's in September 1938. It was an all-boys school for the south half of Kingston, but like most separate schools, its staff was predominantly female. There was only one male teacher on staff. Sister Mary Louise, of the Sisters of Providence, was Carl's Grade 1 teacher and told him in a letter at the end of the school year that she liked his "way of always being ready to help others."[11] No more perceptive comment about the core of Carl's character could have been made. Miss Almon Doolan taught Grades 2 and 3; Miss Kathleen Brady was in charge of Grade 4; Sister Mary Bernardo, a strict disciplinarian who wasn't afraid to use the strap, taught Grades 5 and 6; and Mr. Joseph Carty was the principal and senior teacher, who happened to be the father of Michael Carty, Carl's best friend at St. Mary's and fellow altar boy at the cathedral.[12] The Carty family also lived on William Street. When Mr. Carty was principal of St. Mary's, he was something of a novelty, being only one of twenty-nine laymen teaching in the province's separate schools! Carl's connection with Michael Carty was to last a lifetime. As president of the Association of Catholic High School Boards of Ontario, beginning in January 1970, he was a confidant and ally of Father Carl in the formation of a unified political strategy on completion of the separate school system.

Sadly, Mr. Carty died of a heart attack when the boys were in Grade 5. To replace him, Carl's father chose Miss Doolan. On the day that Carl entered her Grade 7 class, she stood at the classroom door and proudly announced that Carl Matthews, Michael Carty, Fred Flynn, Peter Marson and Joe Mattson were to skip to Grade 8. Carl was ecstatic, his mother was pleased, but his father was not. He picked up the phone and told Miss Doolan that Carl would remain in Grade 7 so that he would not be too young when he entered university. Carl was crushed. C.P. then proceeded to call the parents of the other boys. Only Mrs. Mattson insisted that her Joe stay in Grade 8. Miss Doolan was a sterling teacher. By February of the Grade 8 year, she had covered the curriculum and began to teach her boys the Grade 9 course in subjects such as algebra. More important, she passed on the essentials of the Catholic faith to all her students in a kind, loving and truthful manner that probably helped many of them live their faith as adults. In Carl's eyes, she was marvelous. He was old enough to soak in her influence as a teacher, but too young to understand the degree to which her teaching and example had begun to sketch out and fill in for him a view of life that was profoundly Catholic. Miss Doolan thought that Carl showed great promise. Many years after he had passed through her grade eight class, she sung his praises in a letter to the *Catholic Register*.[13]

When Carl was in Grade 3, a mere nine years old, he became an altar boy at St. Mary's Cathedral. He learned his Latin responses and the many subtle differences between a Low Mass and a High Mass and between a High Mass and a Pontifical High Mass. There was plenty for a young boy to absorb, including a new language and a reverential behaviour one found nowhere else but in the sanctuary, and there were plenty of ways for a greenhorn to make embarrassing mistakes and unsightly blunders while serving Mass. But Carl learned quickly and efficiently and liked being an altar boy so much he stayed on until the end of high school. Indeed, the sanctuary became a second home for Carl and his three brothers. They served Mass many mornings before school and were at the cathedral for funerals any day of the week and for weddings on Saturdays; and they served Mass on Sunday mornings and Benediction on Sunday evenings.[14] On 25 April 1944, Carl witnessed the enthronement ceremony for Archbishop J.A. O'Sullivan. Since there was no room in the sanctuary for the altar boys, Carl was stuck behind a pillar at the rear of the cathedral. Despite this, the Baroque lavishness of the ceremonial was not lost on him. In due time, Carl rose to become the archbishop's mitre bearer and then his master of ceremonies, second only to the priest-chancellor, for Pontifical celebrations.[15]

From St. Mary's Carl went to Regiopolis, the Jesuit-run high school for boys on the other side of Kingston.[16] He rode his bike to school every day and loved every day that he was at "Regi." All his teachers were Jesuits, with the exception of Gerard Belanger (French) and Wilfred Pluard (senior science). Father Clement J. Crusoe, S.J. was the principal and then rector of the college and also taught Latin. He had attended university with Carl's father and was a dinner guest at the Matthews home three or four times a year. At one of those dinners, Father Crusoe left behind a book on St. Ignatius Loyola, the founder of the Society of Jesus. No one in the family was sure if it was for C.P. or for Carl.

Mr. Alfred Colliard, S.J., a scholastic at the time, was the teacher who exerted the greatest influence on Carl. Of the eighty-seven teachers Carl had in his life, Mr. Colliard remained the best. He taught Grades 11 and 12 English literature and composition and Grade 13 Canadian and American history, played many musical instruments and wrote the words of "Football Song" and "Alma Mater" for Regiopolis College. He conducted his classes with genuine and infectious enthusiasm, his arms constantly in motion, as if he were conducting an orchestra, and he was a font of endless encouragement to all his students. Mr. Colliard certainly encouraged Carl to keep writing. On one of Carl's essays, he commented in bold red pencil: "Exceptionally carefully written. See me about it." The topic of the essay was the tercentenary of the Jesuit Martyrs of Upper Canada. If there was any one Jesuit whose life as a religious and a teacher acted as a magnet quietly drawing Carl into the Jesuit community, it was Alfred Colliard. After ordination, he was founding rector of Brébeuf College School in Toronto, in 1963, and later rector of Campion College in Regina, before returning to Toronto as treasurer of the Canadian Jesuits. He died of Alzheimer's disease in 1988, at the age of seventy.

Carl's best subjects were religious doctrine, English and history. He was not much of a science student, though later in life he took a shine to statistical analysis, and Latin and French took him to task. As a scholastic, he barely passed his philosophy courses, all of which were taught in Latin; as a theology student, it was a trial to read the fourth-year text, *De Deo Uno et Trino*. But that lay in the future. Carl loved his five years at Regiopolis, excelling at debating, essay writing, acting and public speaking, all the right foundations for a career in politics or law. The Regiopolis debating club – Carl Matthews, Bill Lundy and Joe Mattson – defeated St. Michael's College School, on 10 February 1950, on a question pertaining to government examinations for high school students. Carl's team defended the negative – that such examinations should not be abolished. One of the St. Michael's debaters was James Jerome, a future Speaker of the House of Commons. Another highlight of Carl's high school days was being one of four Kingston students to win an essay writing contest on "Ottawa, Our Nation's Capital," in January 1951, his senior year. The prize was a three-day trip to Ottawa for the opening of parliament. (This was not Carl's first time in Ottawa. In 1948, he watched the Liberal convention that chose Louis St. Laurent to succeed MacKenzie King as prime minister, and in 1950, he attended King's funeral.)[17]

But Carl's biggest triumph was his lead role as St. Edmund Campion, in Richard Breen and Harry Schnibbe's *"Who Ride on White Horses."* Campion was an English Jesuit martyr put to death during the reign of Elizabeth I. It was a huge role and a real challenge. Since no senior student came forward to audition for the part, Father Joe Driscoll, S.J. turned to Carl, a Grade 11 student. The play was presented on 25 and 26 March 1949. During one of the cast's many after-school and Saturday rehearsals, Father Driscoll remarked to Carl that the man who took the part of Campion at Fordham University in New York City had entered the Jesuits and that David Asselin who played the role at Loyola College in Montreal had joined the community in Guelph. Was it a challenge? A prophecy? An invitation? Carl's reaction was simple and direct: "Well, you won't get me!" For a seventeen-year-old boy, it was the only answer he could give.

Carl ended his days at Regiopolis in fine style. He gave the address of welcome at the convocation on 8 June 1951. His good friend, Michael Carty was valedictorian. Grade 13 would have been a strenuous year, capped by the departmental examinations, a harrowing experience for many of those whose goal was university. But however demanding the daily grind of preparation for those exams might have been, Carl spent much time in the school chapel and at the cathedral praying about his future. The priesthood was centremost in his prayerful speculations. There was little doubt in either his mind or heart that he felt called to the Catholic priesthood. If there was any anxiety or confusion about his decision, it arose from the competing interests and desires of other people. Having watched Carl in the sanctuary for many years, the cathedral priests naturally thought that he should go to St. Augustine's Seminary to train as a diocesan priest. Carl's father, meanwhile, wanted him to consider the Basilians, who had taught him in Toronto and had given him a teaching job while he attended university. Then there were the Jesuits. Among them was Carl's hero, the incomparable Mr. Alfred Colliard. When it came time for Carl's mother to give her opinion, she simply said: "Let Carl go wherever the Lord is calling him." Archbishop O'Sullivan said the same thing. It was good advice.

Carl opted for the Jesuits.[18] On the evening of 14 August 1951, after prayers at the cemetery in the Irish Block outside Owen Sound, his family delivered him to the front steps of St. Stanislaus Novitiate in Guelph, his home for the following four years. There were nineteen novices that year, some arriving in early September. In a letter to his family, dated 28 September 1951, Carl tried to explain his decision to join the Jesuits:

> Tomorrow we begin the Long Retreat. For the past two years I have anxiously, and at times feverishly, awaited this day. It marks the real beginning of my apprenticeship as a candidate for the priesthood in the Society of Jesus. But why have I been privileged to spend thirty days alone with my Creator and Redeemer? Why did Our Lord choose me, the most undeserving of all, as one of three from the whole of Ontario to embrace this exquisitely wonderful life? Why, I know not. All I know is that for many months I had been continually haunted by a voice whispering: "Come follow Me in the Company that bears My Name." Try as I might to ignore and resist it, and try I did, this call kept mounting to a crescendo, all the while my plaintive "Why?" echoed and re-echoed unanswered.
>
> And now, thanks to God's grace and your kind understanding and generosity, I am about to begin the time-hallowed Exercises of St. Ignatius, thirty days in which I hope "to advance in spiritual wisdom and grace before God and men." Today as we await the beginning of the retreat, I am extremely happy and contented in mind and soul.[19]

St. Stanislaus Novitiate was a strict house. Father Brendan Cloran, S.J. was the novice master for 1951-52. His manner was that of a drill sergeant in the army – rarely smiling, never laughing – except that he was preparing young men for the army of Christ. He was a straight shooter, a conscientious leader who through prayer and reflection drew men to the service of Christ and the Church. Father John Swain, S.J., a future Acting General of the Jesuits, was the novice master for Carl's second year of novitiate, 1952-53. He encouraged the novices to be courageous leaders and men of religious conviction, always loyal to the Pope, "come hell or high water," as he was fond of saying. In a manner of speaking, for two years Jesuit novices majored in spiritual formation in the context of the charism of St. Ignatius of Loyola, the founder of the community, and minored in Latin and Greek. They also taught catechism. St. Ignatius had done so and wanted his men to do the same. The novices would leave St. Stanislaus in pairs and walk (never ride) on average from six to ten kilometres to one-room schools where they would teach for forty minutes and then return home. Blizzards were always a special challenge.

Carl, along with thirteen other novices, took first vows as a Jesuit two years to the day of entering the Novitiate, 15 August 1953. To his family, he wrote: "Yippee! The big letter arrived. The body of it only filled four lines but those four lines were the happy climax to the past seven hundred and twenty-two days."[20] Brother Matthews was now Mr. Matthews, S.J. and a scholastic with a Roman collar. The entire Matthews family drove from Kingston to celebrate with him. Although Carl never once considered leaving the novitiate, there were times when he was afraid that he would be sent home on account of his poor grades in Latin and Greek. Fortunately for him, the novice master took a gentle approach to Carl's linguistic deficiencies. Looking at Carl's marks, he said, "Brother Matthews, you can do better than this."[21]

Carl was now in the Juniorate; that too would last two years.[22] This time he majored in the Classics – Latin, Greek, English, French and history – and minored in spiritual formation. The Juniorate was located next door to the Novitiate. Carl continued performing well in English and history but not so well in his language courses. On Tuesdays, members of the Juniorate walked to schools in Guelph to teach catechism. For the school year 1954-55, Carl gave a course called "A Bird's Eye View of Church History," for the thirty-seven Grade 8 students at St. Stanislaus school. The course outline ran to eight single-spaced typed pages and would have been a challenge to present to Grade 9 or even Grade 10 students. Their time together may have been fun for Mr. Matthews, S.J., but for the students, it was a lot of history to absorb.[23]

Next was the Jesuit Seminary at 403 Wellington Street West, near Spadina Avenue, in Toronto, for three years of philosophy and science, leading to a

B.A. from St. Mary's University in Halifax.[24] (Carl would never set foot on the St. Mary's campus, a fact that brought him some discomfort when he applied to the Ontario College of Education in 1958. The registrar took a dim view of such an arrangement and only accepted his application when Carl said that Prime Minister John Diefenbaker had recently accepted an honourary LLD from St. Mary's.) Carl continued to teach catechism; this time, though, he was allowed to take a streetcar to his various assignments. He gave lessons for one hour a week at St. Margaret's school and then St. Anthony's and loved every minute in the classroom with the children. It was a refreshing break from philosophy lectures in Latin. Wednesdays were free days for scholastics. If the Legislative Assembly was in session at Queen's Park, he would take in Question Period. It was a curious hobby, not one shared by his fellow scholastics. Another hobby was serving as master of ceremonies on major feast days and on those occasions when the bishop arrived at the seminary for ordinations. Few Jesuits relished the task, but Carl, experienced in such duties at his home parish, gladly took on the responsibility. On Sunday afternoons, he would attend the "pay-what-you-can" performances of the Toronto Symphony Orchestra at Massey Hall. Needless to say, the orchestra received precious little from Carl or from those scholastics he had cajoled into going with him.

The Jesuit Seminary was an historic place and the subject of Carl's third publication. The property passed from Robert Sympson Jameson, husband of the celebrated novelist Anna Jameson and builder of the original home in 1838, to Frederick Widder, a commissioner for the Canada Company who purchased the home in 1844 and named it "Lyndhurst," to the Loretto Sisters in 1867 who made it their residence and school, and finally to the Jesuits in 1930. Over the years, there had been four substantial additions to the 1838 building. Carl celebrated this history in "The Close of a Chapter at '403.'" Its publication in *The Canadian Scholastic* (May 1958, 1-4) coincided with the decision by the Jesuits to move their philosophy students to Spokane, Washington and to embark on a campaign to build a new seminary. The article, modified to fit circumstances, appeared in the *Telegram* (2 November 1963, 29), to mark the newspaper's new building on the site, and in *The Globe and Mail* (18 February 1974, 5), several years after the *Globe* had purchased the *Telegram* building and turned it into its Front Street headquarters.[25]

Carl's other publications from this period on Wellington West were "St. Ignatius – The Educator" (*Martyrs' Shrine Message,* June 1956, 41-42), a page-and-a-half article that explained the Jesuit system of education, and "The Separate School Question in Ontario" (*The Canadian Scholastic,*

January 1958, 1-10). The article regarding separate schools is the first evidence of his interest in the highly charged issue that would come to dominate his life for more than three decades. Carl's initial contribution to the literature on separate schools, a field of inquiry largely uncultivated by Catholics, managed to work in four significant features in only ten pages: a knowledge of early separate school legislation; a careful parsing of the distinctive features of the separate school system; a reference to Franklin Walker's groundbreaking *Catholic Education and Politics in Upper Canada* (1955); and a convincing argument, based on the Ontario government's own statistics, on behalf of increasing legislative grants as an immediate means of improving the financial footing of separate schools. Whether Carl knew it or not, this brief but authoritative article would provide him an entry into the topsy-turvy world of separate school politics, when the time was right. That time would come within five years.[26]

After philosophy in the seminary, there was Regency, normally a period of three years. Carl was assigned to his alma mater, Regiopolis College in Kingston. However, in order to sign a contract to teach, he required teaching qualifications.[27] To that end, he took a ten-week summer course at the Ontario College of Education, in 1958, and earned an Interim High School Assistant's Certificate, Type B. English, geography and history were his teachable subjects. Life at OCE was different. It was the first time that Carl had shared a class with female students and non-Catholics. For him, it was a new experience, and no one seemed to mind his Roman collar and black suit. Carl was impressed with Professor John McMaster, who did an outstanding job of teaching his students how to teach English Literature to high school students. His lectures were invaluable.

Also attending OCE that same summer was Father J. Kevin McKenna, S.J., who would be principal of Regiopolis College when Carl was stationed there. Father McKenna would have a profound influence on him. One day, when the two of them were walking home to the Jesuit residence at 226 St. George Street, Carl turned to Father McKenna and congratulated him on his splendid and completely unrehearsed presentation to the 400 students in the amphitheatre. The compliment was answered with a shock of realism that was sudden as it was inspiring. Father McKenna stopped and, pointing his finger into Carl's chest, said: "Never, ever, forget, Mr. Matthews, that through the sacrifices of countless people, you have been given first-rate training as a Jesuit. We must share that gift of knowledge every day of our lives. We must seize the opportunity. The Lord and his disciple, Ignatius, expect no less, my friend."²⁸ These words, always remembered by Carl, became a motto of sorts for him. To share with others would be his portion and cup as a Jesuit, a confirmation of his natural tendency to be of assistance to others, as noticed by his first grade teacher, Sister Mary Louise.

Despite some initial reservations about spending his Regency in his hometown,²⁹ Carl embraced life at Regiopolis, which was as close-knit a Jesuit community as it had been when he was a student there. He was returning to a familiar and much-loved place. On staff were thirteen priest-teachers and four scholastic teachers. Carl taught English and Religion in both sections of the Grade 10 class, the first year, and added Grade 13 English to his teaching load, the second year. To his great joy and satisfaction, each one of his Grade 13 students took and passed the departmental examinations, and many of them achieved high honours. Carl's other responsibilities were the debating club, the public-speaking contest, the altar boys and the May 1959 production of the play *Twelve Angry Men.* In a way, it was high school all over again. In addition, Carl supervised the student dormitory every evening. Visits to his parents and siblings at home were limited to three hours, three times a year, which was a relative luxury when one considers that during his first seven years as a Jesuit he had not been allowed to visit his family at home at all.³⁰ Actually, outings of any kind were rare, but, at the request of Father McKenna, Carl made a report on English teaching at Regiopolis at the separate school board office in Kingston. It was the first time he had spoken in public on the subject of education in front of his father.³¹

Carl's Regency came to an end a year early, in June 1960. There should have been a third year and then theology, but Father Gordon George, S.J., the provincial superior, moved him back to the Jesuit residence on St. George Street so that he could pursue full time a master's degree in education at the University of Toronto. Carl specialized in school finance and administration. He took eight courses, earning six As and two Bs, and graduated with a M.Ed. on 2 June 1961. Charles E. Phillips, the dean of graduate studies, invited him to continue his academic work in education on the doctoral level. Armed with Phillips's invitation, Carl had no trouble convincing Father George to delay his entry into theology, even though that would push back his ordination by at least two years. During the 1961-62 school year, he took four more courses – History of Education in Great Britain, History of Education in Ontario, Research in Education and Educational Finance – and audited a course in statistics during the winter term of 1962. His marks were three As and one B. Professor Brock Rideout, who taught Carl the course in Educational Finance, would be the primary inspiration behind Carl's lobbying for the Foundation Tax Plan.

In October 1962, Carl accompanied Father Joseph P. Finn, the director of education for the diocese of London, to the annual meeting of the Diocesan Superintendents of Schools, held that year in Washington, D.C. Knowing Carl's interest in separate school finances, Father Finn wanted his help in presenting a distinctly Canadian reply to John E. Cheal's recent doctoral dissertation from the University of Chicago, *Canadian Provincial School Systems: Their Input-Output Differences.* On the long car trip to Washington, Father Finn and Carl composed their rebuttal. As an extra measure, Carl wrote his own critique of an article by Cheal, "An 'Experiment' in Public Aid to Non-Public Schools," that had appeared in the May 1962 issue of *Administrator's Notebook.* The article was culled from the dissertation. Carl was not shy to take on Cheal. His critique was hard-nosed and tightly argued, revealing several fundamental flaws in Cheal's assumptions and conclusions concerning public funding of Catholic education in Canada. One wonders if Cheal would have been awarded his doctorate, if Carl had been on the committee judging Cheal's defense.[32]

For his own dissertation topic, Carl chose "The Administration of the Ontario Separate School System, with special emphasis on post-war problems accentuated by a tremendous increase in enrolment."[33] At least that is the way that he described it in a letter to the historian Franklin Walker. Carl knew that Walker was writing a follow-up volume to his *Catholic Education and Politics in Upper Canada* (it would be published in 1964 under the title *Catholic Education and Politics in Ontario*), and he did not want to tread on Walker's territory. He was wise to have asked for Walker's imprimatur. Walker assured him that his new book did not deal with the administration of the province's separate schools, but he did suggest that Carl narrow his research to the Metropolitan Separate School Board.[34]

The dissertation was never written. As we shall see in Chapter Two, the acceptance of the Foundation Tax Plan by Premier John Robarts in February 1963 eclipsed any need to write on a problem that would be greatly alleviated by the Plan's successful implementation, beginning in 1964.[35] Another reason for the dissertation's demise was that Carl had begun his theology course, which left him no real time to devote to intensive research and writing.

Carl attempted to resurrect the dissertation in 1966. This time he proposed to write on "The Tiny Township Case (1928) and the Resultant Status of

Catholic Secondary Education in Ontario." The title was to change often. It went from "Controversies about Catholic Secondary Education in Ontario, 1880-1930," to "The Quest for Publicly Supported Catholic High Schools in Ontario, 1860-1930" and finally to "The Separate School Question in Ontario at the Post-Elementary Level, 1910-1930."[36] According to Carl's careful calculations, Walker had devoted a mere thirteen pages to the topic in his two volumes.[37] It looked like Carl had the field all to himself. Once again, though, the dissertation stalled. Years of research in Toronto, Ottawa, Kingston, Hamilton and London that produced more than 1,100 pages of documentation went nowhere.[38] It was one of the few times in his life when his energy and ambition fizzled in the face of a good idea. Perhaps it can be easily explained by the fact that by 1966 Carl had already found his *métier* and it was not in academia. However, it took a long time for him to realize this about himself.

Starting as a graduate student, he had become quite adept at lobbying by letter all the big players in separate school politics, and he was quite bold in the deliverance of his opinions. As a theology student, he devoted his free days to public talks on separate schools in church basements in numerous cities. Invitations to speak were a regular feature of his life. Whether by design or fortuitous circumstance, or a combination of both, he had become a self-appointed front-line advocate of a more forward-looking way of promoting and securing the rights of separate school supporters. Carl was a natural at what he was doing and something of a novelty in separate school circles. Why abandon his position of influence for the drudgery of writing a dissertation? "The insatiable quest for school justice," Carl wrote Bishop Joseph T. Ryan of Hamilton, his good friend, "may be incompatible with getting a doctorate."[39] No one understood Carl's dilemma better than himself. He formally withdrew from the Ed. D. program in September 1972.[40]

In any event, 1966 was a big year in the life of Carl Joseph Matthews. It was the year of his ordination. Progress towards the priesthood began three years earlier when he received Father George's permission to commence his theological studies. "Do it now, Carl," he said.[41] In August 1963, Carl moved to the new Regis College on Bayview Avenue. Theology was more enjoyable than philosophy. Moral theology, scripture, canon law, Church history and liturgy were taught in English. That was a huge relief. Only dogma was taught in Latin, with oral exams also in Latin. That was a burden made all the more trying by the presence of several classmates who could argue in Latin better than in English. But Carl persevered, successfully completing three out of four years of theology. (As was the custom at the time, he did his fourth year immediately following ordination and was duly awarded a Bachelor of Theology from St. Mary's in Halifax. During that year, much to his surprise, Father Carl was appointed the part-time registrar of Regis College, replacing Father David Stanley, S.J., the renowned scripture scholar.)

There were thirteen members of the Regis class in 1966. At the hands of Bishop F.A. Marrocco, Carl was ordained a subdeacon on 4 May and a deacon on 5 May, in the college chapel. Deacons of Jesuit Provinces other than Upper Canada, especially those from the American West, left for their home dioceses. The exception was José Rodriguez from Leon Province in Spain, who remained in Toronto. Ordination to the priesthood took place on 4 June, also in the college chapel. Six Jesuits received Holy Orders that day. They were Bob Gaudet, Carl Matthews, José Rodriguez, Bill Clarke, John LeSarge and John Trainor. The ordaining prelate was Bishop Benjamin I. Webster of Peterborough. Each candidate was allowed twenty-five guests. C.P. and Florence Matthews had waited patiently for fifteen years to see their son elevated to the priesthood. It was a special moment of grace for them to receive his priestly blessing. The Matthews family celebrated with a dinner in the Hunting Room at the King Edward Hotel.

Father Carl's first Mass was the next day, 5 June. All 150 seats in the chapel were filled with relatives and friends. Michael Matthews served, and Father Alfred Colliard, S.J. was the assistant priest. The altar faced the people, and only the Eucharistic Prayer was in Latin, but there remained some traces of what was becoming the "Old Mass." One photograph shows Father Matthews standing, with Michael and Father Colliard kneeling on either side of him, starting Mass with prayers at the foot of the altar. After the Mass, Ursula and Denis O'Connor entertained the family at their home in Stouffville. Father Carl celebrated his first Solemn High Mass, on 12 June, at St. Mary's Cathedral in Kingston, his parish church. It was homecoming for the "old" altar boy. Father Bernard J. Walsh, the cathedral rector, was assistant priest, Father Bill Downey was the deacon, Father Leon Pelletier was subdeacon and Father Colliard delivered the sermon. At the reception, which was attended by 135 people, many people who had been a part of Father Carl's life took the opportunity to speak. Among them were Father Crusoe, S.J., a former teacher, Michael Carty, his high school chum, Edmund Milne, a former student at Regiopolis, T.J. McKenna, on behalf of Catholic high school boards, C.P. O'Neill, veteran Catholic assistant superintendent of elementary education, Paul Matthews, who represented the family, and, of course, C.P. Matthews, the proud father. It was a grand and glorious day.[42]

By way of a postscript, Father Carl made his Tertianship (the last part of the Jesuit training program) at Auriesville, New York, from 16 June 1969 to 15 January 1970, with four months devoted to pastoral ministry (Father Carl was given permission to continue his separate school work in Toronto).[43] He then made his profession of final vows, on 15 August 1971, twenty years to the day he entered St. Stanislaus Novitiate in Guelph. The ceremony took place, fittingly enough, in the chapel of Regiopolis College, but since it was soon to be vacated by the Jesuits, there was a note of irony to the occasion. The Society of Jesus put its approval on Father Carl "as a man who bears the stamp and ideals of St. Ignatius, as they are found in the Spiritual Exercises, in the Institute of the Order, and in the Constitution of the Order, and also as one who will strive continually in this manner in the age in which he lives as a disciple of Christ and a witness of the Gospel."[44]

---

[1] Reverend Carl J. Matthews, S.J. [hereafter known as CJM], Personal Papers, Box 1, File 1 [hereafter known as Matthews Papers]. **NOTE:** unless otherwise stated in the endnotes, all references are to this collection of papers. Therefore the name of the collection – Matthews Papers – will only be repeated if necessary.

[2] Ibid., Genealogical Chart compiled by CJM. Additional information about parents supplied by CJM, Box 1, File 2, "Handwritten Notes to the Author, June 2003" ["Handwritten Notes"].

[3] Box 1, File 1, Newspaper Clipping.

[4] Box 1, File 1, "Handwritten Notes"; Box 2, File 5, CJM to Monsignor Welsh, 2 June 1964. Information confirmed by Gillian Osley, assistant archivist, Archives of the Roman Catholic Archdiocese of Toronto [ARCAT], telephone interview, 14 July 2003.

[5] Box 1, File, 1, Father & Mother, Melancthon, to Charles P. Matthews, Guelph, 14 July 1922.

[6] Information on C.P. Matthews' career as a teacher and separate school inspector was taken from the following sources: "Leading educator dies," *Catholic Register*, 4 March 1978; "Separate School inspector dies," *Kingston Whig-Standard*, 13 February 1978; Memo: my dear parents, from CJM to Friends, 8 October 2001; L.J. Flynn, *At School in Kingston 1850-1973: The Story of Catholic Education in Kingston and District* (Kingston: The Frontenac, Lennox and Addington County Roman Catholic Separate School Board, 1973), 162-63.

[7] Box 3, File 3, CJM to The Directors, Ontario Separate School Trustees' Association, 5 April 1968.

[8] Flynn, *At School in Kingston 1850-1973,* 193.

9 Box 1, File 2, "Handwritten Notes."

10 Box 5, File 4, CJM to Mrs. Fryer, 21 May 1984.

11 Box 1, File 1, Sister Mary Louise, St. Mary's School, Kingston, Ontario, to "Dear Carol," 28 June 1939. Father Matthews changed the spelling of his first name, from Carol to Carl, on his first day of high school and legalized the change on his first visit to Queen's Park, paying a charge of $15. The name Carol was derived from his father's name in Latin, Carolus Patricius Matthews, which appeared on his Varsity diploma. Father Matthews's parents resisted calling their first son Charles Jr. and instead chose Carol.

12 Box 1, File 2, "Handwritten Notes," School days at St. Mary's.

13 *Catholic Register*, 23 September 1972, 6.

14 Ibid., 4 April 1992, 10.

15 Box 2, File 5, CJM to Most Rev. J.A. O'Sullivan, D.D., 24 April 1964; *Catholic Register*, 4 April 1992, 10.

16 Box 1, File 2, "Handwritten Notes," Regiopolis College; Box 1, File 3, "Regiopolis College."

17 Box 4, File 6, CJM to Stephen Lewis, 7 October 1970.

18 Box 1, File 2, "Handwritten Notes," Novitiate; Box 1, File 4, "Novitiate."

19 Box 1, File 4, "Novitiate," CJM to Mom, Dad, Theresa, Paul, Ursula, Victor & Michael, 28 September 1951.

20 Ibid., CJM to Mom, Dad, Theresa, Paul, Ursula, Victor & Michael, 7 August 1953.

21 Box 1, File 2, "Handwritten Notes."

22 Ibid.

23 Box 1, File 5, "A Bird's Eye View of Church History."

24 Box 1, File 2, "Handwritten Notes," Bachelor of Arts.

25 Box 1, File 6, "Copies of *Telegram* and *Globe* articles, plus correspondence."

26 Box 1, File 7, "Copies of publications and other writings from the period of the Scholasticate."

27 Box 1, File 8, "Ontario College of Education, Graduate Work at the University of Toronto, French Language Course at Université de Montréal, Theology."

28 Box 1, File 2, "Handwritten Notes."

29 Box 1, File 8, CJM to Father John Mitchell, S.J., 27 March 1958.

30 Box 1, File 2, "Handwritten Notes."

31 Box 2, File 7, CJM to Father J. Kevin McKenna, S.J., 11 November 1965.

32 Box 1, File 9, "Unpublished Essays and Critiques, 1962"; Box 2, File 3, CJM to Rev. Joseph P. Finn, Ph.D., 31 October 1962; CJM to Very Rev. Gordon George, S.J., 31 October 1962.

33 Box 1, File 8, CJM to Franklin A. Walker, 15 April 1962.

34 Ibid., Franklin A. Walker to CJM, 18 April 1962.

35 Box 2, File 10, CJM to Most Rev. Joseph F. Ryan, Bishop of Hamilton, 17 March 1967.

36 Ibid., CJM to Franklin A. Walker, 4 March 1967; CJM to Very Rev. Angus J. Macdougall, S.J., 20 1967; CJM to Most Rev. Philip F. Pocock, Archbishop of Toronto, 9 September 1967. Box 3, File 15, CJM to Edward Sheridan, S.J., 15 December 1969.

37 Box 2, File 8, CJM to Reverend Raymond Durocher, O.M.I., 19 March 1966; Box 1, File 8, CJM to Willard Brehaut, 20 April 1966.

38 Box 4, File 18, CJM to Mary C. Babcock, Executive Director, Ontario English Catholic Teachers' Association, 5 April 1972.

39 Box 2, File 10, CJM to Bishop Ryan, 4 March 1967.

40 Box 4, File 19, CJM to George E. Flower, Ontario Institute for Studies in Education, 8 September 1972.

41 Box 1, File 2, "Handwritten Notes."

42 Box 1, File 10, "Illustrations," Photo Album.

43 Box 3, File 10, To the Tertians, 14 April 1969.

44 Box 1, File 11, "Final Profession," Sermon by Father Thomas M. Moylan, S.J.

CHAPTER TWO

FUNDING PARITY FOR CATHOLIC ELEMENTARY SCHOOLS

Introduction

Father Carl Matthews' curious career in separate school politics from the promotion of the Foundation Tax Plan, beginning in 1961, to his election as a school trustee, in 1972, was a paradox that allowed him to produce some of the era's best policy statements and political wisdom for the separate school side. It was a time when Catholic leaders in education collectively sought to clarify their own political identity and pedagogical principles in what must have felt like a never-ending and near-hopeless struggle to safeguard the viability of separate schools. Insufficient financial revenues were a perennial problem for all separate school boards. So too was the truncated nature of the system under their administration. Separate school boards had jurisdiction over kindergarten to Grade 10 (elementary grades in the eyes of the government), but numerous boards failed to offer Grades Nine and Ten. Until they did so, however, no government would seriously consider Catholic claims to more public funds or, later, their demands for what became known as separate school completion.

Both issues – financial parity and completion – would come to the fore in the 1960s. To the first, a young and brash Carl Matthews, a Jesuit scholastic, would promote a simple but brilliant solution that produced handsome long-term dividends; concerning the second, as Father Matthews, he would clarify the central issues at stake, pare away false worries over financing completion and offer numerous warnings about the self-destructive nature of threatening politicians or, worse, giving up entrenched constitutional rights for short-term gains.

Father Matthews' career was curious not so much because it was odd, even though it appeared to be just that to many of his contemporaries, but because it was so unique. There was no one remotely like him on either side of the school question. Freelancer par excellence, and blessed with the freedom of Religious life and the constant support of his Jesuit superiors, Father Matthews was a letter-writing, door-knocking and speech-making gadfly of almost infinite energy, ingenuity and creativity. He had an intimate grasp of school history few in the Catholic fold could match (Professor Franklin Walker was a notable exception, but he lived and taught in Chicago). As well, Father Matthews' mastery of the annual statistics generated by the ministry of education spoke loudly and clearly on behalf of separate schools. He loved facts, not rhetoric, and statistics were his favourite facts. In his hands, they became powerful weapons of persuasion that no one in a position of power and influence could ignore. He also demonstrated a practical knowledge of the political game at Queen's Park. He was aware of the difference between strategy and tactics; he had an uncanny ability to go straight to the top of the political pyramid and stay there, year after year; and he knew how to massage political egos, ending up a friend, and at times a confidant, of party leaders, the minister of education and opposition education critics.

Once Father Matthews had made up his mind on a point of policy, or the course of action to be taken or avoided, he was patient in explaining it, tenacious in defending it and fearless in promoting it. He had his admirers and collaborators. Among them were politicians of all stripes, bishops, bureaucrats, trustees, teachers and other separate school stakeholders. They appreciated his knowledge of the issues at hand and his considerable persuasive skills. He knew how to argue a point, and in the days before faxes and e-mails and inexpensive long-distance phone calls, he presented his arguments in tightly scripted letters. Father Matthews also had his detractors, all Catholics it appears. Bitten one too many times by the forcefulness of his opinions, they felt that someone who had no official standing in any association connected to separate schools had no business participating in policy making, regardless of his Roman collar and the sincerity of his motives. And there were those who found his steady stream of letters just too much. (Even Father Matthews' staunchest supporter, Bishop Joseph F. Ryan of Hamilton, thought he had better things to do than write him on Christmas Eve.) For a few, his presence was a threat to their own standing in the Catholic school establishment.

From the curious nature of Father Matthews' career, let us move to the paradox that gave it life and substance and was the primary reason for his every success as well as his Achilles' heel. He was the consummate outsider who by means of skill and timing became the quintessential insider. Put another less generous way, being an outsider and attached to no organization, he was free to express his ideas and opinions and offer plans of action, which he did to great effect on many occasions, but being an outsider also made him vulnerable to exclusion from the inner circle at crucial moments. This was certainly the case in 1970, when the Ontario Separate School Trustees' Association turned a deaf ear to his entreaties about their Implementation Brief. The insider found himself on the outside, pleading in vain.

"I have no position, no status, no weight."[1] That is how Father Matthews described himself in 1965 to Archbishop Philip Pocock. Several years later, he wrote Kevin Power of Ottawa, secretary-treasurer of the Association of Catholic High School Boards of Ontario: "I am on no payroll or expense account. My efforts are just those of a concerned Student of the School Question."[2] True in both instances but hardly the entire picture. Early on, when Matthews was still a scholastic without a theology degree, both Bishop Ryan and Archbishop Pocock considered him the expert on separate schools and did not hesitate to say so publicly. This was high praise indeed, much to the utter exasperation of Father Edward Sheridan, S.J., rector of Regis College, the Jesuit seminary then in Willowdale. He thought that the whole idea of Matthews being an expert on anything was crazy. To that charge, delivered in a dressing down of sorts, Matthews the theology student replied, "For sure, Father."[3] Sheridan's response to that was to recommend that if he wanted to be an expert, he should visit school systems in Europe. On another occasion, in 1964, when Bishop Ryan invited Matthews to speak in Hamilton, Father Sheridan exploded when Matthews asked for his permission to leave the seminary on a regular class day:

> "Doesn't the Bishop realize, Mister, that you are now a student of theology? Why doesn't he ask a prominent person? Don't you realize that you have my Moral Theology exam next week? How are you going to get to Hamilton without missing several lectures? Surely you are not thinking of borrowing my car? If you went, would you embarrass the Jesuit Order in front of Mayor Vic Copps by falling on your face during the talk? You better not, Mister. O.K., go. Take the Rector's car, but heaven help you if you put a dent in it. Your exam here will be postponed two days. This is no way to run a seminary. In fact it is crazy."[4]

Father Sheridan need not have worried. The Hamilton talk went well (and the Rector's car was returned without any dents). Carl Matthews knew what he was doing. He was knowledgeable, pragmatic, and non-partisan; he was diplomatic nearly to a fault; he was a clear thinker and a glutton for hard work, brimming with self-confidence and motivated only by the common good of separate school children; and he kept in regular contact with the bishops' committee on education, with the executive secretary of the English Catholic Education Association of Ontario and, incredibly, with nearly every constituent organization of that association, such as the Ontario Separate School Trustees' Association, the Association of Catholic High School Boards of Ontario, the Federation of Catholic Parent-Teacher Associations of Ontario, the Ontario Catholic Student Federation and the Ontario English Catholic Teachers' Association. Keeping open all these lines of communication was a singular achievement. Indeed, Carl Matthews was so good at trumpeting the separate school side, by 1967, that Bishop Ryan believed that he was "the best informed man on Catholic schools in the Province of Ontario."[5]

But none of these qualities, as admirable as they surely were, could have come together and made the man, if Father Matthews had not taken the words of St. Ignatius himself and turned them into his philosophy of life. "Work as though the entire success of your project depended on you and not at all on God, and at the same time trust in God as if you were not able to do anything yourself and God alone could do everything." These words, deeply rooted in his formation as a Jesuit and a paradox in itself, are the key to unlocking Father Matthews' curious career as a separate school hound.

The Foundation Tax Plan

In July 1961, Carl Matthews was twenty-nine years old and the recent recipient of a M.Ed. degree from the University of Toronto, specializing in school finance and administration. Instead of proceeding to theology, he asked for and received permission to begin a doctorate. He wasted no time and enrolled in Professor Brock Rideout's summer course in educational finance.[6]

Rideout drew up the ministry of education's grant schemes for both school systems. He encouraged Matthews' fascination with school finances and was probably the best versed education bureaucrat on the esoteric topic of the Foundation Tax Plan as a means to raise the annual per-pupil revenue of have-not school boards without having to increase local property taxes. The subject would have rated at least a passing mention in class. More importantly, as a member of the provincial government's powerful cabinet committee, Rideout would champion the concept of the Foundation Tax Plan when it came up for official discussion at Queen's Park in late 1962.

The ivory tower of Varsity, however, could not satisfy all of Matthews' ambitions. They were always more than purely academic; they were practical and even political, so to speak. The workload at the doctoral level should have commanded the lion's share of his time and attention; there was a thesis to write. But armed with one graduate degree and pursuing another, he had to satisfy a long-nourished need to connect with separate school people, so that he could share with them his growing expertise in separate school finances. In short, he wanted to be part of the political dynamic. There is no other way to explain adequately the commencement of a correspondence that would take him deep into the turbulent and uncharted waters of separate school lobbying. If he was unknown and inexperienced, he did not let such things bother him. Nerve was never in short supply.

It began in the summer of 1961 with a letter to Francis G. Carter, a London-based lawyer and president of the Ontario Separate School Trustees' Association (OSSTA).[7] The occasion was the forthcoming OSSTA brief to the Conservative government of John Robarts. Matthews admired the brief but did not mention the inaccuracies in several statistics for fear that criticisms from a total stranger might be taken as unfair sniping.[8] He had an eagle eye and also an ingrained deference to his seniors. Accuracy in statistics, especially if they were the heart of an argument intended to sway the government, became a bugbear for him. The education department was loaded with statisticians who could tear apart any amateurish dabbling in numbers. The OSSTA brief was corrected at the insistence of Dr. R.W.B. Jackson of the department of education, before it was presented to the premier. During the course of rewriting the brief, Robert Laidlaw, OSSTA's executive director, informed Matthews that all corrections had been inserted.

Matthews' next contact was Father (later Monsignor) Vincent Priester. He was the executive director and secretary of the English Catholic Education Association of Ontario (ECEAO) and a veteran warrior in many school battles. Matthews had asked Priester for a loan of Frank Carter's manuscript on separate school legislation and litigation (which was published in 1962 as *Judicial Decisions on Denominational Schools*). This led Priester to invite Matthews to participate in the annual Ontario Conference on Education, scheduled for November 1961 in Windsor.[9] At the conference was Brock Rideout, who spent most of his time promoting the Foundation Tax Plan to the delegates. It emerged as a major recommendation of the conference.[10] For Matthews, the concept of the plan prompted an Epiphany. No longer would separate school supporters have to plead for corporation and public utility taxes, a political impossibility; financial equity could be achieved if the basic formula of the per-pupil legislative grant were changed to a direct inverse ratio to local assessment on property: the lower the assessment, the higher the grant. When the right moment came, he would pitch the plan.

On his return from Windsor, Matthews completed his first "Trends in Ontario Separate School Finance." This initial foray into the analysis of the yearly installments of the *Report of the Minister of Education,* which compared the difference in overall revenue between the two publicly funded school boards, in terms of legislative grants and local taxes, opened doors for Carl Matthews. One of the people to receive a copy of "Trends" was Frank Carter. Impressed, he asked Matthews to participate in a special meeting of the OSSTA executive, in London, on 9 December 1961.[11] The subject was the possible effect of the new secondary school program on separate schools. Next was the publication of "Trends" in the February 1962 issue of *Catholic Trustee.*[12] This was the first of many articles to appear in OSSTA's official periodical. Some positive publicity came courtesy of Father Joseph Finn of London, chaplain of OSSTA, when he told the delegates at the trustees' Easter 1962 convention about Matthews' interest in separate school finances.[13]

Hard work and productivity can establish one's reputation, but if one's reputation is to last and grow it needs connections. Carl Matthews made all the right connections at the very beginning. They were Frank Carter, Bob Laidlaw, Brock Rideout, Father Priester and Father Finn. The name of Matthews had begun to circulate; his byline had appeared in print. Did he have a future in the separate school camp? The answer to that question came soon enough.

October 1962 ushered in a remarkable confluence of events. At the beginning of the month, the two trustee associations, OSSTA, and its French counterpart, l'Association des commissions des écoles bilingues d'Ontario (ACEBO), started to work on their annual brief to the government. Having listened to Matthews in the OSSTA office, on the merits of the Foundation Tax Plan, Bob Laidlaw invited him to draft the second of two sections. The first section would request specific changes in legislation; the second would discuss long-range proposals concerning finance.[14] Matthews told Laidlaw that he intended to propose the Foundation Tax Plan, and Laidlaw gave him the green light to proceed. The separate school strategy would remain the same: financial parity between the two school systems. But adoption by the trustees of the plan would be a radical departure on tactics. That was the gamble.

Never one to tarry, Matthews started work immediately. To the task at hand he added a touch of political lobbying that proved decisive to the success of the trustees' brief. He knew that the Foundation Tax Plan had no chance of becoming Conservative government policy if Catholics in general and the two opposition parties in particular did not openly support it. Being elected by Catholic ratepayers, the trustees would speak for Catholics via the trustee associations. What about the Liberals and the NDP? The latter party under Donald C. MacDonald needed little convincing. MacDonald was already onside. The big question mark was the Liberals, the official opposition, led by John Wintermeyer.

Wintermeyer, a Catholic, was willing to be convinced. Matthews had interviewed Wintermeyer at his home in Kitchener, in August 1962, for his dissertation, and was aware that he was toying with a plan to pool corporation taxes at the local school board level. Matthews thought that that plan had too many disadvantages to survive in the political arena. Alberta had already implemented the purest form of the foundation program for school finances. The implication was obvious: there was no reason, financial or political, for Ontario not to emulate Alberta. On 5 October, Matthews issued an invitation to Wintermeyer to chat, and the two men met in Wintermeyer's room at the Westbury Hotel on 8 and 9 October.[15]

The meetings were strictly secret. The press and perhaps a majority of the public would not have tolerated a Jesuit lobbying the leader of the official opposition, who was also a Catholic, to change his party's policy on financing schools in the province.[16] The press would have had a field day, and the potential for political boomerang on the Liberals was enormous. But secrecy prevailed. By the end of the second day of talks, Wintermeyer agreed to adopt the Foundation Tax Plan as Liberal Party education policy. Matthews left the Westbury in disbelief. Something akin to a political miracle had happened. Now he needed to convince the trustees. He returned to Bellarmine Hall (the Jesuit residence on St. George Street) and resumed work on the brief, invigorated no doubt by the coup he had just engineered. (Wintermeyer lived up to his change of mind. On 4 December 1962, he announced in the Ontario Legislature the Liberal Party's version of the Foundation Tax Plan, and he did not retreat on the issue during the campaign for the 25 September 1963 election.)[17]

During the week of 21 October, thirty-three-year-old Bill Davis was appointed minister of education, an extraordinarily fortuitous choice on the part of Premier Robarts, and on 27 October, the Catholic Bishops of Ontario presented their brief on separate schools to Premier John Robarts. The political gods smiled kindly on Davis. Ahead of this genial, pipe-smoking lawyer from Brampton lay a long and highly successful political career. He was minister of education from 1962 to his election as party leader and premier in 1971 and premier from 1971 to February 1985. He would be front and centre on the stage of separate school politics during those twenty-three years, and standing in the shadows, never too far from him, would be Carl Matthews, the Jesuit expert on separate school finances. A genuine friendship sprung up between them. It was based on mutual respect and trust and an easygoing camaraderie natural to both men that did not exclude frankness and, on occasion, testiness in their ongoing exchange of ideas and opinions.

Bill Davis had scarcely warmed the seat of his ministerial chair at Queen's Park when the episcopacy unveiled their brief. The bishops demonstrated considerable political smarts when they claimed, quite correctly, that financial equity was a necessary condition for equality of educational opportunity, the current mantra of those in the education business, and they reminded the Robarts government that separate school boards were so handicapped from a lack of financial equity with their public board counterparts that many of them were on the verge of collapsing.[18] However, the bishops had no intention of providing concrete solutions. In their collective mind, a plan of action was the proper sphere of the Ontario Separate School Trustees' Association.

Into the breach stepped the executives of the English and French trustee associations. While a storm of controversy erupted in the press over the bishops' brief, the trustees went about their work with little fanfare. They met at the Lord Simcoe Hotel in Toronto, on 20 November 1962. Frank Carter, OSSTA's legal advisor, was first to speak. The centrepiece of his nine-page presentation was the equitable sharing of corporation taxes. Carl Matthews, the Jesuit scholastic, was next. By his own admission, at age thirty, he was "a raw rookie among a group of seasoned veterans."[19] What was then called the Foundation Program was the sole focus of his six-page brief. No one at the meeting, except Bob Laidlaw, had heard much, if anything, about the program, and if any of them had, they had not heard so concise and convincing an explanation of it as that given by Matthews:

> The Ontario Separate School Trustees' Association is pleased to join the ranks of those who have already recommended that all publicly supported schools in this Province be financed on the basis of a Foundation Program. More specifically we request:

(a) that the Provincial Department of Education define in terms of expenditure for specific local services and facilities an adequate standard of education in all schools;

(b) that it meet half the total provincial cost from general legislative grants;

(c) that, to finance its share of the Foundation Program, each school board be required to levy a specified mill rate (to be uniform throughout the Province) on the rateable property of its supporters;

(d) that the legislative grant to each school board be the difference between the product of this specified mill rate and the approved cost of the Foundation Program provided by each board.[20]

The brief ended by re-affirming the local autonomy of school boards and by reminding everyone that the Foundation Program was for all school boards and that its goal was to level up and not down. If the program could work in New York State and Alberta, it could work in Ontario.

There was considerable tension in the smoke-filled room. Matthews' brief had made clear that "school boards that have become accustomed to the lion's share of corporation taxes are in no mood to relinquish an equitable portion to pupils under other boards that are starving."[21] Separate school boards certainly had a right to their share of corporation taxes, but they would never get those taxes. A new remedy had to be found, and that remedy was the Foundation Program. It was as if several generations of heroic struggle were about to be consigned to the dustbin of separate school history. Roland Bériault, executive secretary of ACEBO, ended the impasse. He moved to accept the Matthews' brief as OSSTA's and ACEBO's sole proposal to the government. It was time to make a clean break with past tactics for financing the elementary grades (from kindergarten to Grade 10; no one in 1962 expected a breakthrough on secondary grades). The motion was accepted unanimously. The trustees selected Frank Carter to write the introduction and Carl Matthews to compose the rest of the brief. Matthews presented the basic formula of the Foundation Tax Plan: taking into account weighting factors for urban and rural needs,

1. the Department of Education would determine in dollars and cents the total amount it costs to educate adequately a child in the schools of this Province;

2. this cost would be met in the following manner:
   by a uniform mill rate levied province-wide based on an equalized municipal assessment;
   by legislative grants

The plan presupposes equalized assessments throughout the Province.[22]

On the suggestion of Frank Carter, the brief was printed in English and French, as a show of unified determination. It was a clever move. Chris Asseff, OSSTA president, and Raymond Côté, ACEBO president, presented the brief to Premier John Robarts in a private meeting on 12 December 1962. Although Robarts disagreed with the assumption of a uniform provincial assessment, he did tell the trustees that a solution would be found.[23] That was good news. So too was the fact that the trustees' brief aroused nary a whiff of press-inspired hostility or panic among the politicians.

The name Carl Matthews appeared nowhere on the trustees' brief. Nor was there any acknowledgement of his authorship of the press release dated 12 December 1962, in which he provided replies to seven "Possible Objections to our Proposed Plan for Financing Ontario Schools." Anonymity in these two matters was fine with him. However, that did not stop him from promoting and explaining the Foundation Tax Plan in *Catholic Trustee*. In the November 1962 issue, he contributed "Foundation Program of School Finance as Applied to Alberta," a fortuitous prelude to the writing of the brief, and in the January 1963 issue, he published "Background Comments on the Catholic Trustees' Brief" as well as a second installment of "Trends in Ontario Separate School Finance," this time using tables and a graph to illustrate his figures.[24]

Matthews was on a roll, but not everyone was pleased with this upstart Jesuit, who appeared from nowhere and liked to think that he knew a great deal about financing separate schools. Father Vincent Priester, executive director of ECEAO, had no time for a Foundation Program. Addressing the inaugural meeting of the Oakville Catholic School Board on 14 January 1963, he was adamant that separate schools had a right to their share of corporation taxes.[25] Either before or after this meeting, he gave Matthews a thorough dressing down. At least, it was a one-on-one encounter. T.J. McKenna was another critic. Chairman of the Hamilton Catholic High School Board and a columnist for the *Catholic Register*, he wrote in his column of 26 January 1963 that there was a contradiction in tactics between the bishops' October brief, which he claimed called for legislative changes in the allotment of corporation taxes, and the trustees' December brief, which proposed a Foundation Program.[26]

In due time, Matthews would address both the Priester and McKenna objections, and find vindication for his interpretation of the bishops' brief – that it was an invitation to the trustees to come up with a solution. Matthews found support from no less a person than Bishop G. Emmett Carter, auxiliary bishop of London and the author of the bishops' brief.[27] But the episcopal imprimatur would not arrive in time to save Matthews from a public humiliation at the hands of fellow Catholics. The occasion was a meeting of the Willowdale Serra Club at the Bayview Golf and Country Club, in January 1963. Bishop Francis Marrocco, an auxiliary of the archdiocese of Toronto, invited Matthews to talk on financing separate schools. This is the way that Matthews, many years later, remembers the evening:

> On the very day of the dinner the Bishop was called out of town, and I proudly walked into a room of about fifty lay leaders who were total strangers. The meal was good. My speech went fine. What followed was a nightmare. Man after man rose from his seat and denounced the young pup who had the gall to suggest that corporation taxes were not going to be transferred from public school boards to separate school boards, and there was a much less controversial way to achieve parity. I recall that one man in the bear pit ended his remarks by shouting: "Too bad that Martin Quinn died recently, as he would have given you a piece of his mind." [Martin Quinn was the leader of the Catholic Taxpayers' Association during the 1930s. He died on 8 July 1949.] The knockout blow came when the obvious leader, who wanted all to know that he was a Catholic and a Progressive Conservative, rose to say that this Jesuit seminarian was clearly in bed with the opposition parties, and his leader, Premier John Robarts, would soon dismiss the crazy proposal once and for all. Crushed like an ant, I gratefully accepted a ride home to the Jesuit house at 226 St. George Street.[28]

The "obvious leader" of Matthews' tormentors could not have been more wrong in his prediction. Premier Robarts stood up in the legislature on 21 February 1963 and delivered a lengthy statement on the Ontario Foundation Tax Plan.[29] Moreover, he would make his version of the plan a cornerstone of the Conservative campaign during the election of 25 September 1963, winning 77 seats to 23 for the Liberals and 7 for the NDP. It was a stunning victory. Two weeks after Robarts' bravura performance in the legislature, Archbishop Pocock and Bishop Carter asked Matthews for his opinion.[30] He made some three-dozen marginal comments on his copy of the 21 February 1963 *Debates* and then sent copies of his annotated *Debates* to the two bishops. Pocock and Carter then asked Robert Laidlaw of OSSTA to send copies to the remaining five members of the bishops' committee on education, in advance of their meeting with the Premier in early April. Laidlaw's covering letter to the bishops is interesting:

> According to Rev. Mr. Matthews one major obstacle to financial parity was not mentioned in the legislature. It would seem that the new scheme (except for the Corporate tax adjustment grant) will continue to rely on the system whereby the Department pays a board a percentage of its approved expenditures for the previous year. The only way a board can strive for the "Equality Grants" is one year to budget for a deficit (which is illegal) or to raise the Separate School mill rate (which is odious).[31]

Matthews made public his views on the Robarts Foundation Tax Plan in a talk to the delegates of the annual meeting of OSSTA, on 15 April 1963.[32] His attempt to be fair and balanced in his presentation, in a word non-partisan, provoked one Liberal to accuse him of being pro-Conservative![33] It was a silly and absurd accusation. Matthews had actually favoured the Liberal version of the plan and did not want to see Robarts "beatified as the saviour of Catholic schools."[34] Yet he was also a realist in politics. The Robarts plan may have been imperfect, but it was "a giant step in the right direction."[35]

When Bill Davis, the minister of education, introduced the Ontario Foundation Tax Plan in the legislature on 27 January 1964, he inaugurated a virtual revolution in financing education, without transferring a penny from the tax base of the public schools to that of the separate schools, which were the greatest beneficiaries of the plan. Everything would be done by regulations, the complexity of which guaranteed political peace. In 1963, the year prior to the plan's formal implementation, separate schools (kindergarten to Grade 10) had a per-pupil revenue of $206, of which $128 was in legislative grants and $78 in taxes, for a difference of $83 compared to the per-pupil revenue of public elementary schools. That difference was very real and would never have been narrowed significantly by the standard legislative grants. In 1967, three years into the plan, separate school per-pupil revenue was $395, of which $299 was in grants and $96 in taxes, leaving a difference of $51, a direct result of the Foundation Tax Plan. Financial parity had yet to be reached, but the dramatic upwards narrowing of the gap in per-pupil revenue between the two school systems produced unprecedented "wealth" for separate schools. For the first time in the history of publicly funded education in Ontario, separate schools could plan for the future of their students without having to fear the prospect of financial collapse.

One wonders when the Robarts government would have adopted the Foundation Tax Plan as government policy, if the opposition parties had not agreed to support it and if OSSTA had not petitioned for it in its 1962 brief; one also wonders how long it would have taken the Liberal Party under John Wintermeyer to make the plan his party's policy if Carl Matthews had not spent 8 and 9 October, on his own initiative, convincing Wintermeyer to do so; and lastly one wonders when OSSTA would have petitioned for the plan, if Robert Laidlaw had not invited Matthews to speak to the trustees' provincial executive on 20 November. One wonders.

---

[1] Matthews Papers, Box 2, File 7, CJM to Archbishop Philip Pocock, 2 December 1965.

[2] Box 3, File 6, CJM to Kevin Power of Ottawa, 10 July 1968.

[3] Box 1, File 2, "Handwritten Notes," 18.

[4] Ibid., 23.

[5] Box 2, File 10, Bishop Joseph F. Ryan to George Schneider of Waterdown, 8 February 1967.

[6] Box 2, File 1, CJM to Francis G. Carter, 23 July 1961.

[7] Ibid.

[8] Box 2, File 1, CJM to Francis G. Carter, 21 October 1961.

[9] Box 2, File 1, CJM to Father Vincent Priester, 18 October 1961.

[10] Box 1, File 1, CJM to Father Vincent Priester, 29 November 1961.

[11] Box 1, File 1, CJM to Father Gordon George, S.J. [Canadian Jesuit Superior], 2 December 1961; Robert G. Laidlaw to CJM, 4 December 1961.

[12] CJM, "Trends in Ontario Separate School Finance," *Catholic Trustee* (February 1962), 4.

[13] Box 2, File 3, CJM to Father Joseph P. Finn, 31 October 1962.

[14] Box 1, File 3, CJM to D.F. Dineen, 12 October 1962.

15. Box 2, File 2, CJM to John J. Wintermeyer, 5 October 1962; Box 2, File 4, CJM to Francis G. Carter, 3 September 1963.

16. Box 2, File 10, CJM to Bishop Joseph F. Ryan, 17 March 1967.

17. Ontario, Legislature of Ontario, *Debates,* 4 December 1962, 66.

18. *Brief Presented to the Prime Minister of Ontario and to the Members of the Legislative Assembly by the Catholic Bishops of Ontario* (October 1962).

19. Box 2, File 6, CJM to Roland Bériault, 12 April 1965.

20. Box 2, File 3, CJM, "A proposed draft by Carl J. Matthews, S.J. of a section of the Brief to be presented by O.S.S.T.A. to the members of the Ontario Legislature, November 1962," 4.

21. Ibid., 2.

22. The Ontario Separate School Trustees' Association and L'association des commissions des écoles bilingues d'Ontario, *Brief Presented to the Prime Minister, to the Minister of Education and to the Members of the Legislative Assembly of Ontario* (December 1962), 6-7.

23. *Telegram,* 13 December 1962, 10.

24. CJM, "Foundation Program of School Finance as Applied to Alberta, *Catholic Trustee* (November 1962), 14-15; "Background Comments on the *Catholic Trustees'* Brief," *Catholic Trustee* (January 1963), 34-35; "Trends in Ontario Separate School Finance," *Catholic Trustee* (January 1963), 31-33.

25. *Oakville Journal Record,* 16 January 1963, 4.

26. T.J. McKenna, "The School Bag: Anglicans' Brief: It Could have Been More Definite," *Catholic Register,* 26 January 1963, 7.

27. Box 2, File 3, CJM to Bishop G. Emmett Carter, 8 February 1963; Bishop G. Emmett Carter to CJM, 8 March 1963.

28. Box 1, File 1, "Handwritten Notes," 16. The name of only one of CJM's tormentors that night has survived. He was Thomas J. Day, a lawyer. See Box 3, File 9, CJM to Thomas J. Day, 31 January 1969.

29. Ontario, Legislature of Ontario, *Debates,* 21 February 1963, 911-26.

30. Box 2, File 3, CJM to Father Gordon George, S.J., 2 April 1963.

31. Box 2, File 3, Circular Letter, Robert Laidlaw, OSSTA to _____, 3 April 1963.

32. *Proceedings of the Twentieth Annual Meeting of the Ontario Separate School Trustees' Association Held at the Royal York Hotel, Toronto April 15-16, 1963,* 15-18.

33. Box 2, File 4, CJM to Father Angus J. MacDougall, S.J., 16 September 1963.

34. Box 2, File 3, CJM to Father Joseph F. Finn, 4 April 1963.

35. Ibid.

CHAPTER THREE

THE HIGH SCHOOL CRISIS

The Happy Statistician

Carl Matthews' "Trends in Ontario Separate School Finance" was both a reason for and a justification of his lobbying for a Foundation Tax Plan for the province. "Trends" proved the need for a radical reinvention of the legislative grant as the only realistic means through which separate schools could achieve upward parity with their public school counterparts, and it proved that the Foundation Tax Plan, as flawed as it was, worked wonders. The year 1964 was the best year for narrowing the gap in per pupil revenue, from 70.2 per cent to 78.1 per cent of the public school per pupil revenue. Nineteen sixty-seven was another good year because the Corporation Tax Adjustment was calculated by the minister of education on the proportion of students enrolled, increasing the separate school portion of public school per pupil revenue from 82.7 per cent to 88.2 per cent. The numbers told the story as plain as daylight. For this improvement, Matthews gave all the credit to Dr. Joseph Fyfe of Sudbury, OSSTA's finance expert.

Also, after the first five years of John Robarts' version of the plan, the separate school enrolment statistics in "Trends" became a component in the argument for completion. They showed that the number of students attending separate schools in Ontario increased each year, not always at the same rate, of course, but always without fail, to the point that the political justification for keeping more than 400,000 students in a truncated system that ended at Grade 10 began to ring more and more hollowly. Strength in numbers – that was the trump card for separate schools. For the twenty-first and final issue of "Trends," the word enrolment was added to the title.

"Trends" was accurate, reliable and efficient in reporting. It was all about the facts produced by numbers, and the numbers did not lie; nor did Matthews ever make them lie. Each issue of "Trends" was very clear in its presentation, four pages in length – and thus quickly and easily digestible – and always revealing reading. Simply put, it was solid ammunition on the battlefield of separate school politics, especially in the hands of ambitious education critics in the legislative assembly. At "Education Estimates," in May 1972, Bernard Newman, the Liberal member for Sandwich West, overwhelmed everyone with an avalanche of numbers from that year's "Trends," without revealing his source. Newman delivered a first-rate performance. Bewildered, Thomas Wells, the minister of education, wondered aloud where Newman got his material. "Are these personal figures, or are they figures published in some report," he asked. Newman responded: "No, I am quoting figures presented in a brief, I would assume to the minister, on 'Trends in Ontario Separate School Finance,' by Carl J. Matthews, SJ. I would assume that this was presented to the minister at some time or other. His officials would have this."[1]

Printed every year for twenty-one years, beginning in 1961, "Trends" had two basic aims, which never changed: one, "to give the latest available information on the financial status of the two branches of the public school system"; and two "to put this into perspective by showing how the new figures compare with the old."[2] Inspired by Bob Wilson, the statistician for the Metro Separate School Board, Matthews was the only one in the Catholic education camp who conducted this kind of comparative analysis and shared the results of his labours. He demonstrated the difference between public and separate schools in average daily attendance (ADA), total expenditures, provincial grants and other revenue (mainly local property taxes). Three additional categories were expenditure per pupil, provincial grant per pupil and other revenue per pupil. Although all financial calculations had to be based on average daily attendance, Matthews took the trouble to present total enrolment figures for both systems for a range of years as well as the percentage of increase in enrolment for each system, plus or minus, which was very revealing. Lastly, he broke down the separate school enrolment by grade, from kindergarten to Grade 10.

According to Matthews, total revenue per pupil equaled total cost per pupil, because school boards, whether they were public or separate, typically spent every penny allocated to them. Deficits were illegal, and surpluses were non-existent. This explains Matthews' later adoption of the phrase "Per Pupil Revenue-Cost." The two words were interchangeable. Average daily attendance was changed to average daily enrolment in 1968, and total expenditures became net day school expenditures, in 1974. Over time,

"Trends" featured four new categories of relevant comparison: pupil-teacher ratio; the number of separate school pupils at English-speaking and French-speaking schools; the number of students studying French as a second language; and the relation of per pupil revenue-cost, as a percentage, between the separate and public systems.

The most complete example of per pupil revenue-cost can be found in the twenty-first "Trends" (1981):

	Public (P)	Separate (S)	Relation of S to P
1959	$291	$186	64.0%
1960	309	200	64.7
1961	328	217	66.2
1962	342	234	68.4
1963	371	260	70.2
1964	386	301	78.1
1965	409	329	80.3
1966	456	377	82.7
1967	484	427	88.2
1968	574	506	88.2
1969	641	577	90.0
1970	719	663	92.2
1971	766	730	95.3
1972	837	797	95.2
1973	885	857	96.8
1974	997	968	97.1
1975	1,219	1,213	99.1
1976	1,437	1,422	99.0
1977	1,604	1,576	98.2
1978	1,772	1,750	98.7
1979	1,955	1,924	98.4

"Trends" for 1961 and 1962 were graduate school papers and never published. But, from 1963 onwards, "Trends" regularly appeared in full in *Catholic Trustee* and each issue was given ample coverage in the *Catholic Register*. Before an issue of "Trends" was published, however, Matthews distributed at his own expense copies to the bishops of Ontario, school inspectors, directors, school boards, which would put it on the agenda for the trustees, Catholic organizations across the province and members of the provincial parliament. Archbishop Pocock, for one, was always grateful to receive a first copy of "Trends." One year, he gave Matthews two hundred dollars towards the purchase of typewriter ribbons!

Matthews compiled "Trends" from the annual *Report of the Minister of Education*, which was available to everyone, and starting in 1970 (the tenth instalment), he used raw data from the department of education. He had a contact in the department, who was authorized to act as a liaison. Acquiring the data from her was simply a matter of asking for it. Making the calculations was Matthews' responsibility.

Not once did any statistician in the department of education challenge his figures in "Trends." That happened only when Matthews published "1971 Budgets of Ontario School Boards."[3] Using two documents circulated by the ministry of education, on 23 August and 22 September 1971, which provided for the first time figures on enrolment and revenue for both boards in each municipality, Matthews was able to show that the per pupil revenue-cost of separate school boards ranged from 66 percent to 129 per cent of per pupil revenue-cost of public school boards.[4] However, Matthews failed to include in the enrolment figures the resident-external pupils for the province's smallest boards. It was a minor oversight, but a behind-the-scenes flap followed. It drew in Premier Bill Davis, Robert Welch, the new minister of education, E.E. Stewart, deputy minister of education, J. Arthur Keddy, chief statistician at the ministry of education, and G.D. Spry, the ministry's director of school business administration who confirmed in person Matthews' figures.[5] In the end, Matthews admitted his oversight and offered to amend his figures, but he defied Welch by stating that any amendments would not affect the article's primary conclusion – "that except for the four largest Separate School Boards, all others average out to full parity."[6] It was a conclusion that the government should have welcomed, he remarked with dismay.

Matthews stopped compiling "Trends" in 1981 because the ministry of education could not provide financial data for the same grades in each system. In particular, he needed data for Grades 9 and 10 in the separate schools as if the government did not treat them as elementary grades. In the absence of such crucial data, Matthews found "it incongruous to compare average revenue-cost figures between Junior Kindergarten to Grade 8 on the one hand, and Junior Kindergarten to Grade 10 on the other."[7] For 1977 and 1978, he was forced to "guesstimate" the per pupil revenue-cost of the elementary students, on the one hand, and the Grade 9 and 10 students, on the other. Guesstimating was not Matthews' style.

In between work on the annual "Trends," Carl Matthews published other statistical work for different Catholic audiences. He was the author of "Some Facts and Figures on the English Catholic High Schools in Ontario," for the Association of Catholic High School Boards of Ontario; "How We Have Grown" and "Annual Saving to the Ontario Taxpayer," for the English Catholic Education Association of Ontario; "Closing the Gap" and "Eighty-Five Years Ago," for the Federation of Catholic Parent-Teacher Associations of Ontario; and "The Hows and Whys of School Grants," for the Ontario English Catholic Teachers' Association.[8] The last named was the most readable and authoritative history of school grants to appear in print. Carl Matthews was making a name for himself.

The Peripatetic Freelancer

The years 1963 to 1968 were some of the most energetic and productive in the soon-to-be crowded life of Carl Matthews. He was a theology student for four years and ordained to the priesthood in 1966, after which he completed his degree and served as part-time registrar at Regis College. Studying theology and preparing for ordination would have filled the plate of most of his Jesuit contemporaries, but Matthews had taken on another vocation – that of self-appointed lobbyist for separate schools, who belonged to no organization and was beholden to no political party, but was willing to work with any Catholic association committed to Catholic education and with any politician, regardless of party, who would listen to him. Matthews had struck early and struck big on the Foundation Tax Plan, convincing the separate school old guard and at least one party leader to take a radical turn in policy when it came to financing tax-poor schools. It was an unqualified victory for the Jesuit scholastic. If he had intended to become a player in separate school politics, he was now one, and it would be up to him to decide to what degree and in what fashion he wanted to be involved at the provincial level.

With the blessing of his provincial, Father Gordon George, S.J., and his successor, Father Angus Macdougall, S.J., Carl Matthews chose to stay in the game as a very active student of the school question, mainly behind the scenes, quietly but forcefully influencing policy and political direction, but also on the public platform, educating and rallying the Catholic rank and file. As soon as the Foundation Tax Plan was in place, he shifted his interest in the direction of government recognition of Catholic high schools and the completion of the existing separate school system.[9] He would work on behalf of the executives of OSSTA, OECTA and the Association of Catholic High School Boards of Ontario (ACHSBO), which was founded in 1966; he would maintain regular contact with Archbishop Pocock, Bishop Carter and Bishop Ryan as well as with politicians such as Bill Davis, Robert Nixon and Donald C. MacDonald; and he would accept numerous invitations to speak. It was quite a balancing act, between the private and the public and the religious and the political. He was in the thicket of politicking but always well above the entanglements of party politics.

Carl Matthews was not one to acquire enemies, as a way of doing business, or to hold grudges, as a way of living. After a quiet 1964, OSSTA invited him to be a member of the Finance Group at the annual general meeting in 1965, the Special Advisory Committee on School Finance, also in 1965, the Grants Committee in 1966 and two working committees: one to write the 1966 brief on improvements to the Foundation Tax Plan and the other to write the 1968 brief on larger units of administration. For someone who was not a trustee, let alone a member of the OSSTA board of directors, Matthews was very busy at OSSTA's behest and loving every minute of it, despite his oft-repeated protestations to Chris Asseff and others that his involvement was only a hobby.

Shortly after the appearance of the Ontario bishops' pastoral letter on "Ecumenism and Catholic Truth," Carl Matthews wrote Dr. Joseph Fyfe in September 1965 that "The big guns are still to be heard from; I mean the laymen who pay the costly fees for the thousands of students in our Catholic high schools. Until they are heard from, in an organized way, then we shall get nowhere. I feel that only O.S.S.T.A. can give this leadership."[10] He was right in his assessment but had to wait several years to be vindicated for placing his hopes in the trustee association. It began at a meeting of the Ontario Catholic Education Council, on 5 January 1968. With a thirteen-point memorandum written by Father Matthews, A.E. Klein, OSSTA president, voiced his support of the upward extension of the separate school system. On 2 February 1968, the OSSTA directors followed suit in a resolution drawn up by Father Matthews, who wrote a similar resolution for the consideration of the general membership at that year's annual convention:

> **Whereas** that branch of the public school system known as Separate Schools is presently cut off at Grade 10,
>
> **and whereas** this is five-sixth of the way through an integrated school program,
>
> **and whereas** there is nothing preventing the Ontario Legislature from updating the Separate School structure to meet the changing needs of Ontario children,
>
> **therefore be it resolved**
> that the Ontario Separate School Trustees' Association petition the Provincial Government to permit a Separate School Board to complete the secondary school program where there are sufficient pupils.

Eight hundred trustees unanimously passed the resolution on 27 April 1968.[11]

Matthews was occupied on other fronts in 1965. He represented OECTA at a national conference on school finance in Toronto, on 27 October, and wrote two well-argued memoranda for private circulation. The first one, dated 25 November 1965, argued against Catholic participation in a planned united appeal on behalf of all independent secondary schools for no-strings attached grants. This was no solution to financing Catholic high schools. The second one, dated 3 December 1965, made a vigorous case against shared time or shared services as a solution to the same dilemma.[12] Undergirding both memoranda was the essential belief that any compromise that might bring some temporary relief would inevitably destroy the constitutional autonomy of separate school boards and the Catholic persona of the schools under their jurisdiction. Bishop Ryan, a member of the bishops' committee on education, agreed with him.[13]

The establishment of the Association of Catholic High School Boards of Ontario (Grades 11, 12 and 13) in the spring of 1966 provided Matthews with another organizational outlet to channel his ideas and exercise his growing lobbying skills. T.J. "Ted" McKenna, the association's first president, became a close ally and friend of Matthews, who saw ACHSBO as an instrument to keep OSSTA on the straight and narrow when the time came for the trustees to present their official position on completion of the separate school system.[14] Father Kenneth Burns, C.S.C., principal of Notre Dame College School in Welland, had broached the subject of a high school association as early as November 1964.[15] There was a desperate need to speak with one voice on behalf of the Catholic high school boards and the lay advisory boards.[16] Matthews was in complete agreement. "Something must be done soon before a crisis develops," he wrote to Burns. "At the present time tuition fees are not high enough to enable the school authorities to offer the type of educational services demanded in the mid-sixties, and they are too high to be paid with equanimity by most fathers of families, especially when they are being assessed steep taxes to support the public high schools. The only solution is legislative grants, preferably accompanied by release from taxation for the academic collegiates."[17]

Matthews joined ACHSBO's Research Committee, helped to organize the association's first Study Congress, held in Toronto on 3 December 1966, and in 1967 accepted the chairmanship of a committee to investigate the status of Catholic high schools outside Ontario. His first task as a member of the Research Committee was to draw up a questionnaire for the principals of the eighty-five English-language high schools. The questionnaire was divided into nine sections: enrolment; size of school; large school types; other breakdown of all schools by type; teachers; teachers' salaries; building [physical plant]; revenue Grades 9 and 10; revenue: Grades 11-13. The final question was an open-ended one: "The consensus among the Principals is that Catholic high schools must receive new sources of revenue, or else their quality of education will decline, or they will lose all but the wealthy students, or (especially in the case of the small and medium schools), they will be forced to close."[18] An appendix gave statistics on each of the schools by name. The results, minus the appendix, were published in the OECTA *Review*.[19] In March 1967, Matthews wrote "A Proposed Outline for Case on Catholic High School Question." Divided into six sections, the "Outline" presented the facts and figures on Why Catholic High Schools?; The Historical Background of Senior Separate Schools; The Present Situation in Post Elementary Education; The Anomaly of a System that Ends at Grade 10; A Glance at Developments Outside Quebec; What Ontario Separate School Supporters Seek.[20]

There were 375 delegates and thirteen speakers, including three bishops, at the Study Congress of December 1966. Typical of Matthews, he gave all the credit for the congress's remarkable success to others, in this case to Father Patrick Fogarty, C.S.C., the new executive secretary of ECEAO and also the secretary of ACHSBO, and Ted McKenna, the association's president. Not once in his letters to Archbishop Pocock and Bishop Ryan did he mention his own contribution.[21] Matthews' comments on the Congress are revealing:

> At the dinner Archbishop Pocock "laid it on the line" for the assembled Religious Superiors. He said that public funds would never be forthcoming to the Church, to the Orders, nor even to the

new Lay Advisory Boards. It was the opinion of the Bishops that only elected Separate School boards would be eligible to receive Government money. His Grace said that the Minister of Education was now aware that we wanted the jurisdiction of such boards extended upwards, at least for the academic programs. This declaration came as a shock for some Religious who still dream of bags of money being given to independent schools.

A more general shock came the next day when Frère Omer Deslauriers told the assembly that after six months study, his Association [l'Association des écoles secondaires privées Catholiques Franco-Ontariennes] had the previous day passed a resolution requesting just that: substantial grants-in-aid to (French) private high schools. He called it "Associate School Status," modeled on the Quebec pattern. After the session I told my friend that this goal seemed unrealistic in Ontario. He considers our goal "the ideal," but claims that it is even more unrealistic in the foreseeable future.

So, at the moment, the English and French Catholics are pulling in opposite directions.[22]

Frère Omer's report was 151 pages long. Matthews thought that French Catholics had been "pushed and pulled" by Prime Minister Lester Pearson and Premier John Robarts to leave the Catholic fold and go it alone.[23] He warned Bishop Carter of the potential damage such a defection could inflict on the chances of achieving separate school extension, and he alerted Ted McKenna to the political dangers of using language as a solution to the financial problems of French-language Catholic high schools.[24] Frère Omer himself confirmed Matthews' worst fears, in a letter of 19 October 1966:

To me, it seems that our group throughout the province is ready to accept French Public High Schools with assurances for religion. The urgency is very great because in many places, the graduates from the primary schools cannot integrate fully in the actual English Public High Schools. It does not seem that the majority is ready to wait for a delay and wait for a complete system that would be Catholic because this does not appear feasible at the moment. Also, the relations between the French and English, at the level of the local boards is so tense that French speaking Ontariens do not favour a continuance of the actual set up unless something definite is done in the near future.[25]

On 30 May 1968, Premier Robarts introduced Bill 140 for the provision of public funds for French-language secondary schools within the public school system.

Despite having exams in scripture and dogma, and continuing problems coping with *De Deo Uno et Trino,* Father Matthews received permission to attend the presentation of the Ontario Catholic Education Council (OCEC) to the Provincial Committee on the Aims and Objectives of Education in the Schools of Ontario, on 11 January 1966. Chaired by Mr. Justice Emmett Hall, a judge of the Supreme Court of Canada, and his second in command, Lloyd Dennis, the committee was commonly called the Hall-Dennis Committee. Matthews and Hall had become corresponding friends after Matthews had sent him copies of his two 1965 memoranda on grants-in-aid to independent secondary schools and shared time and services. Three days before OCEC's appearance, Father Matthews wrote to Father Raymond Durocher, O.M.I., one of the presenters of the OCEC brief, that "If the opportunity presents itself I am hoping that you will say something like: 'Just last year the Saskatchewan Government extended the Separate School system from grade 8 to 12, and put the senior academic classes on an equal financial footing with the collegiates.'"[26] Matthews assured Father Durocher that such a statement would please not only Mr. Justice Hall but also Dr. J. Francis Leddy, another committee member, because both of them had been instrumental in laying the foundations for the enabling legislation, Bill 53, that had been passed without a dissenting vote in the Saskatchewan legislature in March 1964.

Along with Father Durocher, the other presenters of the brief were Bishop G. Emmett Carter of London and Dr. Laurent Desjarlais of the School of Education at the University of Ottawa. According to Matthews's report of the encounter:

> Fr. Durocher gave a 15-minute general résumé of the brief. The ensuing silence was broken when the Chairman asked what special area the delegation would like to address. Knowing that the High School Question did not take up much space in the brief, I was pleasantly surprised to hear Fr. Durocher single out this topic. Then they were off the launch pad and on target.
>
> The discussion lasted more than a half hour – longer than any other single topic. All three spokesmen were knowledgeable and persuasive (though they needed some prompting from the Chair to refer to the applicability of the Saskatchewan Plan ....)

At no time did any of the speakers divorce the financial problem of Grades 9 and 10 from that of 11, 12 and 13. Justice and equality for all was their theme. Dr. Desjarlais talked about the handicap of operating a "truncated system" at a time when the Department of Education was trying to integrate the elementary and secondary divisions. In reply to a question, Bishop Carter said that it was taken for granted that public money would be paid only to lay boards acceptable to the Minister.

Just two Committee members (out of 21) expressed basic objections to funds being allocated to Catholic high schools. As expected, my old professor, Dr. Charles Phillips, complained that the entire subject was outside the terms of reference of the investigation. The Chairman seemed pleased with the response given to this by the delegation – namely that Aims and Objectives could not be discussed in a vacuum.

Later, Mr. Muir from Hamilton said that giving grants to one denomination would open the Pandora's box and thus fragment the existing structure, since other denominations would feel entitled to them too. After an embarrassing false start at an answer (namely that Catholics are the largest denomination), the delegates quickly developed the Chairman's hints that the basic structure was not being determined in 1966, but was established prior to 1866. Since that time Quebec has provided equality for "the minority" and Ontario had not.[27]

On Saturday, 15 January 1966, Matthews had a private chat with Mr. Justice Hall that lasted nearly three hours and sent a confidential report on it to the Ontario bishops. Both men agreed that OSSTA had had a difficult time during their session on Friday but that Dr. Joseph Fyfe had been wise to insist to the committee that the trustees sought not public funds for private schools but the completion of the intended structure of the separate school system. Hall gave Matthews a warning intended for other ears that Catholic authorities should wait until the Committee on Aims and Objectives had finished its report before they submitted a brief on the future of separate schools to the government. If they did not wait, Hall would conclude that Catholics had taken the subject out of his field of responsibility.[28] Wait they did. The committee's final report, *Living and Learning,* was published in 1968, and OSSTA presented its "Equality in Education" brief in 1969.

If writing a confidential report on a private meeting looked somewhat Jesuitical, even to Carl Matthews, nothing of the sort could be ascribed to the many speeches he gave from 1965 to 1967. The School Question had become the High School Crisis. Matthews wrote about it often and at length to Bishop Carter, Archbishop Pocock and Bishop Ryan, his three main episcopal listening posts. However, to Catholic parents, teachers and trustees, he avoided the word crisis, even though it was on everyone's mind and lips, and talked instead about financial justice for Catholic high school students and the reasons for keeping their schools thoroughly Catholic. In those early years, he always spoke from a prepared text, in a manner at once professional, historical, factual and hopeful, and after every speech he willingly entertained questions from his audience. Matthews never lost hope, no matter how desperate the current situation might have been for high school students and their tuition-paying parents; nor did he seek or expect payment for his appearances. He was grateful to receive a cheque for twenty-five dollars, a rare occurrence. Quite often, he was sent home with only a box of homemade cookies and bus fare. Among his many stops on the separate school circuit were Barrie, Peterborough, St. Catharines, Hamilton, Kingston, Kitchener, Stratford and of course different venues all over greater Toronto.[29] It was exhausting but exhilarating work, on his "day off" at the seminary.

So impressed was Bishop Ryan with Matthews, the separate school stumper, that the bishop asked him to write a one-page information newsletter for the people of each parish of the diocese of Hamilton. Matthews happily complied. In Ryan, Father Matthews (a priest since 4 June 1966) had an episcopal supporter who would never desert him, and for him Matthews produced a clear and succinct summary of the facts about the High School Crisis that Catholics could use at a moment's notice. The newsletter talked about "Our Rights," "Our Commitment," "Our Financial Needs," and "Our Mandate." It ended with a lengthy and pertinent quotation from the Vatican Council's ratification of the Declaration on Christian Education.[30]

The High School Crisis was most acute and politically embarrassing in Metro Toronto. Bill Davis, minister of education, told Father Matthews as early as February 1965 of his bewilderment that the Metro Separate School Board had yet to accept grants for more than 4,000 students in Grades 9 and 10.[31] These grants were theirs to have and were now more generous than ever because of the Foundation Tax Plan. The implication was obvious: there was no use talking about separate school extension to Grade 13 unless separate school boards took the first step and extended their jurisdiction over Grades 9 and 10, which they could do on their own initiative. As the crisis developed, Father Matthews took his concerns and proposed a "solution" to Archbishop

Pocock in a letter of 26 September 1966. He made sure to pass on Davis's remarks to the archbishop. The letter is worth quoting in full because it amply demonstrates Father Matthews' depth of understanding of what was a terribly complicated issue involving the Metro Separate School Board and the Religious communities who owned and operated the overwhelming majority of the high schools in Metro Toronto. On both sides there were individuals unwilling to embrace the kind of changes necessary to staunch the crisis.

Knowing that the Catholic secondary schools in Toronto are in financial difficulty, I would like to suggest a partial solution to the problem. No doubt, Your Grace has already studied the different possibilities, including the following views. Forgive me for taking up so much of your priceless time.

I believe that every effort of persuasion must be used both on the independent school authorities and on the Metro trustees to have most of our Grade 9 and 10 students supported by provincial grants.

At the present time, only in five of the 18 schools are public funds accepted for the junior classes. This record for Toronto is the reverse of the provincial pattern. Outside of Metro there are 120 regular schools having Grades 9 and 10 (therefore not counting here the five minor seminaries). Of these, 105 are supported by provincial grants; in other words, 87 per cent. This contrasts with 28 per cent in Metro.

Such a marked difference in policy might be understandable if the Toronto Board were in a less favored financial situation. However, the reverse is true. On a per pupil basis it has larger provincial grants (about $263), and greater local revenue (about $184), than any other Separate School board in Ontario. These amounts are my estimates.

Since the year that Michael Power High School reverted to private revenue, the public grants available to it have about doubled. In fact, the "Foundation Tax Plan 1964" has had its greatest effect in Toronto.

I believe that the financial considerations that would affect a rental agreement [between the Metro Separate School Board] with the local schools [owned by religious communities] should be looked at in light of 1967 data, rather than 1963 data.

The major recommendation in the annual brief to be presented to the Government next week by the Ontario Separate School Trustees' Association has a special significance for Grades 9 and 10 in our provincial system. It is recommending that the Corporation Tax Adjustment Grant be calculated on a complex formula involving number of pupils, rather than on the proportion of residential assessment accruing to the Separate School board. Besides increasing by about one-third the C.T.A. Grant for all elementary classes, this formula would benefit for the first time the secondary classes under the Board.

By the way, the C.T.A. Grant for the Toronto Board in 1966 would perhaps average out in Metro to about $58 per pupil. Although this particular grant is higher in the city proper than in the suburbs, this factor is ignored in Metro when the money is being spent. In other words, all pupils are treated alike.

Father Doyle, C.S.Sp., Superior and Principal at Neil McNeil High School is not only satisfied with this agreement with the Board and with the Commission [The Catholic High School Commission of Toronto], but he is enthusiastic about it. He maintains that the agreement has not diminished in any way his authority as academic head of the secondary school. Principals whom I interviewed in Ottawa last month said the same thing.

I believe that it would be unfortunate if provincial grants for our senior classes throughout the Province were not forthcoming, or were delayed, due to differences between local Catholic educators. In February 1965, Mr. William Davis told me *en passant* that it was quite unrealistic for Catholics to expect the Government even to consider giving grants for senior high school classes when available funds were not being used for the junior high school grades.

Of course, no one expects all the Catholic high schools to go under elected boards. Perhaps two or three in Metro might wish to retain their independence at all costs (to themselves that is). In this respect they would be like Upper Canada College or Branksome Hall.

The Religious in Toronto at great sacrifice have operated the secondary schools, and there can be no doubt about their good will. Likewise, the Metro Separate School trustees have shown dedication to the cause of Catholic education by their efforts on behalf of some 60,000 pupils. I know that both groups have the same interests at heart: quality education, both elementary and secondary, in a Catholic environment.

Only dire financial straits made the Toronto Board decide to drop Grades 9 and 10 in 1937 (*Daily Star,* May 13, 1937). In those days of the Great Depression no one imagined that 30 years later the Board's revenue from legislative grants would increase from $8 per pupil to $263.

Knowing the special interest of Your Grace in Catholic high schools, both in the Province and in the Archdiocese, I have written this rather lengthy report. While the decision in this matter rests in other hands, I believe that the wishes of Your Grace will be of major significance. By providing so many new schools in this area, the Archbishop and the members of the High School Commission have more than done their share. Now the time has come, it seems to me, to have part of the financial burden lifted on to the broad shoulders of the Government of Ontario. The average Catholic wage earner has about reached his limit.[32]

Father Matthews sent his opinions on the subject of Grades 9 and 10 to people other than the archbishop of Toronto. Beating drums on multiple fronts, he sent letters, sometimes explanatory, at other times exhortatory, to George Schneider in Waterdown, Bishop Francis Klein of Saskatoon, Bishop G. Emmett Carter, Ted McKenna, Ed Nelligan, superintendent of the Metro Separate School Board (MSSB), and Mr. Justice Emmett Hall.[33] The matter had become something of an obsession for Matthews. He would not give up until he had been satisfied that everyone who should hear him had heard him.

MSSB was central to the success of his lobbying. The board could not ignore forever the pressure from separate school stakeholders who sent their children to Catholic high schools and were in need of financial relief. To that end, the board struck a sub-committee of the finance committee to investigate the possibility of expanding the board's jurisdiction to include Grades 9 and 10. Chaired by Ed Brisbois, a trustee, the sub-committee had three other trustees, including the board chair, Dr. John Andrachuk, four members of the board administration, a representative of the archbishop and Father Carl Matthews. In retrospect, his inclusion was highly fortuitous.

The sub-committee met in June, July, November and December 1966 and made its recommendations to the MSSB at a meeting on 12 January 1967. Dr. Andrachuk was an outspoken supporter of extension to Grade 13 but an equally outspoken opponent of absorbing only Grades 9 and 10.[34] That would be a half-measure, in his way of thinking, and tantamount to perpetual defeat. His opposition had to be overcome. Father Matthews overcame it. At one of the sub-committee meetings, he confronted Dr. Andrachuk with the Bill Davis interdiction against any negotiations on separate school extension so long as the province's largest separate school board failed to exercise its constitutional right to administer Grades 9 and 10. "You mean that we could be holding up the whole Province!" exclaimed Andrachuk at the news.[35] The answer was a simple yes. He changed his mind.

The sub-committee recommended that MSSB assume the operation, finances, educational policy and administration of Grades 9 and 10 in all the schools that had applied by 1 February 1967 to have these grades taken over by the MSSB, and that student admission to these grades be on the same basis as admission to kindergarten and to Grades 1 to 8. The entire board approved these recommendations on 24 January 1967.[36] What Father Matthews argued for in his letter of 26 September 1966 to Archbishop Pocock had come to fruition.

As if to offer practical proof of the sincerity of his own position, Father Matthews worked hard to persuade his own Religious community to transfer Grades 9 and 10 at the Jesuit-run Brébeuf High School to the MSSB. It was an uphill battle. Father Angus Macdougall, S.J., the Jesuit Provincial, applied to the MSSB, on 11 January 1967, to take over the junior grades. Father Matthews was the author of the application.[37] However, Father Robert Meagher, S.J., principal of Brébeuf and a private school man, was determined to prevent the process from proceeding. Then there was a misunderstanding between the board and the Jesuits about the classroom rental fee, which was supposed to have been $250, a figure agreed upon prior to submitting the application, but which was reduced to $200. A stalemate ensued that was ended by Father Percy Johnson, a trustee, who persuaded the board to reinstate the $250 fee, not subject to negotiation. But not even this could stop Father Macdougall from withdrawing the application on 5 May. Hearing this news from Ed Nelligan, a shocked Father Matthews wrote Father Macdougall, telling him that Brébeuf stood to lose $455 per student in its Grade 9 and 10 classes. Such a loss in revenue would be devastating to the hundreds of parents of Brébeuf students who had a very large stake in the community's decision. The letter changed Macdougall's mind. He re-applied and Brébeuf's Grades 9 and 10 were shifted to MSSB.[38] The near fiasco involving Brébeuf was hardly unique. In general, religious superiors supported upward extension but some principals, fearing loss of control, were dead set against it![39]

Things were going swimmingly for Father Carl Matthews. In April 1967, he published "Catholic High Schools – Our Right, our Heritage," a paper he had delivered at the first ACHSBO Study Congress.[40] It examined the history of various legal initiatives, including the Tiny Township Case, to have Catholic secondary education recognized as part of the separate school system. In May 1967, at the request of Lloyd Dennis, co-chair of the Hall-Dennis Committee, Father Matthews submitted a one-page outline of his ideas on separate school completion.[41] Dennis was grateful for Father Matthews' previous co-operation in supplying the committee with pertinent historical material, and he was toying with the idea of having Matthews appear in person before the committee. That would have been a feather in Matthews' cap, but it was not as important as his success in gaining the ear of Robert Nixon, leader of the Liberal Opposition in the Legislative Assembly.

It began with a letter from Father Matthews to Nixon, dated 22 March 1967. It was typical Matthews. He gave Nixon some historical and statistical material on Catholic high schools and suggested a "background" chat on the subject. In reply, Nixon invited Matthews to help the Liberal Party prepare for the education estimates that would be before the Legislative Assembly in about six weeks.[42] (Never one to play political favourites, Matthews also wrote Donald C. MacDonald, leader of the NDP, in much the same vein.)[43] Matthews finally met Nixon at a private reception for him at the Willowdale home of Barnett "Barney" Danson, on 30 August 1967. Father Lionel Stanford, S.J., rector of Regis College, was a friend of Danson and invited Matthews to come along, on the eve of his annual retreat. Although the house was crowded, the two priests easily made their way over to Nixon. They exchanged views on many things: Premier Robarts' 24 August 1967 announcement on French-language high schools (Nixon: they were long overdue); so-called French ridings in the province (Nixon: the Liberals would only have to take four out of the ten; Matthews: Nixon would need all ten to form a government and would have to trump the premier on French high schools, if he wanted to win them); religious guarantees for the French high schools (Nixon: he would look into the matter after the election); and the status of English Catholic high schools (Matthews: the problem could be solved by extending the jurisdiction of the Separate School boards) and the expanded terms of reference for the Hall-Dennis Committee (Nixon: if the committee made a recommendation concerning Catholic secondary education, "he would welcome it as having merit.")[44]

Nixon actually made this last remark in an address to all the guests. There was nothing private about it. This prompted Father Matthews to tell Father Patrick Fogarty about Nixon's remarks. Father Fogarty told Archbishop Pocock and Ed Brisbois and recommended that Father Matthews inform Mr.

Justice Hall and make a record of his visit to Danson's house[45] Matthews wrote a memorandum and in a letter informed Nixon of it. He also reminded Nixon of his pledge to support a solution to the crisis in Catholic secondary education "if perchance one is proposed in the future Hall Report."[46] This was potentially dangerous stuff, with a provincial election on the horizon. Nixon replied with a three-page letter explaining his past actions and present views on the dicey topic of Catholic high schools.[47]

Six days after the Danson gathering, Premier Robarts called an election for 17 October 1967. The Liberals suffered yet another defeat at the hands of the Conservatives, but the Liberal Party had not forgotten the Catholic high school question. In November, the party's education committee invited Father Matthews to answer a list of eleven questions.[48] He readily agreed. For two consecutive afternoons at Queen's Park, he spoke without notes into a Dictaphone on the status of separate schools in the other nine provinces. The tapes were later transcribed and copies were made for each member of the Liberal caucus.

While the election was being fought, Father Matthews was writing a speech for Arthur Maloney, a prominent Conservative and criminal lawyer from Toronto. "It was a once-in-a-lifetime opportunity," Matthews told Father Macdougall, "which I dared not bungle."[49] Maloney had been invited to address ACHSBO's second annual Study Congress, on 4 November 1967. His acceptance had been quite a coup for the association. However, he had three murder trials on his docket and no time to write his speech. Having seen some of Father Matthews' letters to the *Globe,* Maloney asked him to be his ghostwriter. Matthews took up the task with relish, even though he would have to remain anonymous. Only three or four people ever knew that he was the real author. Except for the third last paragraph and the final one, as well as several minor additions and changes to the text, Matthews was responsible for the composition of "A Reasonable Solution to the Problem Facing Catholic Public Schools in Ontario." He described the Maloney speech this way: the "approach had to be reasonable, factual, aggressive, yet conciliatory. Simply, the appeal had to be to common sense."[50]

The four hundred delegates loved what they heard. Several times they interrupted Maloney with applause, and at the end, they gave him a standing ovation. John Wintermeyer, the former leader of the Ontario Liberal Party, introduced Maloney, and Archbishop Pocock, who had just returned from Rome, thanked him. Gordon Duffin, representing the minister of education, sat quietly during the speech, embarrassed by all the hoopla.[51] One could not have blamed him if he thought that this speech like most speeches would die at the doorway after everyone had left. But it did not. ECEAO distributed more than 51,000 copies throughout the province.[52] The Maloney speech was Matthews' first bestseller. (Father Matthews also wrote a second speech for Arthur Maloney, "Our Heritage – Kindergarten to Grade 13," which he gave to the Federation of Catholic Parent-Teacher Associations of Ontario, on 21 March 1969.)[53]

All this fine progress in a unified separate school agitation came close to disintegrating with the news that the London Separate School Board and the Catholic Secondary School Board were negotiating with the London Board of Education the terms for merging Catholic Central Secondary School in London into the city's public school system. Any agreement would commence on 15 August 1967. In return for giving up the administration of the school and accepting General Vanier Secondary School as the school's new name, the Catholic Secondary School Board [the governors of Catholic Central] would retain the following rights: to decide academic staff and student enrolment, subject to approval by the board of education; to conduct the religious education program in the same manner; to have its religious and priests who were teachers wear their usual attire; to have clergymen and trustees considered "visitors" to the school; and, if not satisfied with the agreement, to return to the status quo with six months notice. The clincher to the proposed deal, of course, was that operational and capital costs concerning the school, then in serious financial difficulties, would be borne by the London Board of Education. Students in Grades 11, 12 and 13 would no longer have to pay fees.[54]

News of this astonishing and disturbing development came from none other than Bishop G. Emmett Carter. John Bennett was a trustee for both the Separate School board and the high school board. He originated the idea and moved the discussions along while Carter was at the Synod of Bishops in Rome. Soon after returning to London in late October or early November, Carter became Bennett's most enthusiastic backer. In a strictly confidential letter of 7 December 1967, to Father Patrick Fogarty of ECEAO, Bishop Carter described the draft agreement, which had yet to be signed by any of the parties or approved by the government, the "first real break in the Ontario high school picture ... it gives us practically everything we need to continue our role in high school education, without, at the same time, being obliged to continue to carry the crippling and increasingly impossible burden of finance."[55] He went on to say that "I do not consider this to be in any way opposed to the present movement but, on the contrary, a complement to it and perhaps a most important advance."[56]

There were many in the movement who did not share that opinion. Bishop Ryan, for one, was horrified that a brother bishop could break ranks on separate schools, and Carter was miffed that Ryan got hold of a copy of his confidential letter of 7 December.[57] In all likelihood, Father Fogarty informed Bishop Ryan of Bishop Carter's letter, since Bishop Ryan was the bishops' representative on the board of ACHSBO and Carter wanted to give people a chance to comment on the draft agreement, a copy of which he promised to send to Fogarty in a few days. It was probably Bishop Ryan who told the news to Father Matthews.

No one in London knew that Matthews was aware of the negotiations, and he was successful in keeping his name out of the ensuing controversy until the big meeting of all concerned in Toronto on 5 January 1968. When he wrote Father J. Harold Conway, O.M.I., principal of Catholic Central, he made only one fleeting allusion near the end of his letter to the scene in London. Instead, Matthews used the occasion to remind Father Conway of ACHSBO's recent resolutions supporting completion of the separate school system and to inform him of Brock Rideout's comments on Premier Robarts' announcement in Galt, on 14 November 1967, concerning the government's plan to merge elementary and secondary school boards into larger units of administration – for the most part, county-size boards of education. A necessary component of this plan was the integration of Kindergarten to Grade 13. This was the future for Boards of Education across the province. According to Rideout, who was in charge of changes to the annual legislative grant, there was good reason that the same future might some day belong to separate schools. Implied in Father Matthews' letter to Father Conway was a question that he wanted Father Conway to ask himself. Where would separate schools fit into this new administrative and educational scheme, if the London Separate School Board and the governors of his own school were willing to give up any hope of completion in exchange for financial relief for just one Catholic high school?[58]

In the meantime, once more courtesy of Father Fogarty at ECEAO, Father Matthews received a copy of the draft agreement, on 11 December 1967, and he immediately set about analyzing it at the request of Bishop Ryan. Finished two days later, the analysis was a thirteen-point memorandum. Points 4, 5 and 10 were the strongest:

(4) Premier John Robarts and Education Minister William Davis have said time and again in the past year that Boards of Education

must administer all the grades from kindergarten to 13 in the Public School system. With the professional staff for such an integrated program, the schooling could correspond to the unity of a child's mental growth.

(5) The Separate School system in Ontario is constitutionally guaranteed as part of the public domain ... Therefore the Government has an equal responsibility to children in this system. To solve an inseparable problem, the Government may have to extend the Catholic system so that it is not left dangling without a top [Grades 11, 12 and 13].

(10) A separate School Board has no more right to turn over the operation of the Catholic Grades 9 and 10 to a Board of Education than it has such right for Grades 1 and 2. This is a policy matter of the greatest significance and would require, at the least, the approval of the Ontario Separate School Trustees' Association.[59]

Father Matthews also hammered away on another theme: that if a Board of Education was allowed to administer a Catholic high school, there was no stopping it from demanding to administer the elementary grades. It would be the end of separate schools, a frightening prospect.

Father Matthews sent copies of the memorandum to Bishop Ryan, Archbishop Pocock, Ted McKenna, Father Fogarty, Ed Brisbois and A.E. Klein, the president of OSSTA.[60] Klein, in North Bay, was so impressed by what he read that he changed his mind on the matter. A week earlier, he had written that the transfer of Grades 11, 12 and 13 was fine with him and OSSTA, but not the transfer of Grades 9 and 10. Now he asked Father Matthews if he could send a copy to Bishop Carter under his own name and that of OSSTA. Matthews said yes, and the thirteen-point memorandum became known as "Mr. Klein's Position Paper."[61]

Father Matthews wrote his own two-page position paper, "The London High School Proposal and the Future of the Separate School System," finishing it on 31 December 1967. English and French Catholic leaders were scheduled to meet with the London Separate School Board and the governors of Catholic Central Secondary School, on Friday, 5 January 1968. The meeting, sponsored by the Ontario Catholic Education Council, would take place in Toronto (not London as Bishop Carter wanted). "To help forestall an argument over details of the Agreement," Matthews wrote to Father Macdougall, "I have tried in the enclosed paper to get to the heart of the matter."[62]

Thirty-five people were invited to what was a showdown. Archbishop Philip Pocock chaired the proceedings. John Bennett delivered a nineteen-page speech, vigorously defending the proposal, and eight people, including Father Matthews, made brief replies to Bennett. It appears that Pocock, prepped by Matthews, gave a cold shoulder to the London proposal. It also appears that ACHSBO, supported by A.E. Klein of OSSTA, re-affirmed its support for separate school completion. The trustees, in particular, would understand the value of accepting larger units of administration. Once they were in place for separate school boards, the question of the integration of Kindergarten to Grade 13 for separate schools, called continuous learning, would naturally fall onto the government's lap.[63] It made little sense to have one without the other. (The Hall-Dennis Committee, busy writing its final report, *Living and Learning,* would re-affirm this basic logic – without having to seek unanimity among its members on separate school extension. The committee tabled its report on 28 June 1968.)

John Bennett and his supporters left the meeting unconvinced, but they met their match in the London Board of Education. It would not accept the teaching of religion during regular school hours.[64] That was non-negotiable, and on that the negotiations floundered, despite repeated attempts by the separate school board and the board of governors of Catholic Central to keep them going. The crisis was over.

Even before the London imbroglio had begun, Father Matthews had urged OSSTA's directors, in a letter of 17 November 1967, to fall in line with Premier Robarts' announced intentions to amalgamate school boards. Larger school boards in the public system, a fait accompli, dictated larger school boards in the separate system, which, by constitutional right, could not be forced into amalgamation but had to ask the government to pass the appropriate legislation. In fact, it was amalgamate or perish, replied Frank Carter to Father Matthews, ten days later.[65] On 26 November 1967, in a speech to the St. Catharines Diocesan Council of the Catholic Parent-Teacher Association, Father Matthews said that regional boards based in cities or large towns should administer separate schools.[66] The days of township school boards were numbered. In mid January 1968, Dr. J.R. McCarthy, the deputy minister of education, asked OSSTA for recommendations on the establishment of larger areas of administration for separate schools. OSSTA responded by striking a working committee on 16 January. Members of the committee were Joe Fyfe, chairman, Father Raymond Durocher, O.M.I., Francis G. Carter, Ed Nelligan, Hank Lottridge and Father Carl Matthews,

S.J. Also participating in some meetings were A.E. Klein, Chris Asseff and C.P. O'Neill from the department of education. The committee held six weekly sessions between 24 January and 11 March, each meeting lasting from three to four hours.[67]

Father Matthews made many contributions to the process of writing the brief that OSSTA presented to the government 27 March 1968. He wrote a nine-page "Confidential Report," a four-page essay on "Reasons for Enlarged Jurisdictions" and an entire draft brief for the committee's consideration.[68] He succeeded in persuading his fellow committee members to include in the brief the concept of continuous education from Kindergarten to Grade 13 for separate school students and a recommendation for combined county boards, where necessary. He believed that OSSTA should propose not only outward extension – the county as the basic administrative unit – but also upward extension – completing the separate school system – and that OSSTA should demonstrate that the two were inextricably linked. However, Father Matthews did not support the idea that OSSTA should ask only for outward extension if the Robarts government immediately promised upward extension. That would have been bad politics.[69]

But success for Father Matthews came at a steep price. It was a real tug-of-war to convince some members of the committee, especially Father Durocher, that inclusion of the K to 13 concept in the brief was appropriate and even vital to the future of separate schools. Father Durocher was his biggest nemesis, fighting him every inch of the way.[70] For Matthews, this brief was the right opportunity for OSSTA "to break new ground" and "to tell the legislators that 400,000 Ontario school children deserved to have their Catholic public schooling continued after Grade 10."[71]

"An Act to Amend the Separate School Act" (Bill 168) was given Royal Assent in July 1968. It brought about radical change in the administration of Ontario's separate schools. The number of school boards was reduced from more than 450 to 63; the priest as treasurer-secretary of the local school board became a thing of the past; the one-room rural schoolhouse, a leftover from the nineteenth century, was abandoned forever; and directors of education and superintendents replaced the venerable school inspectors. This was a new era for Catholic education. Now would the Robarts government listen to OSSTA's plea for upward extension?

Father Carl Matthews was not about to wait for the ruling Conservatives to ask themselves that question. He wanted OSSTA to take the next step in the political process and prepare a brief that would deal with the completion of the separate school system. "Completion" was the word that Father Matthews used in a letter of 31 March 1968 to Nick Mancini, a Hamilton member of the OSSTA executive committee. Within three weeks, A.E. Klein, the president of OSSTA, would have to make a decision on whether to proceed, and Matthews was convinced that Mancini was "the best man to influence that decision."[72] It is not clear if Mancini took the hint and pressured Klein in the direction of Matthews' thinking, but the fact remains that OSSTA executive did establish a working committee on completion.[73] Matthews' instincts were right again, but he was not invited to be a member.

Not one to stand idle while others were carrying the separate school banner, Father Carl Matthews delivered one of the best speeches of his life on 14 May 1968 to MSSB student teachers. "Let's Finish the Job" was his personal manifesto on separate school completion. It was published in the OECTA *Review* and then in the *Catholic Trustee,* gaining wide circulation among teachers and trustees.[74] Walter Pitman, MPP, the stand-in education critic for the NDP, told Matthews that he thought the speech was "the first time that he had ever seen a good case [for completion] made on educational grounds."[75] Those words gave Matthews the kind of hope he needed to carry on.

The Equality Brief

On 15 July 1968, OSSTA invited all interested parties to submit briefs on the high school question. In its search for unity and consensus, the trustees' association would consider each brief in the course of its deliberations on the contents of its presentation to the government in the spring of 1969.[76] Meeting at Bishop Joseph F. Ryan's residence in Hamilton, on 9 August, the executive of the Association of Catholic High School Boards of Ontario chose Father Carl Matthews to write its submission. Ed Brisbois of Toronto moved and Frank Kovacs of Welland, who was president, seconded the motion; the vote was unanimous.[77] Aside from Father Patrick Fogarty, Matthews was the obvious choice. He readily accepted on condition that the association explain to his Jesuit superior the necessity of his having to spend time away from his doctoral thesis, provide him with a Dictaphone, a typist, transit tickets and expense account, and agree that the format and contents of the initial draft was his responsibility. Matthews did not ask to be paid (which was a mistake) and did not shy away from the executive exercising their right "to tear the draft apart, to the extent that they feel necessary."[78] The executive had no problems meeting these conditions, which were modest in the extreme. They paid him an honorarium of $250.[79]

Since the deadline for submissions to OSSTA was 31 October 1968, Father Matthews began work the very day he was chosen. He wrote from 9 August to the 28 September, as much as eighteen hours a day, including a forty-five-hour session over the Labour Day weekend.[80] Even though Matthews gratefully acknowledged that earlier material from Ed Nelligan and his committee was instrumental in helping him compose the brief in such a short span of time, the brief was all Matthews from start to finish, except for the ten-page summary at the beginning, which was prepared by Frank Kovacs.[81] When the 150-page brief was ready, the executive asked him to make minor changes to only twenty-three pages.[82] Father Fogarty suggested the only major change – that Parts I and II be switched around. It was a wise suggestion.[83]

Of the twenty or so submissions to the OSSTA Working Committee, *Completing Their Schooling* was the lengthiest and most comprehensive. It was also the most sustained and best-written work of Matthews' career. The unifying theme of the brief was completion of the last sixth of the separate school system. There were no side questions, such as "How should the Government finance Catholic High Schools?"[84] That was for the government to decide at some future date. Completion was in the title, with a purposeful focus on the students themselves – the brief was all about *their* education and *their* future as Catholic students in a Catholic system of education. Part I was titled The Case for Completion. Up to that point, no one in the Catholic camp had presented such an airtight argument on behalf of completing the separate school system. This was Matthews at his finest. OSSTA should have adopted Part I for its own brief. Part II dealt with the historical background, the present situation and the changing scene in Ontario. It addressed and effectively demolished a host of diversionary issues: grants-in-aid to private schools; shared time; shared services; released time or religious instruction in public schools; the demand for one school system; and affiliation with public boards of education. And lastly it dealt with the political factor. The remainder of the brief was made up of five extensive appendices: the status of Catholic schools in other provinces; elementary and secondary school enrolment by municipality; facts on individual high schools; a questionnaire to owners of present high schools; and principals' views on a solution.

Bishop Ryan rightly called *Completing Their Schooling* "compelling and instructive."[85] Francis J. MacNamara, a member of the board of governors of

ACHSBO from Sault Ste. Marie, thought that the brief's "greatest value is a source book for any protagonist of our Catholic educational cause. I find that it has all the answers I need to be totally prepared to discuss and argue the cause of Catholic education, put together in easily accessible fashion."[86] Among the governors, he was not alone in his praise. Grayce Manese, John Moher and Mary L. Rudden added their own encomiums.

Only Father Matthews could have defended ACHSBO's submission, which he did on 5 February 1969, at the invitation of the Working Committee. In his general remarks to the committee, and during the question-and-answer period that followed, Matthews was adamant that any demand for "local taxes for our purposes would be suicidal." He claimed (correctly, as events in 1986 would prove) that minor changes to the already existing corporation tax adjustment grant and the Foundation Tax Plan would provide the necessary funds to begin completion of the separate school system. Matthews also insisted that in Ontario there existed two public school systems – not one school system with two branches (C.P. O'Neill of the department of education backed him on this). On other matters, he argued that province-wide completion, one grade per year (not one board at a time, as his friend Ed Nelligan proposed), would be a suitable compromise, that any history in the brief should be limited to one paragraph and that there should be no mention of umbrella school boards (a very serpentine proposition), the abolition of Grade 13, French high schools, alternative plans or religious education.[87] Concerning religious education, Matthews argued that members of the Legislative Assembly would say, "That is not our concern but the concern of Catholic educators who should address it themselves."

Father Matthews' contribution to the process of shaping OSSTA's brief was a positive one and did not end with *Completing Their Schooling*. He may have been shunted to the sidelines by the drafter of the brief, OSSTA's research director, Father Raymond Durocher, OMI, but Matthews had his allies on the Working Committee and Advisory Board who were anxious to hear his opinions on different drafts of the brief. A.E. "Ab" Klein, Nick Mancini and Francis Kovacs, unbeknownst to each other, sent him copies of the second, third and fourth drafts, with instructions from each one not to communicate with any one else![88] The situation was ludicrous, but Matthews shrugged it off and went to work.[89] Ed Brisbois, another ally, also knew that Father Matthews was reading the brief-in-progress.[90] In February 1969, even Father Fogarty, a member of the Advisory Board, shared with Father Matthews his insider's observations on the slowly emerging brief.[91] The following month, committee chairman A.E. Klein asked Father Matthews to provide him with the political antecedents to the 1920s Tiny Township case. Impressed by Matthews' two-page rendition of the facts, Klein invited him to appear before the Working Committee on 26 March 1969, so that the entire committee could hear him and decide if any mention of the case should be included in the brief.[92] For someone who was officially on the sidelines, Father Matthews was certainly engaged at the centre of things.

From his typewriter there came a steady stream of praise, criticism and warnings on each of the drafts.[93] His two chief worries were that OSSTA would demand an immediate overhaul of local taxes to finance completion, and that it would present alternative proposals to the government. Ed Nelligan was the major force behind the idea of local financing. He steadfastly opposed the use of the Foundation Tax Plan to finance Grades 11, 12 and 13. He did not even want to use it to finance any transition period.[94] On the subject of alternative proposals, Father Matthews was blunt. "That is just not done," he wrote to Nick Mancini, "since politicians will never consider a greater if the petitioner is obviously prepared to opt for a lesser."[95]

On 26 May 1969, OSSTA delivered its long-awaited brief, "Equal Opportunity for Continuous Education in Separate Schools in Ontario" (often referred to as "Equality in Education"), to Queen's Park. That same day, Father Matthews wrote to his friend, Robert Nixon, leader of the Liberal Opposition. Matthews distanced himself from certain parts of the brief, telling Nixon that he did not accept paragraphs 34 to 37, that there was no need to amend any Act other than the Separate School Act and that "the last sixth of the Separate School system can best be completed one grade at a time."[96]

The Campaign for Completion

The OSSTA executive met with Premier John Robarts and Bill Davis, his education minister, for fifty minutes. To everyone's relief, they did not say "No" to the "Equality Brief." In the best Canadian tradition, they promised to study the whole question. For them, it was also a political matter – they would have to face re-election. The trustees responded by saying that they too had to gain re-election – in December. They came away from the meeting with no firm assurances about anything connected to the brief but believing that the premier would give them an answer before the next municipal election.[97] After speaking with Robarts and Davis, the delegation met for ninety minutes with Robert Nixon and the Liberal caucus. An unfortunate mix-up delayed their meeting with the NDP caucus until the following morning.

That the OSSTA executive presented the brief to the two opposition parties immediately after their presentation to the government was due to last minute lobbying by Father Matthews. Elie Martel of the NDP had invited Matthews to meet with the NDP caucus on 6 May. Eight members attended what turned out to be a two-hour conversation. To Nick Mancini, OSSTA president, Matthews described the meeting this way:

> They knew that the Trustees' Brief is to be presented on May 26th ... At different times they argued with one voice as follows: "Everyone knows that on such a contentious 'Catholic' issue, the Government will never give in until the two Opposition parties first go on record in favour of 'completion.' It was thus in 1962-63 on a breakthrough in elementary school financing; it was thus in Saskatchewan in 1963-64 on extending the Separate School system upwards. So the Separate School people need our support and Liberal support now. We are generally sympathetic to the case, but if we are bypassed on May 26th we shall conclude that our help is not wanted. If that much-heralded Brief is addressed only to Robarts and Davis, and if the delegation does not troop into Nixon's office and MacDonald's office the same day, then good-bye to any possibility of endorsement, from any Party." That was their unanimous feeling.[98]

This time the message was crystal clear, and Matthews' advice was heeded.[99]

Separate school supporters had to wait more than two years and for another premier for a "definitive" response to the "Equality in Education" brief. During that period, OSSTA and its partners in education orchestrated the Campaign for Completion.[100] As for Father Carl Matthews, he had returned to Toronto in late August 1969, from the first three months of his Tertianship in Auriesville, New York. For his mandated pastoral ministry, that would last the next four months, he was allowed to continue to work on behalf of separate schools. After that, however, his future appeared uncertain. "My Provincial Superior," he wrote to Nick Mancini, "says that it is time for me to begin paying back the Order for the tens of thousands of dollars it has invested in my studies towards a doctorate in Education at the University of Toronto."[101] Almost thirty-eight years old, Matthews had yet to complete the doctorate, and there was a reasonably good chance that he would be sent out of Ontario, as early as January 1970, most likely as a principal in a Jesuit high school. But he had no desire for such a posting. He had dedicated his life to the School Question and wanted to remain available to OSSTA. To prove his sincerity, Matthews told Mancini that he had turned down two handsome job offers in the ministry of education:

> A year ago May, the Minister of Education called me in and suggested that I join his Department. I was flabbergasted, though cool to the idea. Only two people know of that proposal: Father Fogarty and Mr. Nelligan. The very next day Father advised against it, as he felt that the Honourable Mr. Davis was simply trying to silence me. "Remember what happened to J. Bascom St. John a few years ago?" I remembered. When he joined the Department's Policy and Development Council, his writings against Departmental policy [in the *Globe and Mail*] came to a firm halt.
>
> Last June I told Ed Nelligan about the Minister's suggestion. His reaction was expressed in the same words. "Remember what happened to J. Bascom St. John? Don't bite. Keep your integrity as a Catholic writing on the School Question."
>
> So I put the thing out of mind. Then a few days ago, for the first time in 16 months, the Minister [Bill Davis] called me in again. In an hour's private chat he begged me to join the Education Dept. I reminded him "that all he knew about me during the [past] seven years, he had gotten from conversations, articles, reports, memorandums, speeches, on one single theme: parity for Separate School pupils. Therefore if he wanted me, he must have been impressed by that work. Well, I felt an obligation in conscience to continue that work. It could be done on the Trustees' team; it could not be done as a Civil Servant. No matter what senior officer was my boss, he would not be a Catholic school man, and would prohibit all lobbying for parity for kids in Catholic public schools."
>
> To make a long story short, I said to the Minister of Education, "Thanks for the nice offer, but my ties are with O.S.S.T.A. in the future. There I can do more good than here, as much research on aspects of the School Question still has to be done."[102]

In a letter to Bishop Ryan, Father Matthews claimed that the salary for the job that he had turned down was worth $22,000 a year![103] Since he had earned only $2,100 from 1967 to 1969, as income for work on the School Question, this was quite a refusal. During those years, not a nickel had come his way from Father Fogarty at ECEAO.[104] Thus began a series of begging letters to be hired as OSSTA's research specialist, now that Father Raymond

Durocher's workload had increased after he became acting editor-in-chief of the *Catholic Register*.[105] Any objective person would have seen that Father Carl Matthews would have been ideal for the position, a real asset. He had a proven track record of research and publications, including the indispensable "Trends in Ontario Separate School Finance," and he was on excellent terms with all the right people in the three political parties at Queen's Park.

Objectivity, however, was not forthcoming. Neither was gratitude. All that OSSTA offered him was employment, "from time to time, at a fee, for specific research."[106] It was not much but Matthews took it because at last OSSTA would begin to pay him consultant's fees for his professional services to the trustees. For the first time in his career, he had at least semi-official status and felt free to have a business card describing himself as a "Consultant on Ontario Separate Schools." OSSTA sweetened things, in October 1970, by paying him $1,000 for past services.[107] A bargain, it was long overdue and much welcomed. Obviously given in good faith, it might also have been issued as a salve to help ease the pain that Father Matthews had experienced earlier in the year when OSSTA's Working Committee had criticized him for sending copies of a commissioned work to Archbishop Pocock, Bishop Ryan and Des Burge, the Director of Information for MSSB.[108] (At the time, the Working Committee, sometimes referred to as the Equality Committee, was writing a brief to the government on implementing the recommendations of the "Equality in Education" brief.) The work in question was Father Matthews' dissection of a January 1970 brief to the government by the Ontario Public School Trustees' Association.[109] "A Unified Secondary School System for Ontario" was OPSTA's official response to OSSTA's "Equality in Education." It was a potentially dangerous document, especially if the Conservatives decided to use it in their own defense. Matthews' twelve-page critique was the perfect tonic, yet it was all but ignored in the rumpus over what was at worst an honest mistake.

Living with OSSTA was not easy. How ironic, then, that OECTA was far more generous. Mary Babcock, executive director, was more than happy to pay Father Matthews a retainer of $3,500 a year, for research articles on completion and for book reviews, starting in September 1970.[110] That OSSTA would not even match this offer, in November 1970, was a terrible letdown for Matthews, but it appears that it was not enough of a blow to convince his Jesuit superiors to transfer him out of province.

So much for making a living and for staying in Ontario. Father Matthews knew that Premier Robarts' public hostility towards completion would make it difficult to keep everyone in the separate school camp marching in the same direction. The longer he was hostile, the more likely some Catholics would break ranks and offer solutions other than completion. He summarized the situation in a letter to Chris Asseff:

> Those on the right (notably some high school principals), will be all for aligning with private schools of any denomination, in order to seek grants-in-aid. That would weaken our case.
>
> Those on the left will advance the merits of shared time, umbrella boards, or federation with the collegiates. That would wreck our case. Of even greater consequence in the long run would be the effect on our Separate School Boards in the operation of Grades K to 10. Their hard-won autonomy would be put in jeopardy by any such scheme ....[111]

Father Matthews would end up fighting two very lonely battles with his separate school colleagues – on immediate local taxes to fund Catholic secondary education and on joint or umbrella school boards – as OSSTA's Working Committee wrote their Implementation Brief, which was presented to the government on 8 June 1970. On both issues, Matthews' delivered a resounding no. To insist on local taxes, as opposed to an extension of the Foundation Tax Plan, would torpedo the "Equality in Education" brief. To agree to joint school boards would destroy the autonomy of separate school boards. Indeed, over time, separate schools would vanish at the hands of a veto vested in the public school boards. However, since Matthews was not a member of the Working Committee and did not see any part of the brief until August, and then only Part I,[112] he had a frustrating time making himself heard and having his Catholic friends take him seriously. He was forced to turn to hectoring by letter, which always carries with it the possibility of making oneself a pest to the very people one wants to convert. Matthews came perilously close to just that as he hammered away on both fronts.

Ed Nelligan, MSSB director of education, was the strongest advocate of using local taxes as the means to finance extension. His close ally was Joe Fullerton, a member of the board.[113] Nelligan had convinced OSSTA to insert a local taxes demand, albeit obliquely, in their brief of May 1969. As soon as Matthews had returned from his Tertianship in August, he responded with a five-page position paper written over the Labour Day weekend and dated 1 September 1969. After sitting on it for a week, for fear that he had been hasty, he sent copies to OSSTA directors as well as to the Ontario bishops. Believing that it was the best thing that he had ever written,[114] he framed the debate as between "Some Local Financing" versus "No Local Financing" and came down on the side of the latter for the following ten reasons:

1. only it is politically possible;
2. only it is economically possible;
3. only it does not require amendments to the Board of Education Act and the Assessment Act;
4. only it provides for completing the schooling of pupils presently in Catholic public classes; only it keeps the spotlight off students presently in private classes;
5. only it provides for phasing in the program one grade per year for three years;
6. only it does not favour Boards in the few largest cities;
7. only it does not complicate the Franco-Ontarian situation, or keep the latter from exercising a veto over any Separate School breakthrough beyond Grade 10;
8. only it has the felicitous precedent backing it of the Foundation Tax Plan, 1964, as presently revised by the Rideout formula;
9. only it will make it possible for the Ontario Government to bring in enabling legislation on completion of the Separate School system;
10. only it will work in practice, for all.[115]

It was "No Surrender" time for Father Carl Matthews. Two weeks later he sent a slightly amended version of the position paper to each County and District Committee for Equality in Education. He reduced the ten reasons to eight and put them on the first and second pages. The response to his paper from separate school officials, in particular those from outside Metro Toronto, was generally positive.[116] One person whose mind was changed was Bishop G. Emmett Carter of London, chairman of the Ontario Bishops' Committee on Education. To A.E. Klein, Carter wrote:

> I was particularly impressed by the position paper of Father Matthews concerning the tax base. You will recall that in our long and interesting conversation in North Bay [where Klein lived], when the ["Equality in Education"] Brief was in embryo form, I took a rather strong position on yielding our tax base.

> Since my present views represent a shift in my convictions, I think it only fair to acquaint you with the fact that this change is taking place. Although I tend to hold my opinions rather strongly, I hope I shall never be slow to change them when someone produces conclusive arguments. I find Father Matthews' arguments quite conclusive.[117]

Matthews was ecstatic. "Coming at this time," he wrote Carter, "it meant more to me than any letter I had received in my life."[118] This was Matthews at his hyperbolic best. Converting Carter, a kingpin in the Ontario hierarchy, was a major coup. "In Toronto I have been thrown to the wolves, and it seems that my friends here are afraid to stand up and defend me. People at the Toronto School Board say I have undercut the Cause! Father Durocher has bitterly assailed both the Position Paper and my sending it out."[119]

The Jesuit had let his guard down, and the bishop took it all in stride. Indeed, Carter's letter of reply is striking in its affirmation of Matthews' argument against asking the government for local taxes:

> Just in case my letter to the Trustees did not come through clearly enough on the subject, I want you to know that the opinion I expressed appeared to be the unanimous opinion of all of the bishops assembled at the Canadian Conference of Ontario. There was no formal statement or motion passed but there was not a single dissenting voice when I presented my position on your Paper. The only bishop missing was Archbishop Plourde of Ottawa, so you can consider that you have the practically unanimous support of the bishops, at least for the general position you have taken and their appreciation of your stand.[120]

Bishop Carter's letter to A.E. Klein must have had some effect on the trustees. On 22 November 1969, OSSTA decided that a local tax base, as a funding source for Catholic secondary education, was as *an ultimate goal.*[121] Ed Nelligan then forwarded a copy of the trustees' proposal for a five-year phase-in programme for local taxes.[122] Father Matthews thanked him for his courtesy but was dismayed to understand that by continuing to insist on local taxes, the separate school trustees were still willing to disrupt the financing of the public secondary and elementary schools.[123] The public school trustees would never accept that, he warned them. However, for the trustees even to entertain a five-year phase-in was partial victory for Matthews.

Nothing of the like, though, could be said about Matthews' battle over umbrella school boards. The crux of the matter was OSSTA's Implementation

Brief that was presented to the government on 8 June 1970. Central to the brief were four projections or options for financing completion. Projection I would have adjusted the assessment to allow separate school ratepayers to opt into supporting K to 13. Projection II was Father Durocher's proposal for umbrella boards. Projection III sought the application of the Foundation Tax Plan. Projection IV was Ed Nelligan's proposal for local taxes plus grant financing of secondary education.[124] Projections I, III and IV allowed the independent operation of separate school boards, free from interference of any kind from the local Board of Education. Projection II did not. Its most perilous part, according to Father Matthews, was paragraph 18: "An Inter-Board Committee to consolidate these respective appropriations as well as deal with sharing and phasing-in, subject to approval of respective boards before finalization of joint decisions."[125] The vote to approve the insertion of Projection II was 14-3, with Michael Carty, president of ACHSBO, Father Frank Kavanagh, O.M.I., 1st vice-president of OECTA, and Bishop Joseph F. Ryan of Hamilton opposing the resolution. Bishop Ryan subsequently resigned from the committee over the issue. If implemented, the Board of Education would have a veto over the capital and operational expenses of the separate school board. It would amount to the biggest giveaway in the history of separate schools.

Father Matthews waged war against Projection II, paragraph 18 on many fronts. OSSTA had to remove the embarrassing passage from the 8 June 1970 Implementation Brief to preclude any attempt by either the government or the public school trustees from taking political advantage of it. He wrote letters (many lengthy) to Bishop Ryan, Ed Nelligan, A.E. Klein, N.A. Mancini, Father Patrick Fogarty, the OSSTA Directors, Dr. Joe Fyfe, Bishop Thomas B. Fulton, the bishops' representative on the K-13 Working Committee, Mary E. Robida, president of the Federation of Catholic Parent-Teacher Associations of Ontario, the K-13 Working committee and even Bill Davis, the minister of education.[126] All to no avail. Projection II remained a part of the brief.

Complicating matters for Father Matthews was a mistake in the official recording of the vote on Resolution No. 47 at OSSTA's annual general meeting on 9 April 1970. The resolution stated, "the Ontario Separate School Trustees' Association explicitly affirms that the autonomous existence of Separate School boards is not negotiable with any body."[127] Father Matthews had written the resolution as a pre-emptive strike against Projection II in the forthcoming brief, and the Frontenanc-Lennox and Addington County RCSS Board sponsored it at the AGM. There is no doubt that Resolution No. 47 passed, but for some inexplicable reason, the *Catholic Trustee* claimed that it had not been approved.[128] It was an egregious mistake, but OSSTA refused to correct it.[129]

Father Carl Matthews had a good objective reason for defending the jurisdictional independence of separate school boards, aside from the fact that umbrella school boards would have been impossible for more than one-third of the county separate school boards because by design their boundaries were not coterminous with their public school counterparts. Rather, it was a question of why would OSSTA want to undermine the policy positions of the NDP and the Liberals on the subject of completion. By the end of 1969, both parties had come out in favour of it, and their respective positions assumed the autonomy of separate school boards.

On 16 October 1969, the NDP published a discussion paper called "The Financial Crisis in the Catholic High Schools." Prior to its appearance, Father Matthews had worked hard to convince Donald MacDonald, the NDP leader, to reject the concept of umbrella boards.[130] Matthews succeeded. MacDonald's rejection held fast when the twenty-three-member NDP caucus announced its official policy on completion on the heels of a two-day meeting in December. The party's main condition for full grants to Catholic students from Kindergarten to Grade 13 was that "Separate School Boards and Public School Boards join in planning shared facilities and services to meet the needs of all students in every community."[131] Father Matthews could live with that condition. There was no mention of umbrella boards in the December document and no mention in Donald MacDonald's remarks to the Ontario Legislature on 3 March 1970, which was subsequently published as a pamphlet under the title "Equality for Separate Schools." Before his retirement as NDP leader, in October 1970, MacDonald praised Matthews:

> We in the New Democratic Party have tried to deal with the issue on its merits, in as completely rational a manner as possible. I think we have succeeded to some degree in helping to create that kind of climate for its consideration. But if we have succeeded in doing so, it has been (speaking for myself) because of the help which people such as you have given us. It has not only been unstinting, but of such a quality that my understanding and respect for your views has grown throughout the process.
>
> In fact, without your assistance, the course of political events might have been very much different. I am personally very grateful ....[132]

Robert Nixon and the Liberal Party, the Official Opposition at Queen's Park, were next on board. The Liberal caucus published its "Statement" on separate schools on 4 November 1969. It stressed the pedagogical and administrative reasons for completion, never straying into the murky waters of local taxes or umbrella boards. Father Matthews spent most of that day in his favourite place – the Speaker's Gallery at the Ontario Legislature. Nixon generously acknowledged Matthews' assistance, particularly during the three weeks leading up to the unveiling of the "Statement." Matthews could not hide his enthusiasm for the document. "It is cogently and dispassionately argued," he wrote to the Liberal leader, "and merited the top headlines it got in today's newspapers."[133] Matthews continued:

> At different times over the weeks and years it was my privilege to discuss the matter with you. We hit it off well. The statement's reference to the "factual and statistical summary of the situation which was completed in November 1967" brought back memories of talking into your Dictaphone for four hours then, faced only with a list of factual questions from staff-lady Wendy Hansen. Three months earlier we had had a spirited and delightful exchange at the home of Mr. Barney Danson. Then there was the lunch at Stop 33, and the phone call a week ago to check out some statistics.
>
> The policy statement of November 4, 1969 puts hundreds of thousands of Separate School children and their parents in your debt. Ontario education will be the better because of the stand of your Caucus and the Liberal Party.[134]

Nixon placed his leadership of the Ontario Liberal Party on the line at the party's February 1970 convention, when he defended caucus's stance on separate schools.[135] It was a bravura performance, in the face of considerable grumbling and even some outright hostility. Father Matthews appreciated and applauded his courage, quietly and privately.[136]

The recipe for political success was starting to take shape. Two out of three parties at Queen's Park had finally sided with separate school aspirations. They had adopted completion of the system as party policy. It was time to work on the ruling Conservatives and their supporters in the media. Father Matthews, ever the strategist, put forth his ideas for the final phase to Chris Asseff, OSSTA executive secretary:

> If we can convince the Premier and his Cabinet and the editors that Catholics are concerned with the common good, that we have no intention

of weakening the Public high school system, that we don't intend to build a secondary school in every town with a Separate elementary school, that most of the 69 private school buildings would be handed over free, that we realize that some technical programs will be too expensive to provide even in the cities – then I believe our case can be won.[137]

Time would prove Father Carl Matthews' political instincts to have been right. It was the greatest irony of his separate school career that during 1969 and 1970 he had a far more harmonious and productive relationship with the NDP and the Liberals than he did with OSSTA. But if that bothered him to any discernable degree, he never dwelt on it for too long. Matthews was a good soldier. Despite the debilitating infighting with the trustees and others, many of whom he counted as good friends, and not just colleagues, he never quit the team.

That is why when asked to contribute to the public campaign for completion, he did so willingly and cheerfully and often anonymously. For ACHSBO, he wrote three capsule comments on the School Question. They were "A Historical and Legal View"; "A Financial View"; and "A Solution." (Ed Nelligan wrote the other three, which were "The Reason Why"; "Steering the Ship"; and "The Inside Story.")[138] ACHSBO distributed hundreds of thousands of copies of these commentaries. He also wrote "A Talk in the Parish Church at Sunday Mass," to be delivered by a layperson.[139] For the separate school rally at Maple Leaf Gardens, on 25 October 1970, Father Matthews wrote the address given by Jerry Collins, president of the Ontario Catholic Student Federation. Collins was too busy organizing the rally, which was attended by 20,000 people, to write his own speech. He turned to Father Matthews, who kept it to four tightly written pages that eschewed attacks on the government and delivered a message that was positive and hopeful.[140] No one at the time knew that he had written the speech. His next assignment came from OECTA. In May and June 1971, he produced five one-page bulletins on various aspects of completion, a total of 300,000 copies which were distributed on successive Wednesdays, beginning 12 May.[141] Later that year, he added three more.[142] Also for OECTA, he gave two articles for the *Completion Campaign Handbook 1971*. They were "Excerpts from the Historical Background of Catholic Education in Ontario (Secondary)" and "The Hows and Whys of School Grants."[143] To this body of writing should be added three other articles: "Funding Catholic Schools: A Canadian Way," which appeared in the Jesuit weekly *America*, "Richard W. Scott: Architect of the Catholic School System in Ontario," and "We Want a Vigorous System" (on Thomas O'Hagan), both of which were published in the OECTA *Review*.[144] Father Matthews sent copies of the article in *America* to the premier and his twenty-three cabinet ministers and to Robert Nixon and Donald MacDonald. MSSB made copies of the Richard W. Scott piece for each Grade 8 student in its schools.

The Conservatives took 823 days to respond to OSSTA's "Equality Brief." Bill Davis, who had become premier in February 1971, was the one to give the answer. He called a special caucus meeting for 27 August. An election was pending. It would be Davis' first as leader of the Conservative Party of Ontario. The overwhelming opinion of the caucus was that if the party adopted separate school completion as policy, voters, especially those who lived in rural areas, would punish the Conservatives at the polls. Davis had no stomach for defeat, and he had no intention of losing an election over separate schools. His political instincts told him to follow his caucus. In a prepared statement, given at Queen's Park on 31 August, he unequivocally rejected completion. Although he admired Ontario's separate schools, appreciated their role in the history of education in the province, and was committed to protecting their constitutional rights, as premier he was determined to uphold "the principle of a free, non-denominational and non-sectarian secondary school system, accessible to all and supported by all."[145] There was no side to Bill Davis: he sincerely believed what he said.

The premier called an election for 22 October 1971. The Conservatives won 44.5 per cent of the popular vote and more importantly, 77 out of 117 seats. Crushed were both the Liberals and the NDP, supporters of completion. The Liberals dropped from 27 to 20 seats, and the NDP from 21 to 19 seats. The campaign for completion came to a dead end. Or so it seemed that day.

There was no one more shocked by Davis' announcement than Father Carl Matthews. He certainly was not surprised by the election results, having long considered Davis the province's most masterful politician. But Matthews expected statesmanship, not political cleverness, from his good friend when it came time, as he saw it, for the Conservatives to join forces with the Liberals and NDP in the name of equality for Ontario's 400,000 separate school students. He felt let down by the premier, and therein we have the story of Father Carl Matthews, Jesuit priest, and Bill Davis, Protestant politician, or Carl and Bill, as they came to address each other in their letters.

1. Ontario, Legislature of Ontario, *Debates,* 26 May 1972, 2858.

2. Matthews Papers, Box 1, File 12, "Trends in Ontario Separate School Finance," the third (1963), the fifth (1965) to the fifteenth (1975), seventeenth (1977) to eighteenth (1978), and the twentieth (1980) to the twenty-first (1981).

3. CJM, "1971 Budgets of Ontario School Boards," OECTA *Review* (December 1971), 22.

4. Box 4, File 17, CJM to E.E. Stewart, 22 December 1971.

5. Box 4, File 18, CJM to E.E. Stewart, 10 January 1972; J. Arthur Keddy to CJM, 10 January 1972; CJM to Robert Welch, 13 January 1972; Robert Welch to CJM, 21 January 1972; E.E. Stewart to CJM, 27 January 1972; William G. Davis to CJM, 15 February 1972.

6. Ibid., CJM to Robert Welch, 13 January 1972.

7. Box 1, File 12, "Trends in Ontario Separate School Finance," the twentieth (1980), 2.

8. Box 2, File 13, 14 November 1967, CJM, "Some Facts and Figures on the English Catholic High Schools in Ontario, 1967-1968"; CJM, "English Catholic High Schools in Ontario 1968-1969," OECTA *Review* (December 1968), 52-54; "Some Facts and Figures on the English Catholic High Schools in Ontario, 1968-1969," *Catholic Trustee* (March 1969), 11-14; "How We Have Grown," ECEAO, *The Spotlight: News & Views on Catholic Education* (Autumn 1967), [2]-[3]; "Annual Saving to the Ontario Taxpayer," ECEAO *The Spotlight: News & Views on Catholic Education* (October 1968); "Closing the Gap," CPTA, *Echo* (February 1971), 6; "Eighty-Five Years Ago," CPTA, *Echo* (February 1972), 6-9; "The Hows and Whys of School Grants," OECTA *Review* (March 1971), 38-40.

9. Box 2, File 6, CJM to J.W. Fyfe, president, OSSTA, 24 March 1965.

10. Box 2, File 7, CJM to Dr. J.W. Fyfe, 7 September 1965.

11. Box 3, File 2, CJM to N.A. Mancini, 21 January 1968; attached to the letter is "A Draft Resolution for the O.S.S.T.A. Convention, 1968." See also: Box 3, File 15, CJM to Monsignor B.J. Walsh, 31 January 1970: "To this day only two people know that the resolution putting O.S.S.T.A. on record for K to 13 originated with M."

12. Box 2, File 7, CJM, "A Memorandum Concerning a United Appeal to the Ontario Government on Behalf of all Independent Secondary Schools," 25 November 1965, and "A Memorandum Concerning Shared Time or Shared Services as a Solution to the Financial Disabilities of Catholic High Schools in Ontario," 3 December 1965.

13. Box 2, File 8, Bishop Joseph F. Ryan to CJM, 6 January 1966.

14. CJM to the author, in reply to a fax from the author dated 7 August 2003.

15. "Catholic High Schools: Joint Front Ask," *Catholic Register,* November 1964, 1.

16 If a Religious community owned the high school, its operation was in the hands of the community and its board was strictly advisory. The main task of advisory boards was to find the ways to fund the salaries of lay teachers. At one time, religious communities owned thirty-five out of thirty-six Catholic high schools in Metro Toronto. If the diocese owned the high school(s), the high school board gave direction to the principal and looked after lay salaries. All boards were members of ACHSBO.

17 Box 2, File 5, CJM to Father Kenneth Burns, C.S.C., 23 November 1964.

18 Box 2, File 9, "Report on the 1966-67 Questionnaire to the Catholic High School Principals," 5.

19 CJM, "Report on 1966-67 Questionnaire to Catholic High School Principals," OECTA *Review* (April 1967), 45-46.

20 Box 2, File 10, "A Proposed Outline for Case on Catholic High School Question," March 1967.

21 Box 2, File 9, CJM to Archbishop Philip F. Pocock, 11 December 1966; CJM to Bishop Joseph F. Ryan, 11 December 1966.

22 Ibid., CJM to Mr. Justice Emmett M. Hall, 19 December 1966.

23 Ibid., CJM to Bishop Joseph F. Ryan, 11 December 1966.

24 Box 2, File 8, CJM to Bishop G. Emmett Carter, 7 January 1966; Ibid., CJM to T.J. McKenna, 1 April 1966.

25 Box 2, File 9, Frère Omer Deslauriers to CJM, 19 October 1966.

26 Box 2, File 8, CJM to Father Raymond Durocher, O.M.I., 8 January 1966.

27 Ibid., CJM, "A Report on a Public Hearing which discussed, among others, the subject of integrating Catholic High Schools in Ontario."

28 Ibid., CJM, "A Report to the Episcopal Committee on Education re a conversation with Mr. Justice E.M. Hall, Chairman of the Committee on Aims and Objectives of Ontario Education, January 15, 1966."

29 Box 2, File 7, CJM, "Financial Justice for Ontario Catholic High School Students" and "Should We Keep Our Catholic Schools?"

30 Box 2, File 10, "A Newsletter," 27 March 1967.

31 Box 3, File 3, CJM, "Some background notes concerning the 1968 chats with the Minister of Education." The meeting between Davis and Matthews took place on 26 February 1965 and lasted 100 minutes. See Box 2, File 6, CJM to Roland Bériault, 12 April 1965.

32 Box 2, File 9, CJM to Archbishop Philip Pocock, 26 September 1966.

33 Ibid., CJM to George L. Schneider, 1 November 1966; CJM to Bishop Francis Klein, 19 November 1966; CJM to Bishop G. Emmett Carter, 22 November 1966; CJM to T.J.

McKenna, 25 November 1966; CJM to Ed Nelligan, 25 November 1966; Box 2, File 12, CJM to Mr. Justice Emmett Hall, 23 August 1967.

34 "Extension through Grade 13 urged for separate schools," *Globe and Mail*, 4 January 1967, 5. Andrachuk made these comments at the inaugural meeting of the MSSB. His comments ignited a storm of controversy in the *Globe* and caused considerable hand wringing from Father Matthews. He felt obliged to respond to a *Globe* editorial of 10 January 1967 with a letter to the editor, 1 February 1967, and to write to Bill Davis. See Box 2, File 10, CJM to Bill Davis, 7 January 1967.

35 Box 3, File 3, CJM, "Some background notes concerning the 1968 chats with Minister of Education."

36 Box 2, File 9, "Report of Sub-Committee of the Finance Committee Concerning Expansion of the Grades 9 and 10 Programme," 12 January 1967; "Metro School Action Aids Plea for Grants," *Catholic Register*, 4 February 1967, 1.

37 Box 2, File 10, Father Angus J. Macdougall, S.J., to The Catholic High School Commission of Toronto, 11 January 1967.

38 Box 2, File 10, CJM to Father Angus J. Macdougall, S.J., 19 February 1967; Box 2, File 11, CJM to Angus J. Macdougall, S.J., 12 May 1967.

39 Box 2, File 11, CJM to Archbishop Philip Pocock, 15 May 1967.

40 CJM, "Catholic High Schools – Our Right, Our Heritage," OECTA *Review* (April 1967), 8-11, 62.

41 Box 2, File 11, CJM to Lloyd Dennis, 16 May 1967.

42 Box 2, File 10, CJM to Robert Nixon, 22 March 1967; Robert Nixon to CJM, 23 March 1967.

43 Ibid., CJM to Donald C. MacDonald, 22 March 1967; Donald C. MacDonald to CJM, 29 March 1967.

44 Box 2, File 12, "A Memorandum of Remarks of Ontario Liberal Leader, Robert Nixon, Aug. 30 1967, re Catholic High Schools."

45 Ibid., Father P.H. Fogarty, C.S.C. to CJM, 1 September 1967.

46 Ibid., CJM to Robert Nixon, 4 September 1967.

47 Ibid., Robert Nixon to CJM, 7 September 1967.

48 Ibid., CJM, "re Liberal Caucus," [no date].

49 Box 2, File 14, CJM to Father Angus J. Macdougall, S.J., 30 November 1967.

50 Ibid.

51 Ibid., CJM to Mr. Justice Emmett Hall, 15 November 1967.

52 ECEAO, *The Spotlight* (October 1968).

53 Box 3, File 10, Arthur Maloney, "Our Heritage – Kindergarten to Grade 13."

54 Box 3, File 1, copy of a draft agreement, 1967.

55 Ibid., Bishop G. Emmett Carter to Father Patrick Fogarty, C.S.C., 7 December 1967, 1.

56 Ibid., 2.

57 Ibid., Bishop Joseph F. Ryan to Bishop G. Emmett Carter, 11 December 1967; G. Emmett Carter to the Bishops of Ontario, 12 December 1967.

58 Ibid., CJM to Father J. Harold Conway, O.M.I., 9 December 1967. Father Matthews, Mike Carty of Kingston, Jim Murphy of Toronto, Jack LeSage of Tweed and Mary Ruddin of Cornwall drafted the ACHSBO resolutions. See Box 2, File 13, "Resolutions Passed at the Second Annual Study Congress of the Association Held on November 4th and 5th, 1967."

59 Ibid., CJM, "Memorandum Re a Possible Agreement Between a Board of Education and a Catholic High School Board."

60 Ibid., CJM to Bishop Joseph F. Ryan, 9 December 1967.

61 Ibid., CJM to Archbishop Philip Pocock, 13 December 1967.

62 Ibid., CJM to Father Angus J. Macdougall, S.J., 2 January 1968.

63 Ibid., Father Patrick Fogarty, C.S.C., to A.E. Klein, 22 January 1968.

64 "London board rejects plan for RC aid," *Globe and Mail*, 9 January 1968.

65 Box 2, File 13, Francis G. Carter to CJM, 27 November 1967.

66 "Regional Separate School Boards May be Next Step in Province," *St. Catharines Standard*, 27 November 1967.

67 Box 3, File 3, CJM to Bishop Joseph F. Ryan and T.J. McKenna, 12 March 1968.

68 Ibid., CJM, "A Confidential Report to the Special Committee on Larger Areas, to the Executive and the Directors of O.S.S.T.A.," 2 February 1968; "Some possible thoughts for inclusion in the middle part of the O.S.S.T.A. Brief on Larger School Areas," 16 February 1968; "A draft tabled by Fr. Matthews," 4 March 1968.

69 Ibid., CJM to Patrick J. Whelan, 29 April 1968.

70 Ibid., CJM to Dr. J.W. Fyfe, 6 March 1968; CJM to Bishop Joseph F. Ryan and T.J. McKenna, 12 March 1968.

71 Ibid., CJM to The Directors, Ontario Separate School Trustees' Association, 5 April 1968.

72 Ibid., CJM to N.A. Mancini, 31 March 1968.

73 Box 3, File 4, CJM to A.E. Klein, 4 June 1968.

74 Box 3, File 4, CJM, "Let's Finish the Job," 14 May 1968. See also CJM, "Let's Finish the Job," OECTA *Review* (October 1968): 25-28; CJM, "Let's Finish the Job," *Catholic*

Trustee (November 1968): 15-19.

75 Ibid., "A memo for my records," 1968, 4.

76 Box 3, File 6, OSSTA to Father Mathews, 15 July 1968.

77 Box 3, File 5, Francis J. Kovacs to CJM, 14 August 1968; Box 3, File 6, CJM to Father Patrick Fogarty, C.S.C., 10 August 1968.

78 Box 3, File 6, "A Memorandum," 9 August 1968.

79 Box 3, File 5, Father Patrick Fogarty, C.S.C., to CJM, 14 November 1968; CJM to Father Patrick Fogarty, C.S.C., 17 November 1968.

80 Box 3, File 10, CJM to F.J. Kovacs, 6 March 1969.

81 Box 3, File 5, CJM to Bishop Joseph F. Ryan, 15 August 1968; handwritten addition at the bottom of the second page of the letter.

82 Ibid., CJM, Memorandum to the Twenty-man Board of Governors of ACHSBO," 6 November 1968.

83 Ibid., CJM to Francis Kovacs, 16 October 1968.

84 Box 3, File 6, CJM to Kevin Power, 10 July 1968.

85 Box 3, File 7, Bishop Joseph F. Ryan to CJM, 21 October 1968.

86 Box 3, File 5, Francis J. MacNamara to CJM, 10 December 1968.

87 Box 3, File 9, Francis Kovacs to Father Patrick Fogarty, C.S.C., 20 February 1969, "Re: February 5, 1969 Meeting, 3-7. See also, Ibid., CJM to Francis Kovacs, 23 February 1969. On the subject of umbrella boards, see Ibid., CJM, "A Memorandum Requested by Francis J. Kovacs: Some Thoughts on Umbrella School Boards, and on David M. Cameron, M.A., of O.I.S.E.," 24 February 1969.

88 CJM, interview by author, 30 October 2001.

89 Box 4, File 1, CJM to N.A. Mancini, 1 March 1970.

90 Box 3, File 8, CJM to Ed Brisbois, 24 November 1968.

91 Box 3, File 9, CJM to Father Patrick Fogarty, C.S.C., 19 February 1969.

92 Box 3, File 10, Albert E. Klein to CJM, 5 March 1969; CJM to Albert E. Klein, 11 March 1969; Albert E. Klein to CJM, 13 March 1969.

93 The letters from CJM concerning the brief are too numerous to cite or even list. They are located in Box 3, Files, 8, 9 and 10. For one excellent example of his commentary on the brief, see Box 3, File 10, 1 March 1969, "General Comments on the Draft Brief."

94 Box 3, File 8, CJM to Francis Kovacs, 24 November 1968.

95 Ibid., CJM to N.A. Mancini, 30 November 1968.

[96] Box 3, File 11, CJM to Robert Nixon, 26 May 1969.

[97] Ibid., CJM to Francis Kovacs, 27 May 1969. This letter is an in-depth account of 26 and [27] May 1969. It covered three meetings - Robarts-Davis; the Liberal Caucus; and the NDP Caucus (27 May) - and the Premier's statement to the House on 27 May.

[98] Ibid., CJM to N.A. Mancini, 7 May 1969.

[99] Ibid., N.A. Mancini to CJM, 9 May 1969.

[100] Franklin A. Walker, *Catholic Education and Politics in Ontario*, vol. 3 (Toronto: Catholic Education Foundation of Ontario, 1986), 308-65; Michael Power, *A Promise Fulfilled: Highlights in the Political History of Catholic Separate Schools in Ontario* (Toronto: Ontario Catholic School Trustees' Association, 2002), 421-44.

[101] Box 3, File 13, CJM to N.A. Mancini, 13 September 1969.

[102] Ibid., 2-3.

[103] Box 3, File 14, CJM to Bishop Joseph F. Ryan, 14 October 1969.

[104] Box 3, File 16, CJM, "Income for Work on the School Question, from the time I came to Bellarmine Hall," 31 January 1970.

[105] Box 3, File 13, CJM to N.A. Mancini, 28 September 1969. See also, Box 3, File 15, CJM to N.A. Mancini, 18 November 1969.

[106] Box 3, File 15, Chris Asseff, executive secretary of OSSTA, to Father E.F. Sheridan, S.J., 25 November 1969.

[107] Box 4, File 6, OSSTA to CJM, 26 October 1970.

[108] Box 4, File 2, CJM to Edward J. Brisbois, 5 March 1970.

[109] Ibid., CJM, "Re The Brief Presented to the Government of Ontario, January 21, 1970, by the Ontario Public School Trustees' Association," 15 February 1970.

[110] Box 4, File 5, CJM to Mary Babcock, 19 July 1970.

[111] Box 3, File 12, CJM to Chris Asseff, executive secretary of OSSTA, 29 July 1969.

[112] Box 4, File 5, CJM to Bishop Joseph F. Ryan, 20 August 1970.

[113] Box 4, File 8, CJM to N.A. Mancini, 2 January 1971.

[114] Box 4, File 4, CJM to N.A. Mancini, 10 June 1970.

[115] Box 3, File 13, CJM, 'Memorandum on a Method of Financing Completion of the Separate School System in Ontario," 1 September 1969.

[116] Box 3, File 13, CJM to Bishop G. Emmett Carter, 27 September 1969.

[117] Ibid., Bishop G. Emmett Carter to A.E. Klein, 19 September 1969 [copy to CJM].

[118] Box 3, File 14, CJM to Bishop G. Emmett Carter, 2 October 1969.

[119] Ibid.

[120] Ibid., Bishop G. Emmett Carter to CJM, 7 October 1969.

[121] Box 3, File 15, Francis J. Kovacs to CJM, 25 November 1969.

[122] Box 4, File 1, B.E. Nelligan to CJM, 30 January 1970.

[123] Box 4, File 2, CJM to B.E. Nelligan, 3 February 1970.

[124] Box 4, File 6, CJM to Bishop F. Ryan, 26 October 1970.

[125] Ibid.

[126] CJM to Bishop Ryan: Box 4, File 5, 20 August 1970, File 6, 26 October 1970, File 7, 4 November 1971, 24 November 1970, 29 December 1970, File 9, 17 March 1971; to Ed Nelligan: Box 4, File 3, 28 April 19670; to A.E. Klein: Box 4, File 3, 28 April 1970, File 8, 24 February 1971; to N.A. Mancini: Box 4, File 4, 7 May 1970, 10 June 1970; to Father Patrick Fogarty: Box 4, File 5, 16 August 1970, File 7, 20 November 1970, File 8, 14 January 1971; to OSSTA Directors, Box 4, File 7, 1 November 1970; to J.W. Fyfe: Box 4, File 7, 16 November 1970; Bishop Thomas B. Fulton: Box 4, File 8, 7 January 1971; to Mary E. Robida, Box 4, File 10, 16 April 1971; to Bill Davis: Box 4, File 7, 17 December 1970; to K-13 Working Committee: Box 4, File 9, 10 March 1971.

[127] Box 3, File 16, "Resolution No. 47."

[128] *Catholic Trustee* (September 1970), 36.

[129] Box 4, File 7, CJM to The Directors of OSSTA, 1 November 1970; CJM to Bishop Joseph F. Ryan, 4 November 1970; CJM to Directors of OSSTA, 21 November 1970.

[130] Box 3, File 7, CJM to Donald C. MacDonald, 7 June 1969; Box 3, File 13, CJM to Donald C. MacDonald, 14 October 1969.

[131] Box 3, File 15, Walter Pitman to CJM, 23 December 1969; attached to the letter was a copy of "NDP Policy on the Financing of Catholic High Schools."

[132] Box 4, File 7, Donald C. MacDonald to CJM, 28 September 1970.

[133] Box 3, file 15, CJM to Robert Nixon, 4 November 1969.

[134] Ibid.

[135] *Toronto Star,* 21 February 1970, 2.

[136] Box 4, File 1, CJM to Robert Nixon, *Telegram*, 21 February 1970.

[137] Box 3, File 16, CJM to Chris Asseff, 11 January 1970.

[138] Box 3, File 9, ACHSBO, Capsule Comments, 5 February 1969.

[139] Box 4, File 7, CJM, "A Talk in the Parish Church at Sunday Mass," [no date].

[140] Box 4, File 6, CJM, "Address by Jerome Collins," 25 October 1970; Box 4, File 10, Jerry Collins to CJM, 23 April 1971.

[141] Box 4, File 10, CJM to Mary Babcock, 16 April 1971 and the 24 April 1971; Box 4, File 12, CJM to A.E. Klein, 1 June 1971.

[142] Box 4, File 11, OECTA, "Separate School Supporters," 12 May 1971, 19 May 1971, 26 May 1971, 2 June 1971 and 9 June 1971; File 14, "Separate School supporters," 6 October 1971, 13 October 1971, 20 October 1971.

[143] OECTA, *Completion Campaign Handbook* 1971 (20 May 1971), 4-9 and 19-23.

[144] CJM, "Funding Catholic Schools: A Canadian Way," *America* (September 1969), 231-32; "Richard W. Scott: Architect of the Catholic School System in Ontario," OECTA *Review* (October 1969), 5-8; "We Want a Vigorous System," OECTA *Review* (December 1970), 40-41.

[145] Honourable William Davis, "The Question of Extended Public Assistance to the Separate School System," (Tuesday, 31 August 1971), [5].

CHAPTER FOUR

FRIENDSHIP WITH THE HON. BILL DAVIS

Father Carl Matthews recognized a good man and a potential ally on separate school matters in the person of Bill Davis, who was minister of education from October 1963 to February 1971, when he became premier of Ontario. The two men are close in age (Davis was born in 1929 and Matthews in 1932), and they share the same basic temperament (friendly always, frank when necessary and forthright in their opinions and feelings). Whenever an opportunity arose to correspond or to meet in private at Queen's Park for one of their occasional chats, they were honest and up front to a degree that might surprise and even annoy those cynical of clerics in collars and politicians in suits cozying up to one another. That old chestnut about the separation of church and state, now adopted by so many Canadians, never entered the picture to spoil a perfectly legitimate friendship. Neither man practiced guile. Rather, each was a convenient sounding board for the other. For Father Matthews, the outsider, his communications with Davis were a chance to hear the word as it was spoken and acted upon in the inner sanctum of power and influence; for Bill Davis, surrounded by aides and advisors, and cooped up for long periods in the legislative hothouse, his chats with Father Matthews and his letters to him were good opportunities to air hypothetical scenarios or to draw lines, as he saw fit, separating the possible from the impossible, knowing that his Jesuit interlocutor, having received good political advice from the top, would not hesitate to share it with his separate school confreres.

Between 1965 and 1972, Matthews and Davis exchanged a total of fifty-three letters, fifteen of which were written by Davis, and they met on five different occasions: 26 February 1965, 7 February 1967, 2 May 1968, 28 May 1968 and 4 September 1969. These meetings lasted anywhere from thirty-five minutes on one occasion to more than two hours on another. For three of them, Father Matthews wrote detailed and revealing accounts. What began as a polite and diplomatic discourse evolved into a bond of friendship, one that was sufficiently strong and durable to survive the disastrous fallout of 31 August 1971.

On one side of the conversation stood Matthews, the self-described student of the school question. He was the supplicant, so to speak, always digging ever so gingerly and steadily to see if he could discover and bring to light Bill Davis' true feelings about separate schools, always taking the time to thank him and Premier John Robarts for the Foundation Tax Plan, always ready to defend Davis against all critics, especially those loose cannon Catholics who had little or no political sense and were inclined to attack Robarts and Davis on every public platform.[1] Matthews began one letter to the *Catholic Register* with these words: "Poor Mr. Davis. On the school question he is taking it on the chin from both those who are against and those who are for extension. This school year with a decision teetering in the balance it seems incongruous for Catholics to treat men like him as foes."[2] Father Matthews even attended the Conservative Party convention that selected Davis as their leader, in the early hours of 13 February 1971. He sat near the Davis family, at one point helping the photographer Dick Loek of the *Telegram* get a shot of the Davis daughters.[3] After Davis won on the fourth ballot with 812 votes, he kindly autographed Matthews' tally sheet.

On the other side of the conversation was Davis the political survivor, who was willing to listen and debate but never made empty promises or gave away his strategy. Any hint of hope on separate schools was inevitably wrapped in layers of caution. He liked Father Matthews because, as he told him, "we talk the same language on the same wave length."[4] This was high praise indeed. Interestingly, not once but twice did Davis offer Matthews a position in the administrative branch of the department of education, first in May 1968 and then in September 1969.[5] His offer was either a recognition of Matthews' considerable knowledge of education policy and history, from a separate school point of view, or a ploy to silence him into civil servant servitude. After reading their correspondence, one can only believe that Davis's offer was absolutely sincere. Flattered, even flummoxed the first time the offer was made, Matthews declined on both occasions, citing his independence and desire to keep working on behalf of separate schools.

They wrote and talked about many matters, such as grant regulations, the promotion of Catholics in the department of education, the minister's *Annual Report,* the state of Matthews' doctoral dissertation, the Hall-Dennis Committee, the annual OSSTA convention, larger units of administration, Premier Robarts, Matthews' more recent publications, including the annual

"Trends," and a host of pleasantries about the Davis's family vacations in Florida and the like. But the only real topic on Father Matthews' mind was the completion of the last sixth of the separate school system. His goal was to convince Bill Davis of the unassailable merits of completion; he dearly wanted Davis to be known by posterity as the premier who finally gave justice to separate school children after more than a century of political agitation. Father Matthews' hopes were high, but he was bound to be disappointed. His enthusiasm for the cause and his loyalty to Davis blinded him to the political realities of winning an election in 1971.

Let us listen to Father Carl Matthews and the Honourable Bill Davis in their own words, in a selection of letters leading up to and away from 31 August 1971.

17 December 1970

Dear Bill,

All best wishes. I have long believed that you are the logical successor to Mr. Robarts. Many separate school people, prominent and otherwise, tell me that they remain to be convinced that you are the man for the job. I am trying to convince them.

As a fan of yours I have been troubled by a speculative story passed on by a R.C. leader. It goes like this: if Mr. Davis wins the Leadership in February, he will appoint a French-speaking separate school supporter, e.g. Fern Guindon or René Brunelle, as Minister of Education. Then before the general election they will announce that "extension" will be permitted under terms of local umbrella school boards.

Let me explain, briefly, the problem with that solution.

Separate school boards have local autonomy from kindergarten to grade 10. You will agree that, by and large, they are doing a good job, without causing the Cabinet concern about exorbitant spending of provincial funds. To judge how effectively umbrella boards might operate, one need read only the brief a year ago from the Public School Trustees' Association. It was totally negative in tone. From that evidence there can be no doubt that members of Boards of Education would veto or simply shelve vital matters affecting progress for the local separate School Board. Even as recently as this

Fall, O.P.S.T.A. went on record in telling the Prime Minister [Premier John Robarts] in a widely circulated letter: "Sir, the long range position of this Association is that there should be only one educational system in the Province of Ontario."

Separate school trustees will not join forces at the municipal level with people who actively seek their demise. That would be foolish, to say the least. So, just extend their local autonomy for the final sixth of a normal program.

To save money, you can do it a grade per year, beginning with grade 11 next September. To diminish controversy, you need not transfer a dollar of realty taxes away from the Boards of education. Your grants plan will do the job....[6]

5 January 1971

Dear Father Matthews,

... I was deeply moved by your kind remarks. You are one of the few people who have kept an eye on me for the past eight years or so since I assumed my present portfolio, and I am proud to count you among my friends as well as an honest and objective, but sympathetic, critic. It means a great deal to me to know that my stewardship in this office has gained your approval. I have tried to do the things that I felt needed to be done and I am grateful for the splendid co-operation I have received from so many people, both in the Department and in the whole field of education....[7]

The following telegram from Father Matthews was a reaction to a 22 January 1971 front-page story in the *Toronto Daily Star*. The headline read, "Davis rules out extended aid to separate schools."

24 January 1971

I have praised and defended you through thick and thin. So this friend is deeply offended if you are the first against completion. You were going to win the Party leadership anyway. Now you have cinched it....[8]

7 February 1971

Dear Carl,

...It had been my hope that the matter of extension of the Separate School system would not become an issue during the present leadership campaign, and no one regrets more than I do [that] this hope was not realized.

Prime Minister Robarts has made a tremendous contribution not only to Ontario but to all of Canada through his calm and reasoned approach to many matters which could otherwise have proven divisive. His administration has been particularly sympathetic and generous to the Separate Schools of this province, a fact which is totally rejected by the vast majority of Roman Catholics who have written us regarding this matter.

The demands made by the Separate School supporters have come at a time when high costs coupled with "tight money" do not make the taxpayers very receptive to any suggestion which might be construed, even remotely, as cause for further tax increase. Then, too, I am sure you will appreciate that there is a large group of people who feel very strongly that the education system should not be further fragmented. I have no doubt that, given time, the Government could sort out all these opinions and counter-opinions, financial and philosophical problems, etc., and reach at least a compromise.

Unfortunately, the more militant Separate School supporters have focused attention on this very sensitive matter at a most inopportune time. Several meetings during the campaign at which I have spoken have been picketed – which I understand completely. However, at the Ottawa meeting a person in the audience became quite insistent that I should at that moment give an unqualified "yes" or "no". My reply was "at the moment – no". The press was there; the incident received wide publicity and the whole issue has polarized public opinion.

You have known me for some years, Carl, and I believe you are aware that I have always believed that more can be accomplished by a "low-key approach". Many of the reforms credited to me have been developed along these lines, and this is the way I must continue to work. I will not be pushed – especially during a political convention when everything I say is particularly vulnerable to misinterpretation.[9]

Bill Davis was now premier of Ontario.

21 May 1971

Dear Father Matthews,

... So far as the problems that face us with regard to additional financial support for the Separate School system are concerned, I share your hope that this may be resolved before long and I sincerely trust that the results will find a reasonable degree of acceptance by all.[10]

6 July 1971

Dear Mr. Prime Minister,

Greetings. I can hardly wait. It won't be long now. For it was on April 23rd that you promised "a definitive statement within three months." In Windsor.

The other day while searching through old files for something else, I came upon a memorandum about our discussion on Feb. 7 1967. It had been written that evening. Reading it 4½ years later, we can chuckle together – on the eve of the Grade 10 breakthrough....[11]

24 August 1971

Dear Mr. Prime Minister,

Greetings. After such a busy Session of the Legislature, you will have welcomed the break, if not the rest, of recent weeks. Last Friday, while visiting my brother in Ottawa, I just missed by a few minutes your stroll down the Sparks Street mall.

Since receiving your encouraging letter of May 21, I have been waiting, more or less patiently, for the long-awaited announcement on the school question. Except for Joseph Fullerton, Separate School confreres of mine have "cooled it", in order that you can announce the breakthrough. Hopes are high. That letter was good news for those of us who have tried over some years to present the case for "completion" in a reasonable way, on educational [pedagogical] grounds.

Theresa, the future nun, and Carl, the future priest

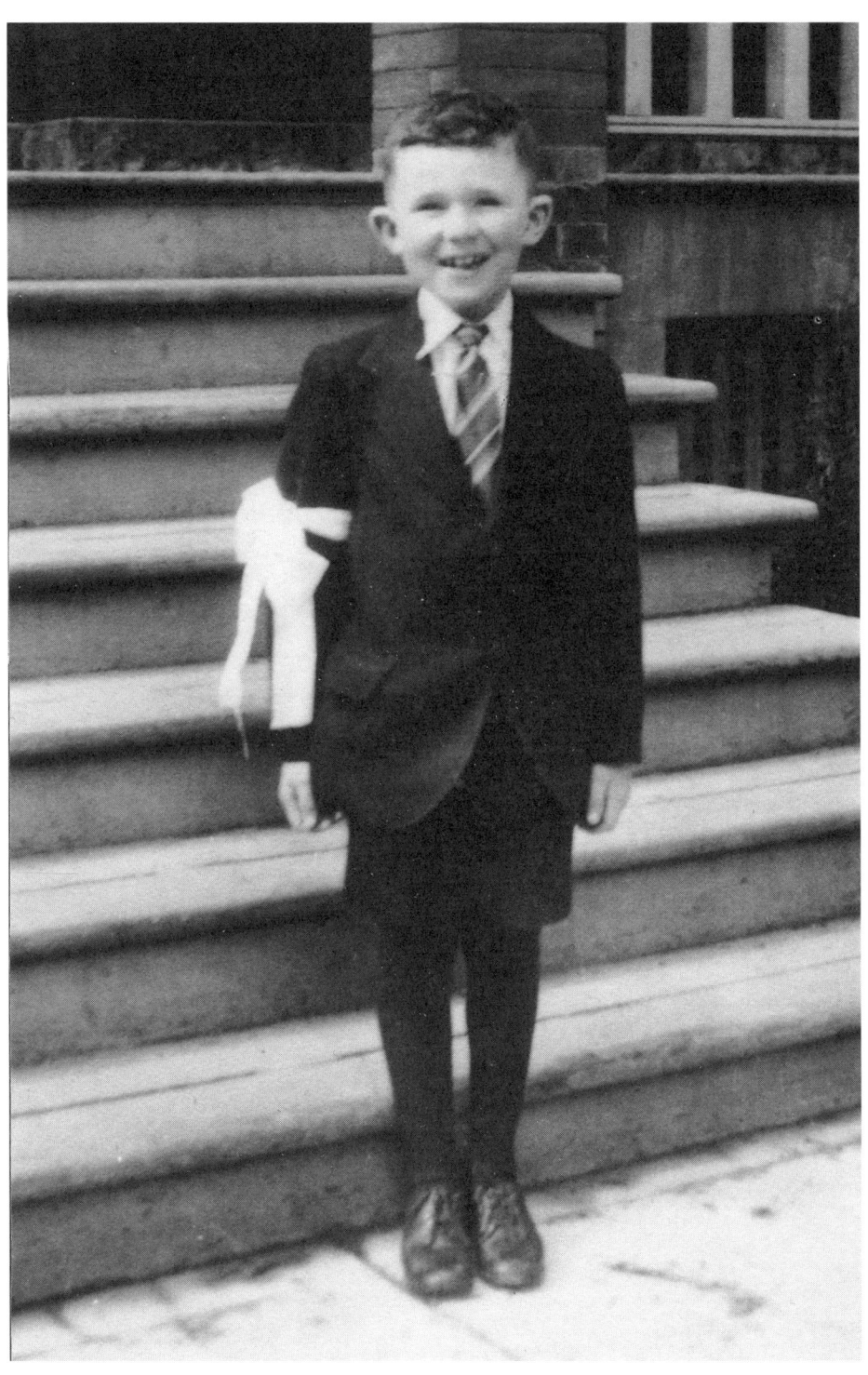
Carl on his First Holy Communion, St. Mary's Cathedral, Kingston, 28 May 1939

The Matthews Family, Christmas 1941

Director of the drama *Twelve Angry Men*, at Regiopolis College, Kingston, May 1959

Floyd Patterson, World Heavyweight Champion,
with Carl (upper right hand corner) and some of his Jesuit confreres,
at the Jesuit residence in Toronto for Mass, 3 December 1961.
It was the day before his seventh defense of his title

Ordination Photograph of
Father Carl J. Matthews, S.J., 4 June 1966

Father Carl gives the main address at the blessing of Sir Richard Scott Catholic School in Toronto, 1 June 1969.
Also on stage, left to right: C.P. O'Neill, chief inspector of the English Catholic schools in Ontario; Monsignor Percy Johnson, chairman of the Metropolitian Separate School Board; Archbishop Philip Pocock of Toronto

Father Matthews in the cathedral tower,
Piazza San Marco, Venice, May 1975

Hon. Bill Davis
Photo Credit: Peter Canton, Gerald Campbell Studios

Father Carl's tally sheet at the Ontario Conservative Party Convention, Maple Leaf Gardens, 13 February 1971. It was signed by Bill Davis, the winner

Father Carl leaves Our Lady of Lourdes parish, 11 December 1988, after ten years on the staff

Members of the Philippine community at Our Lady of Lourdes bidding farewell to Father Matthews

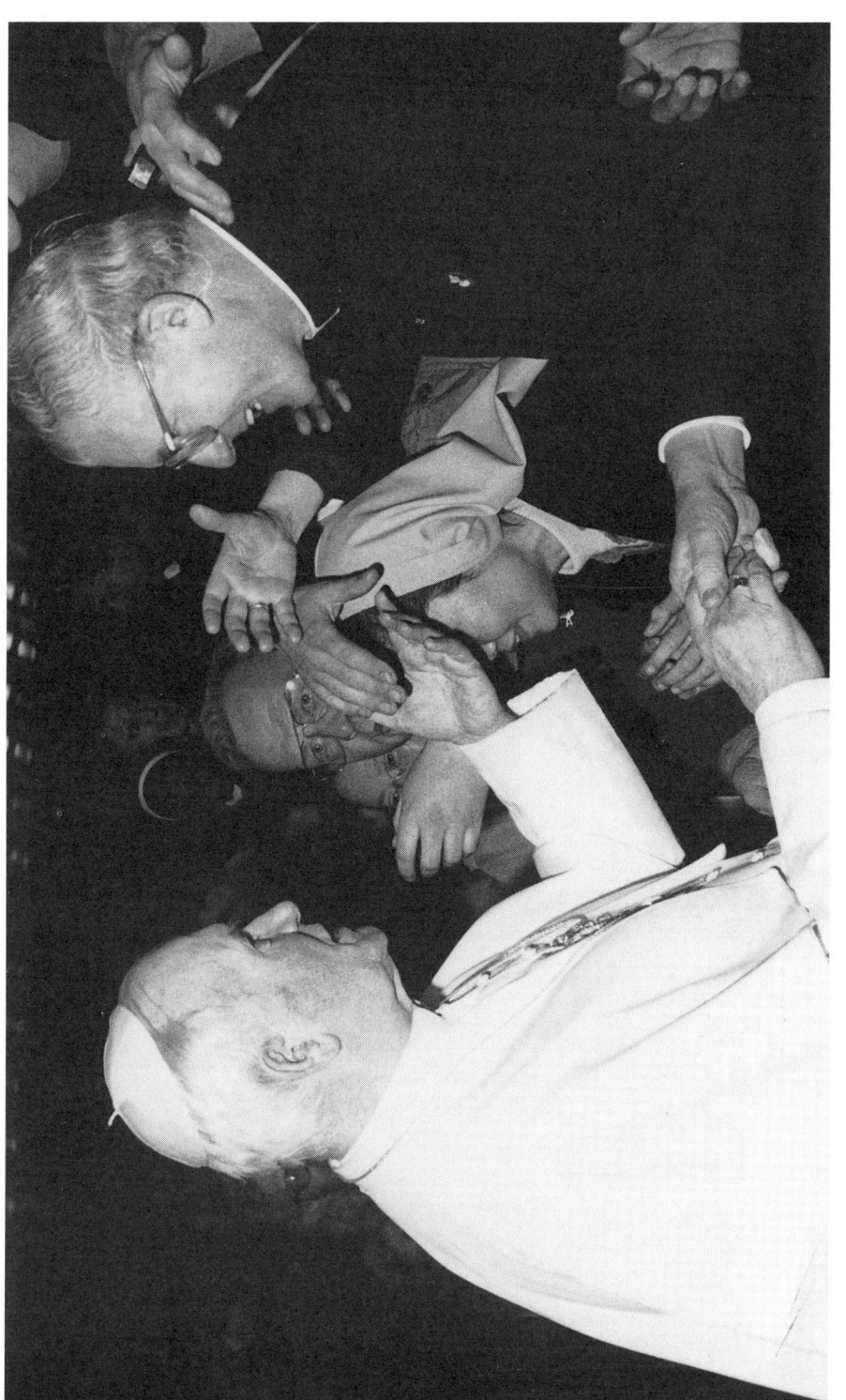

Father Matthews and John Paul II, Rome, May 1989. *L'Osservatore Romano*

Editorial

Why vote No?

On the 26th of this month we Canadians will be making history. In a rare national referendum we shall pass judgment on the Charlottetown accord signed by our political leaders in August.

The polls show it going down to defeat. Many westerners say the accord gives too much to Quebec, and must be rejected. More massively, Quebecers say the agreement gives far too little to them, and must be torpedoed.

Pierre Trudeau and Jacques Parizeau, Preston Manning and Judy Rebick, are leaders of the No forces - though they have nothing in common other than a two-letter word.

And that's what is so worrisome. How can we possibly build a nation, how can we even keep it from breaking up like Yugoslavia, if Canadians of different polarities interpret a No result as a victory?

Such a result will only bring lasting bitterness from one end of the country to the other.

Premier Robert Bourassa will be repudiated at home, and the platform of *indépendance* could then prevail in Quebec's general election next year. The upshot would be the physical cutoff of the Maritime provinces.

More immediately, international investment will flee the troubled country, countless jobs will be lost, mortgage rates will devastate families.

These are not threats. They are consequences.

The issue this week is not Prime Minister Brian Mulroney. A No response will not hasten his departure from office. Why should it? The accord is supported by all three federal parties, by all 10 premiers, by the aboriginal leader, by the Territories, by business and labor.

Where the Yes forces have faltered is in their mindless commercials and in their boring repetition in print of the entire text of the agreement.

Our dear nation of Canada was built on compromises. John A. MacDonald, George Brown and Georges Etienne Cartier were political enemies when they sat at that conference table in Charlottetown on Sept. 1, 1864. But they hammered out an agreement called Confederation.

Sadly, their regional supporters saw it as a selloff to another part of the land. So it probably would not have survived a referendum. And we would still be colonists of England.

To keep Canada together, to respect our differences still, 128 years later, takes courage and generosity.

Whether we like it or not, we do have a referendum next week. It is time to pray. It is time to act. For the sake of Canada - not any region, but our nation - this national weekly, *The Catholic Register* urges readers to vote Yes.

Catholic Register front-page editorial, 24 October 1992

Father Matthews with Tom and Shirley O'Hara, life-long parishioners of St. John's parish in Waubaushene, on their Golden Wedding Anniversary, June 2004

Cover of St. John's parish bulletin, 8 May 2005

Father Carl hitching a ride for Mass on Christian Island

Father Carl and Angelita Galicia, 92,
Mexico City Shrine of Our Lady of Guadalupe, April 2003

Ontario

Congratulations

FATHER CARL MATTHEWS, S.J.
50th Anniversary as a Jesuit

On behalf of the Government of Ontario, I am pleased to congratulate you as you celebrate the 50th anniversary as a member of the Society of Jesus.

As friends pay tribute to your work and dedication to the Catholic Church, to your community, and to the advancement of education in Ontario, I am pleased to extend my warm, best wishes for many more years of happiness and fulfilment.

Mike Harris
Premier

August 15, 2001

Fiftieth Anniversary as a Jesuit. Signed by Premier Mike Harris, 15 August 2001

The Grade 10-11 breakthrough will take courage on your part. But as Prime Minister you showed that courage when you insisted on a consistent age for majority, even when backbenchers were opposed to lowering the age for drinking. Hence I am confident of your big decision this week on the Separate School question.[12]

The Conservative caucus had met on 27 August and rejected completion.

28 August 1971

Dear Mr. Prime Minister,

The events of the past weeks have left me depressed. One has only to re-read the frenzied editorials to realize that this Province, which has been so peaceful for twenty years, is moving towards the most awful of all conflicts, sectarian strife. Only you can nip it in the bud. Only you can head off it next week.

Public observers, like John Zaritsky, speak much of your prowess as a political opportunist. But - as they did for Mr. Frost and Mr. Robarts - they do not speak of you as a statesman. That realization must hurt you deeply, for, as I stood beside you in the Gardens [Maple Leaf Gardens] in your moment of triumph last February, I saw that you are a sensitive man. That night I saw up close what makes a man.

Forgive me if I recall two events of the most distant past. In December, 1950, the Hope Commission unanimously (except for the R.C. members) recommended that Separate Schools be cut back to Grade 6. Editors took up the cry. Ontario was headed for a religious war. But there was none, simply because Premier Frost stood up at the O.E.A. [Ontario Educational Association] Convention the next spring and said, "no." It took political guts. It helped make him a statesman. Catholics cheered, and no group hurt Mr. Frost at the polls. He met the Separate School system's need of the times.

The problem facing Mr. Robarts was different, though just as grave. He and you met the needs of the time in 1963 by implementing a Foundation Tax Plan. Peace prevailed in the Province. And the subsequent election was not lost as a result of "giving in to the Catholics." And the fact of history is that Mr. Robarts became known as a statesman.

If next week you say that the separate public school system must be left at what was formerly known as Grade 10, you will probably win countless votes, especially in the 55 rural ridings. It may even assure a landslide victory at the polls. But neither John Zaritsky of *The Globe* nor anyone else will hail you as a statesman. There was a day in late summer of 1971 when you as Premier could have prevented Ontario from being torn apart by sectarian strife in the newspapers. You could have but ....

In season and out of season, I have urged fellow Catholics to "cool it." Militancy strikes me as unseemly and unproductive. Being a champion of yours has not been easy. But how long can I keep telling my friends ... that he will prove to Separate School people that he is as much a statesman as his predecessors.

Frankly, are you listening to the right advisors? Why I ask is because the lead item on the 11 o'clock news last night on CFRB said that the seven Catholics at the Caucus meeting were opposed to completion. Gosh, how can they speak for English-speaking Separate School supporters in this Province when they want only French separate schools for their people? The man who wrote that letter on "no more grades" in Friday's *Star*, Robert Welch [the minister of education] understands the situation and can help you through the present crisis.

With considerable hesitation, I have written this letter from the heart. It was made possible because you wrote me last January 5th: "You are one of the few people who have kept an eye on me for the past eight years or so since I assumed my present portfolio, and I am proud to count you among my friends as well as an honest and objective, but sympathetic, critic."

Of little value as they are, Mr. Davis, be assured of my prayers and my support.[13]

29 September 1971

Dear Carl,

I realize that my announcement of the Government's decision regarding the extension of the Separate School system must have come as a keen disappointment to you. However, while we may disagree on this one matter, admittedly an important one, I sincerely hope that this will in no way affect our friendship which I highly value.

Needless to say, I wholeheartedly concur with you that both my immediate predecessors fully merited the appellation "statesman", but I would not agree that these worthy gentlemen achieved this distinction solely on the basis of their treatment of the Roman Catholic Separate Schools. Rather, I believe they acquired this stature over their respective terms of office by giving exceptionally good government to the people of this province and in making a substantial contribution to the development and prosperity of Ontario (and Canada) and to the unity of Canadians.

During my years in previous portfolios I believe I had some measure of success and since assuming my present Office my Cabinet has submitted to the Legislature what I feel is a wide range of progressive and comprehensive legislation. I now believe I should seek a personal mandate from the people and, the electorate willing, I will continue to make every effort to develop legislative programs which are in the best interests of all the people of this province. I must leave it to others and to history (I cannot agree that one particular newspaperman should be the final arbiter) to assess my leadership and the accomplishments of my administration.

May I just return for a moment to your comments regarding the admirable way in which Mr. Frost and Mr. Robarts defended the rights of Separate Schools in Ontario. I endorsed and still endorse their position. As a matter of fact, I was very intimately associated with Mr. Robarts (as Minister of Education) in the development of the Ontario Foundation Plan which gave new life to the Separate Schools, and I have taken some considerable pride in their tremendous progress since that time. I have been somewhat nonplussed with what might be considered rather short memories of some Roman Catholics who have chosen to reject this fact and have decided to actively campaign against the government which has treated them more fairly and more generously than has been the case through over a century of existence.

I have gone over this with you many times before, Carl, and when I began this letter I did not intend to be repetitious. However, I do want you to be assured that the Government's decision was a team decision; it was not taken lightly, it was most certainly not made with anti-Catholic prejudice; and, despite certain accusations, it was not intended as an election issue.

I will continue to look forward to your straight-from-the-shoulder and thought-provoking letters. Please keep in touch.[14]

Their friendship did not suffer; sectarian strife occurred only in the newspapers; Bill Davis went on to electoral victory on 2 October 1971; and Father Matthews continued to correspond with him in the same frank and friendly fashion as before. However, if the decision in 1971 to say "No" to completion was a team effort, as Davis claimed, his return to the High School Question thirteen years later would produce an answer that came from him alone, prompted by his conscience rather than his politics. Until then, a long interregnum in separate school agitation set in, and Father Matthews, sensing a cooling political climate, set about looking for another avenue to assist students. In October 1972, he decided to seek election as a trustee for the Metro Separate School Board.

---

[1] Matthews Papers, Box 3, File 10, CJM to Bill Davis, 21 April 1969.

[2] Box 4, File 7, CJM to the Editor, *Catholic Register*, 14 November 1970.

[3] Box 4, File 16, CJM to William G. Davis, 2 November 1971.

[4] Box 3, File 4, CJM, "Conversation with the Minister of Education, May 2, 1968," 2.

[5] Ibid.; Box 3, File 13, CJM to N.A. Mancini, 13 September 1969.

[6] Box 4, File 7, CJM to William G. Davis, 17 December 1970.

[7] Box 4, File 8, William G. Davis to CJM, 5 January 1971.

[8] Ibid., CJM to William G. Davis, *Telegram*, 24 January 1971.

[9] Ibid., William G. Davis to CJM, 7 February 1971.

[10] Box 4, File 11, William G. Davis to CJM, 21 May 1971.

[11] Box 4, File 13, CJM to William G. Davis, 6 July 1971.

[12] Ibid., CJM to William G. Davis, 24 August 1971.

[13] Box 4, File 17, CJM to William G. Davis, 28 August 1971. Some may wonder if this letter was a partial prelude to Davis's stunning reversal in policy in 1984. See Steve Paikin, *The Life* (Toronto: Penguin Books, 2001), 49: "'I think he always felt a little

guilty about the '71 election victory, being on the backs of the separate school issue,' says Hugh Segal. His fellow Big Blue Machine alumnus, Norman Atkins, agrees. 'There was something about his success in that campaign that bothered him,' he says, 'something he wanted to correct.'"

[14] Box 4, File 14, William G. Davis to CJM, 29 September 1971.

Father Carl Matthews, S.J., chairman of the Metropolitan Separate School Board, Toronto, and his fellow trustees, 1986

CHAPTER FIVE

TRUSTEE AND TORONTO BOARD CHAIRMAN

*F*ather Carl Matthews was a trustee of the Metropolitan Separate School Board (MSSB) for fourteen years. He was the first Jesuit in Canada to be elected to public office of any kind. As a priest and a member of a religious community, he needed permission to join the race not only from his local superior and his Jesuit provincial but also from the archbishop of Toronto. Permission was always immediately and happily granted. They did not consider school trustee a political office in the ordinary sense of the word: because no candidate was running under a political banner, there was no political partisanship to taint a member of the clergy. Father Matthews ran in six elections, was acclaimed three times and lost only once. School board elections took place on the same date as municipal elections, either in November or early December, every two years and beginning in 1982 every three years, with the new term of office commencing in January. This made for a crowded field of candidates, from mayor on down, a sometimes-confusing ballot or ballots and a predictably low turnout. It was not unusual for as few as twenty-five percent of separate school supporters to vote for a trustee in their ward. If there were a contest, the margin of victory could be slim and could be determined by the popularity of a candidate in his home parish. Each big ward had several parishes.

In 1972, there were twenty-one MSSB trustees, including the board chairman. At that time, a trustee's annual stipend was $2,400, plus ten cents a mile for mileage when on board business. This was rather modest, especially in light of the fact that a single MSSB trustee could represent a ward that was the size of two or even three city of Toronto wards. For example, MSSB Ward 9 covered city Wards 10 and 11. It had the largest number of separate school electors, around 16,000, who lived in an area that stretched along the north side of Bloor Street from the Don Valley Parkway on the east to Ossington

Avenue on the west and north to the then city boundary. By way of comparison, four public school trustees represented the same area. In anticipation of the 1976 election, the ward was enlarged and renamed Area 5, comprising city Wards 5, 9 and 10. A larger ward meant more schools to visit, more graduations and PTA meetings to attend and more ratepayer problems to listen to and solve. All these commitments were in addition to the once-a-month board meetings that usually lasted five hours and numerous committee meetings that could gobble up one's evenings week after week.

The job of trustee was a thankless but necessary task. Only a Catholic wholly committed to the ideals and hopes of separate school education would want to fight an election so that he or she could be a school trustee, a position often considered the bottom rung of the political ladder leading to nowhere. Father Matthews was obviously committed to separate schools and did not care a wit what others thought of school trustees. Along with his commitment, though, he had a highly personal motive for running. His days as an outsider in separate school politics were behind him.

****

Father Matthews and eleven other Jesuits lived in MSSB Ward 9. Their home was Bellarmine Hall at 2 Dale Avenue in Rosedale. A residence for Jesuits who were taking advance degrees at the University of Toronto, it was a huge house that produced handsome separate school property taxes, an item that Father Matthews included in his campaign literature. Wanting to avoid charges of being a carpetbagger, he wisely chose to run in the ward where he had lived since 1967. However, the incumbent was Vince Pellettier, a six-year trustee and a former chairman of the MSSB management committee who was so well known in Blessed Sacrament, St. Monica's and Perpetual Help parishes that he boasted to Father Matthews on nomination day that he would win the election in a walk. Scared of losing, Matthews ran all the way to the finish line, as he told Premier Bill Davis. He left no detail to chance.[1]

The first detail was his nomination paper. Father Matthews needed ten names of separate school electors in his ward; he collected fourteen. Among them could be found the signatures of Morley Callaghan, the novelist, Norman DePoe, the CBC broadcaster, and John Wintermeyer, the former leader of the provincial Liberal party. Matthews thought that the city hall elections people would be impressed; they were not. To them, the nomination paper was just another piece of paper; they took it and filed it. Matthews was flummoxed by their flippancy but not for long. He threw himself into the election with all the fervour of a first-time candidate.

The second detail was Matthews' promise to Pellettier in writing that he would not speak ill of him during the campaign.[2] He repeated that promise in a letter to Norman Kelly of District 29 of the Ontario English Catholic Teachers' Association (OECTA). At the time of the election, there was a contract dispute between MSSB and its teachers. OECTA invited each of the candidates for trustee to a teachers rally on Friday, 17 November at the O'Keefe Centre. Pellettier had declined to attend. So too did Matthews, who told Kelly in reply to his telegram that he could not support a walkout on a regular teaching day. He also said, "Mr. Pellettier is an honourable man. Rather than say one word against his person, I would rather lose with honour. I shall repudiate anyone who speaks ill of my opponent."[3] Nothing further was said on the subject.

The third detail was the campaign itself. Father Matthews participated in the five all-candidates meetings, visited 1,100 homes, phoned another 400 and organized a team of volunteers who distributed thousands of election fliers. They featured quotes from Robert Nixon, Donald C. MacDonald, the journalists Harold Greer and Martin Dewey and Almon F. Doolan, Father Matthews' grade seven and eight teacher in Kingston. On the sidelines quietly cheering him on stood none other than William A. Allen, the chairman of Metro Toronto Government. He was very impressed by reports from friends that Matthews was knocking on doors as late as 10:00 pm on Saturday evenings.[4] One wonders what people thought when they saw a priest at their door at that hour.

Election day was 4 December 1972. Father Matthews won by a mere 542 votes, receiving 2,605 votes to Pellettier's 2,057. Premier Davis congratulated Matthews on his victory and confidently predicted that he would make "an exceptional contribution to the undertakings of the Metropolitan Separate School Board."[5] Immediately after the election, Matthews got his own phone line and answering service at Bellarmine Hall and asked his provincial, Father T.G. Walsh, S.J., for permission to buy a small used car. Permission was granted.

****

Trusteeship gave Father Matthews an official platform from which he could continue his involvement in separate school politics. He was faithful in his attendance at board meetings, missing only one in his first four years. He treated regular attendance as a minimum prerequisite to political legitimacy. Of the four permanent committees on which trustees could sit (property, finance, management, and planning and development), Matthews chose planning and development and became its vice-chairman. This committee dealt with site acquisitions, new schools and additions to existing ones. Because the 1970s ushered in an era of extraordinary expansion in separate school enrolment in Toronto, the planning and development committee was constantly assessing needs, which seemed to be in a perpetual state of flux, and plotting strategies and tactics to be used by the board in its bargaining with politicians and bureaucrats. Matthews was also chairman of a special committee that worked out a five-year action plan for the MSSB, and he was the board's representative on the City of Toronto Planning Board in 1973.

Outside of the interminable meetings at the board office – meetings he seemed to anticipate and enjoy with relish – Matthews paid close attention to his own ward. He visited each school at least once a month, wrote countless letters of recommendation for students seeking summer employment, sent congratulatory letters to retiring principals and teachers and every September, at the start of the school year, he distributed copies of his own newsletter to his constituents. Four pages in length, it featured ward news, recent board business and always several photographs. Father Matthews was the first Catholic school trustee in Toronto to produce such a newsletter.

All this constituted the nitty-gritty of trusteeship. MSSB duties were onerous enough for the average trustee, many of whom had outside jobs and families to support, but the work of a trustee hardly satisfied Father Matthews' appetite for bigger issues. He had hardly warmed his trustee's seat at the board office, at the inaugural meeting of the new board, on 3 January 1973, when he raised a red flag concerning the autonomy of separate school boards. And by keeping that flag aloft until the end of 1974, Matthews forced trustees to deal with an issue many of them had little stomach to confront. In the process, divisions arose among them, and critics of Matthews' aggressive and seemingly unrelenting style began to surface.

The first and most immediate issue was a motion that two members of MSSB, one of whom would be the chairman, would become members of the Metropolitan Toronto School Board. Under provincial legislation, the custom had been for MSSB to appoint three non-trustees to that board. Lately they had been Donald Clune, Jack Hale and James Murphy. These appointees had a right to vote on motions before the Metropolitan Toronto School Board, but their voting, especially if it were on the losing side, did not require any response on the part of MSSB. Expectations in that regard might change if MSSB trustees voted as members of the public board.

Matthews addressed the motion with a formal statement to his fellow trustees:

> After much thought since last May, after attending meetings of both Boards, after discussing the matter with individual trustees on the Toronto and borough Public school boards, I believe that if we send down there [College Street offices of the Metropolitan Toronto School Board] our chairman and another trustee, it will mean that in a short time – within 5 years – our Catholic Board will lose much of its autonomy, with disastrous consequences for our Separate School system across the Province.
>
> Contrary to the belief of the man on the street, the Toronto City Board of Education is not a sovereign board. Far from it. It must seek permission of another local board for most of its building expenditures and some of its operating costs. That other board is the Metro Public Board. They send a few trustees to it. So do the borough boards. Hence it is an umbrella board. Mr. Chairman, the motion before us would put this Catholic board under the umbrella, in some way, for the first time.
>
> ...if our Chairman is on the losing side of a vote, you can be sure that his fellow co-chairmen of area boards will expect him to bring the decision back here, just as they must do. Sir Richard Scott, the father of the Separate Schools Act, would turn over in his grave.[6]

The motion passed by a vote of 16 to 5. The rookie had lost his initial skirmish. As things turned out, the MSSB did not forsake much, if any, of its autonomy, as Father Matthews had so confidently predicted. But his speaking so strongly against this motion in 1973, when Catholics had little reason to hope for completion of the separate school system, was really a warning about the potential of the seemingly innocuous to cause great harm at some point in the future. In politics, this is known as the law of unintended consequences. And Father Matthews remained true in his opposition. When he became MSSB chairman in December 1985, he politely but firmly declined to accept a position on the Metropolitan Toronto School Board. As chairman, the position on the Metropolitan Toronto School Board and the additional stipend that went with it were his by right, but he would not participate in decisions of a public board that might have a bearing on the implementation of full funding for separate schools.[7] Uproar followed, with five trustees vying for the position. Matthews quietly stayed out of the fray.

Father Matthews did not have to look far to see the tremendous power of government to regulate public institutions out of existence. On 12 January 1973, the Conservative government of Premier Bill Davis announced the closing of the province's fifty-six nursing schools, including the eleven Catholic ones, and the transference of diploma nursing programs to the provincial colleges of applied arts and technology beginning in September. Writing in the *Catholic Register*, Father Matthews lamented the disappearance by regulation of Catholic schools of nursing. "There will be nothing Catholic or spiritual about nursing education. Students will be taught, for example, that life is not necessarily sacred, that there will be many occasions when society will be best served by terminating the life of a child in the mother's womb."[8] (This was one prediction that became true in short order.) Matthews proposed that each nursing school be allowed to remain in existence as an autonomous body within the colleges, along the lines of the federated colleges of the University of Toronto.

His article provoked a caustic response from M. Josephine Flaherty, a nurse-educator. In the final paragraph of her reply, also in the *Catholic Register*, she wrote:

> Father Matthews would have done well to consult the profession and the educators before making his unsubstantiated generalizations. He might have been surprised to learn that some Catholic schools of nursing have been studying this issue for years and are leaders in the planning for new patterns of nursing education in Ontario. Had he a little more confidence in the ability of Catholics to carry out their missions outside the cloister of Catholic institutions, he would be helping to set the pattern rather than trailing along behind.[9]

"Behind whom?" Father Matthews asked in a letter to the *Register*. "Those who would phase out Catholic schools, elementary, secondary and post-secondary?"[10] He was dismayed that Catholics would play an active role in the demise of one of their own institutions – in this instance, nursing schools – and he was not about to collaborate in the demolition of any other kind of Catholic schools.

Father Matthews sent a copy of his *Register* article to Bill Davis. If his aim had been to prod his good friend the premier to re-consider his government's announcement on nursing schools, he must have been sorely disappointed (but not too surprised) to receive a two-page defense of government policy.[11] All that Matthews could do in response was to thank Davis for his genial reply and politely remind him that the Ontario Catholic Hospital Conference was one interested organization that did not side with the government on this issue.[12]

There the matter ended for Davis, but not for Matthews. What to do about the "Report of the Study Team on the Sharing or Transferring of School Facilities," which the ministry of education made public on 27 February 1973. The concluding paragraphs of that Report recommended the formation of a committee to study the question of the abolition of separate school boards. Matthews was not about to let that go unchallenged. To his fellow separate school trustees across Ontario, he wrote a memorandum, dated 20 March 1973:

> For your information I am enclosing a copy of a letter of February 21, 1972 from the Premier, and another of March 2, 1973 from the Minister of Colleges and Universities. They explain how it happened that the Ontario government announced on January 12th past that it would be "transferring" the Catholic nursing schools (among others) to the secular community colleges.
>
> Apparently, a few influential Catholics have been quietly urging the move in recent years. Their counsel fell on receptive ears at Queen's Park. Hence the Catholic nursing schools are to disappear across the Province.
>
> But what of our Separate School boards? Are they the next to go? Not likely. However, if Catholic trustees and teachers are not vigilant, it could happen. Who would have thought just a month ago that a Ministry Study Team would recommend that a committee be established to study the advisability of abolishing Separate School boards! (to express the essence of the concluding two paragraphs).
>
> As one reads the smooth letters from Mr. Davis and Mr. [John] McNie, it is not hard to visualize that the date at the top is a few years hence, and the Premier and appropriate Minister are explaining how it happened that "sectarian separate schools" are henceforth to be managed by the local Boards of Education. "...The guidelines governing the transfer provide for the recognition and continuation of the unique qualities of sectarian programs and it is hoped that the sectarian educators will work to preserve those qualities in the integrated programs" – to quote the premier [in his letter of 21 February 1973].

Such an announcement about Separate School boards would be many steps away. However, in the practical order, people are powerless to stop the last steps. Surely, though, it is within our power to stop the first steps.

At the provincial level, the time to do it is April 5th and 6th at the annual meeting of the Ontario Separate School Trustees' Association. There is a provision in the rules for adoption of urgent motions. I can recall some such during the 14 conventions of OSSTA that I have attended. This year I have a vote, and want to use it in union with hundreds of other Catholic trustees who were shocked by several of the recommendations in the Study Team report publicized by the Minister of education on February 27th.

I believe that if we permit encroachments on our autonomy now, Separate Schools shall, within a decade, go the way of the Catholic nursing schools in 1973. Let us be diplomatic, but firm. We have a heritage to hand on.[13]

Both Lambton County and Frontenac-Lennox and Addington County asked Father Matthews to write a special resolution in defense of the autonomy of separate school boards for OSSTA's April 1973 convention.[14] An individual trustee might author a resolution but only a board could present it at the annual general meeting. As it turned out, the Ontario County board presented seven special resolutions concerning various aspects of the Study Team Report. The seventh resolution was the work of Father Matthews:

"WHEREAS the conclusion of the Report of the Study Team on the Sharing or Transferring of School Facilities, released at the Ontario Legislature on February 27, 1973, recommends the establishment of a committee to investigate the advisability of abolishing Separate School boards, and

"WHEREAS autonomous Separate School boards were guaranteed in the Parliamentary enactment that made possible the creation of Ontario as a province of Canada, and

"WHEREAS, to fulfill a function, such boards are as necessary as the legislature itself,

"THEREFORE BE IT RESOLVED that the Ontario Separate School Trustees' Association in annual assembly inform the Minister of Education that the establishment of any committee to discuss weakening the autonomous structure of Catholic school boards is out of the question."¹⁵

All seven special resolutions were referred to the OSSTA Executive. No action was taken by OSSTA because no government with Bill Davis as premier had any interest in meddling with the existence of separate school boards. Such a move in 1973 would have been pure political folly. By forcing the issue onto the convention floor, Matthews put his fellow trustees on high alert for the next threat to separate school autonomy. That threat became apparent at the very same OSSTA convention.

Earlier in the year, the government had established a Task Force on the Consolidation of the School Acts. The principal aim of Bill 255 (reintroduced as Bill 72) was to repeal a total of thirty-one acts that dealt with education and replace them with one unified Education Act. Among those thirty-one acts were five that could be classified as strictly education acts, and among those five was the Separate Schools Act. At an OSSTA panel discussion that took place on 5 April, David Dehler, an Ottawa lawyer hired by OSSTA, claimed that the elimination of the Separate Schools Act would not endanger separate schools. Father Matthews replied in a memorandum of 3 May 1973. What Dehler said was true, but it was only true in relation to the Courts, he wrote. "Surely the risk, though, comes not from the Courts but from a [future] Cabinet. Even at the present time it is not the Courts which are urging shared schools and shared signatures on forms; it is servants of the Ontario Cabinet."¹⁶ If the Separate Schools Act was suppressed, with the obliging consent of separate school trustees, some future government might use that fact as a pretext to suppress the entire separate school system. Once again, Matthews wanted his fellow trustees to think about the possible consequences of their actions.

On 12 April 1973, Father Matthews made a written submission to the Task Force, in which he offered a simple solution to the "problem." He asked the Task Force to leave out Parts IV and V from the Education Act, "preface them with the pages of "interpretation," bind the pages between matching cardboard covers, and entitle the booklet 'THE SEPARATE SCHOOLS ACT, 1973.' Alternatively, I respectfully propose that you bind everything into one book, with that particular Act at the back (or, if you prefer, at the front)."¹⁷ He went on to tell the Task Force that if Catholics had spoken up at the beginning of the process that had led to the closing of Catholic nursing schools, those schools might still be in existence.

Father Matthews then took the fight to the September 1973 meeting of the MSSB. He proposed this resolution: "That the Ontario Separate School Trustees' Association be advised that the Metropolitan Separate School Board wishes the Minister of Education to retain an identifiable Separate Schools Act." After forty minutes of debate, the resolution passed by a vote of 20-1. The chairman, Joe Marrese, cast the lone vote against it. The resolution was immediately sent to OSSTA.

On 30 November 1973, Thomas Wells, the minister of education, gave first reading of Bill 255. Ed Nelligan, the MSSB superintendent of education, and Father Matthews witnessed Wells' performance from the Speaker's Gallery at the legislature. Afterwards, Bill Copps, a CBC reporter, asked Nelligan his opinion of the Bill. He deferred to Father Matthews. "Well, as a Trustee on the Metropolitan Separate School Board," Father Matthews said, "I'm concerned that for the first time in over 100 years, since prior to Confederation, there would be no Separate Schools Act as an identifiable Act in the new provision." Copps asked: "What does this mean that you are giving up then?" Father Matthews answered: "Well, the danger, I think, is there for the future, if any effort were made by some future Government to consolidate the two school systems in this Province that it might be said that Separate School people acquiesced in the abolishment, the suppression, of a Separate Schools Act in the year 1973-1974."[18] This exchange was aired on the Channel 5 late night news.

The OSSTA directors, however, remained unmoved by the September 1973 resolution of the MSSB and unconvinced by Father Matthews' now very public argument on behalf of the retention of the Separate School Act. On 18 January 1974, they voted to accept the principle of one Education Act, and gave Father Raymond Durocher, OMI, research director for OSSTA, the task of defending that decision.

Matthews' next move was to write a letter to the *Catholic Register* in which he argued at length to save the Separate Schools Act from extinction.[19] The letter appeared in the *Register*'s 9 February 1974 issue. Matthews forwarded a copy to Premier Davis, under a covering letter of 5 March 1974 that spoke to Davis's sense of fair play: "If you were to keep an identifiable Separate Schools Act in the new Bill before it reaches 2nd Reading, I would be re-assured that you don't mean any harm to our Separate School system – even in the long run."[20] Davis replied a week later:

> I can assure you, Carl, that you need not fear the effect of Bill 255 with regard to Separate Schools.
>
> Bill 255 does not repeal the Separate Schools Act. Its purpose is solely to consolidate the five education acts, which include the Separate School Act, and to eliminate anachronistic wording and material. Neither will Bill 255 take away any of the guarantees made under The British North America Act.
>
> I might add that prior to 1954 there were 13 Education Acts in the Province of Ontario and in that year this number was reduced to 5. It is now our intention to reduce this to one act, as is the case in other Canadian Provinces.[21]

Davis's strong suit was his comment about separate school guarantees in the BNA Act. No provincial law by itself could erase them. But on the claim that Bill 255 did not repeal the Separate School Act, he was at best fudging, and Matthews continued the correspondence on that point, replying on 22 March 1974:

> With all due respect, Mr. Premier, nothing could be further from the truth. The last page of Government Bill 255, which received first reading on November 30, 1973, explicitly states that one of the Acts being repealed is the Separate Schools Act. A photocopy of the documentation is attached.
>
> If you re-introduce Bill 255 in its present form, there will no longer be an Act called a Separate Schools Act. Is that not so?
>
> We have had an Act by that name continuously since before Confederation. Hence, even though you are my friend, I must protest strongly your proposal to de-list, to repeal it.
>
> When Premier [Leslie] Frost in 1954 consolidated 13 education Acts into 5, is it not so that there continued to be an Act called a Separate Schools Act? Is it also not so that some Catholics in Ontario had taken strong exception to the recommendation of the majority on the Hope Commission "...that all statutory provisions relating to education in Ontario be consolidated into one Education Act"?
>
> Because of that concern from some Catholic educators, Mr. Frost did not de-list the Separate Schools Act. I earnestly hope that you will show the same statesmanship in 1974 as your distinguished predecessor did in 1954.

Please give serious consideration to a proposal that would permit you to proceed with the re-introduction of an amended Bill 255, and at the same time would keep in the statute books an Act entitled *The Separate Schools Act* ....

There is no one in Cabinet from the English-language Catholic community to plead against the erosion of our [Catholic] institutions. And you are the only Premier we have got. I hope and pray, Bill, that you won't let me down.[22]

Father Matthews ended his letter with a postscript: "What you did for our schools through the Foundation Plan was admirable, and I sincerely thank you." His appeal to statesmanship and to the past did not work. Davis took until early May to reply. Although he acknowledged that Bill 255 did indeed repeal a number of Acts, he insisted that "these Acts are being repealed only to better integrate and consolidate them into one Act. It is our belief that this will in no way adversely affect Catholic education in Ontario, and this belief, I might add, is shared by many prominent Catholic educators."[23]

While Father Matthews was corresponding with the premier, he took his case to the Waterloo County Separate School Board, in February 1974, winning many converts such as John Sweeney, the board superintendent; and to a special meeting the next month of more than fifty trustees at St. Jerome's High School in Kitchener.[24] Billed as an information session, the Kitchener gathering pitted Father Matthews, who argued for the retention of the Separate Schools Act, against Father Durocher of OSSTA, who defended OSSTA's intention to side with the government on consolidation. Because their positions were mutually exclusive, leaving no room for a middle ground, the trustees must have left the meeting bewildered.

Another audience willing to listen to Father Matthews was the North York members of OECTA. He addressed them at a dinner on 6 March 1974. After talking about the Foundation Tax Plan, government-imposed ceilings on expenditures, grants and building costs, the restoration of the Corporation Tax Adjustment Grant and the Hall-Dennis Committee Report of 1968, he finally arrived at the matter of the imminent eradication of the Separate Schools Act. "Of all people," he told his OECTA audience, "we trustees and teachers who were given a Separate Schools Act in trust by our forefathers surely have a duty to safeguard it. If we don't, who will? Certainly no non-Catholic is going to lift a finger to help us if we ever lose interest in helping ourselves."[25] An edited version of this talk was given a generous spread in the 1 April 1974 issue of the

Globe and Mail under the provocative title "The Separate Schools Act: keeping the faith."[26] It appeared just in time for OSSTA's annual April convention.

A heated debate on the consolidation Bill erupted among the delegates at an information session, and right in the middle of it was Father Matthews. He warned the trustees that "Those who are opposed to separate schools are watching carefully the actions of trustees at this convention. Unless the OSSTA executive reverses its position, they will make much of the fact that the repeal of the Separate Schools Act was made at the wishes of our trustees."[27] John Sweeney sided with Father Matthews, saying that consolidation was another step towards the abolition of separate schools. Opposing Matthews was Dr. Nick Mancini, a Hamilton trustee and a former OSSTA president, Bob Dixon, separate school director in Brantford, and Frank Gilhooly of the Ottawa Separate School Board. Dixon pointed out that separate school rights did not depend on provincial legislation but were found in the BNA Act. By the end of the session, it was clear to all that OSSTA had voted in favour of consolidation and found no reason to change its collective mind.

Defeated but undaunted, Father Matthews, the lone wolf, decided to participate in the legislative process for the Education Act, 1974. He convinced the Social Development Committee and consequently Thomas Wells, the minister of education, to amend Sections 244 and 245 of the Act by adding the words "to the board." The amended version presently reads that a director of education "is responsible to the board for the development, implementation, operation and supervision of educational programs in the schools."[28] Without the words "to the board," a school board would have had no control over its own director of education. As important as this intervention was, it paled in comparison to the fact that Father Matthews also persuaded the government to insert a peculiar but very protective preamble to Part IV of the Education Act. Section 79 of the Act reads: "This Part applies to separate schools for Roman Catholics now or hereafter established and shall have the same effect as if this Part were a special Act respecting separate schools for Roman Catholics."[29] The Separate Schools Act may have passed on into history, but its essence continued to live on in the statute books as if it had never died.

****

Father Carl Matthews was a workhorse. He never tired of the topic of separate schools, and he never thought that his work for MSSB or his more public involvement with broader separate school issues were sufficient outlets for his ambitions. As an MSSB trustee, he was able to enter into the work of other trustee organizations. Opportunities, denied to him before his election, quickly presented themselves. On 5 April 1974, his fellow trustees elected him to OSSTA's board of directors, which in turn made him chairman of its legal committee and an OSSTA voting officer of the Ontario School Trustees' Council. The Council was the co-ordinating body for all public and separate school boards in the province. Two years later, Matthews was elected chairman of the Council's legislation committee.

Father Matthews' most successful work for the Ontario School Trustees' Council came as its representative on the board of directors of the Ontario Federation of School Athletics Associations. The appointment was an odd one, but in the end it was quite fruitful for high school athletics in Ontario. It was odd for several reasons. The federation was a secondary school organization, and Matthews was a trustee of a school board that was prohibited by provincial law from operating secondary schools. Also, Matthews had never had anything to do with organized athletics. Regardless, he graciously accepted the January 1975 invitation to sit on the board and the February 1976 request to renew his appointment.[30] It was a fortuitous act of generosity on his part.

The federation had a budget of $90,000, a third of which came from the provincial government and the rest from a seven-cent per-student levy that had to be approved by each school board. The budget was no larger than that of athletic organizations in Manitoba and Saskatchewan, which had much smaller secondary school populations. By 1976, the federation needed a substantial increase in money and was reluctant to ask the school boards to increase the per-student levy. In previous years, the federation's requests to Queen's Park went unheeded. The executive turned to Father Matthews, the only one on the board with any experience in writing briefs to the government. He agreed. The May 1976 brief from the Ontario Federation of School Athletics Associations to Thomas Wells, minister of education, was classic Matthews. Tightly structured, factual and focused on a single request, the brief asked for $35,000 a year from lottery proceeds to subsidize the travel costs of high school athletes who participated in provincial championships. It worked – to everyone's astonishment. The government agreed to fund one-half of the travel costs of seventeen regional teams to twenty-three provincial championships. Matthews thought that the subsidy could be worth up to $50,000 a year![31]

In 1976, OSSTA elected Matthews to its executive and gave him the task of organizing the first-ever seminar for newly elected trustees, which took place on 14-16 January 1977.[32] The seminar was a huge success and became a regular event after each school board election. During OSSTA's annual convention, in April 1977, Matthews was elected 2nd vice-president, by acclamation, which surprised him, and he was made one of two OSSTA representatives on the board of the Canadian Catholic School Trustees' Association (CCSTA).[33]

Almost immediately following his appointment to the CCSTA, Father Matthews was named chairman of its national committee on the status of Catholic schools in the Canadian constitution.[34] There was some urgency to the appointment. Prime Minister Pierre Trudeau's Victoria Charter of 1971, his negotiated blueprint for a revised constitution, retained Section 93 (1) of the BNA Act, which guaranteed denominational rights in education. Without Quebec's agreement, the Victoria Charter died. In 1977, Trudeau revived public interest in the constitution with the establishment of a National Task Force on Canadian Unity, co-chaired by Jean-Luc Pepin, a member of Trudeau's cabinet, and John P. Robarts, the retired premier of Ontario. Public chatter, some if it originating from the Task Force itself, about the substitution of linguistic rights for denominational rights in education prompted Catholic school stakeholders to make formal representations to the Task Force.

The Federation of Catholic Education Associations of Ontario, in the persons of Father Patrick Fogarty, C.S.C. and Donald McDonald, presented a four-page submission to the Task Force on 28 November 1977. Father Matthews, ever the watchdog, was the document's author. He left the submission's key claim to the second last paragraph. It was simple and direct: "Education rights, new rights, for the linguistic minority in Canada can be enshrined in the future Constitution without amending in any way the present and longstanding rights granted to the denominational minority."[35] If there had to be two sets of rights in education, they could live side by side in any revamped constitution. Section 93 (1) of the BNA must stay.

CCSTA took the identical position but made their point in a more personal way and to more than one audience then working on the constitution. On 10 January 1978, C.F. Gilhooly, president, Father Patrick Fogarty, executive secretary, and Father Matthews met Pepin in person in Ottawa. They also had a meeting with Gerard LaForest.[36] He was director of research for the Canadian Bar Association's Committee on a New Constitution. A third person that the CCSTA troika had wanted to see while in Ottawa was Frank Carter.[37] A senior civil servant, he was a member of a three-person committee that was established by Trudeau to advise him on the constitution. The other members were Donald Thorson, a former deputy minister of justice, and Gordon Robertson, secretary to the cabinet and thus the senior civil servant in Ottawa. Matthews had proposed a meeting to Carter in a letter of 1 December 1977. Carter responded by telephone on 12 December. He told Matthews that after consulting the other members of the committee, he could say (but not put in writing) that "there is no thought at all of taking away the rights of the denominational minority, as enunciated in 93 (1) of the BNA Act." He continued:

> It is not in the cards, not at all. In fact, if it became even a discussable prospect at this level, my resignation would be on the Prime Minister's desk immediately. I say that, Father, not as a Catholic – which I am – but as one who professionally values the heritage of this country ....
>
> Your book highlights the fact that hundreds of thousands of Canadian citizens would have rights taken away from them if Section 93 in its present form were repealed. No, that is just not in the cards.[38]

The book Frank Carter referred to in his letter was *Catholic Schools in Canada*, published in 1977 by CCSTA and edited by Father Matthews. The chapter divisions were according to province and territory, with a different author for each chapter. Matthews contributed the chapter on Ontario. Bishop G. Emmett Carter of London, then president of the Canadian Conference of Catholic Bishops, provided the Foreword. The book closed with an appendix that showed the Catholic population of Canada, by province and territory, according to the census returns of 1861, 1951 and 1971. Approximately 7,000 copies were sold, at a dollar a copy. It was a surprise best seller, and Matthews made sure that inscribed copies found their way into the hands of bishops and politicians, including Prime Minister Trudeau.[39]

Father Matthews' other trustee-related activities were many and various during the years 1973 to 1978. He was a member of the education minister's committee on financing schools, from November 1976 to April 1977; he was the Catholic representative on the provincial cabinet's advisory committee on property tax reform and submitted a Minority Report dated 14 April 1978; he was appointed to the board of governors of the Ontario Institute for Studies in Education (OISE), in 1977, representing the Ontario School Trustees' Council, and within two months he had a detailed plan for the re-organization of OISE's governing structure.[40]

****

In his first six years as an MSSB trustee, the peripatetic Father Carl Matthews had fashioned a high profile for himself among his fellow trustees and his constituents. Hard working, productive and controversial at times, he seemed to be everywhere doing everything for separate schools. He continued to have the occasional by-line in the *Catholic Trustee* (in addition to his annual "Trends in Ontario Separate School Finance") and also in the *Catholic Register*. For his sermon to the parishioners of Holy Spirit Church in Scarborough, as part of MSSB's twenty-fifth anniversary celebrations, he made special mention of the heroic labours of trustee James Culnan to bring Catholic schools to the parish.

Father Matthews was acclaimed in the 1974 and 1976 elections, a testimony on both occasions to his popularity. But acclamation, and hence no campaign flyers, twice in a row was his undoing when he was forced to contest the 13 November 1978 election. Father Matthews won the polls in four of the ward's five parishes but not by margins large enough to overcome Michael Flanagan's twenty-to-one landslide in his home parish of Holy Rosary. The thirty-two-year-old Flanagan beat the veteran Matthews by 130 votes (2,805 to 2,675).

Father Matthews was in a state of disbelief. Was it the end of his career in Catholic education? Many parents sent letters or made phone calls expressing their disbelief and disappointment. Even his mother wrote to him the day after the election, telling him not to be too disappointed. "Almighty God always has a plan for us," she wrote, "although at times it is hard to understand, so we have to accept it."[41] If her words were not enough to ease the embarrassment of losing, the wise words of Archbishop G. Emmett Carter of Toronto should have consoled him:

> By now I am sure you are quite convinced that any form of politics is a pretty strange and puzzling proposition. Why you should have been defeated in your candidacy for the Separate School Board has to remain a mystery. If you have any clues, I should like to know what they are.
>
> But you are not only an expert on education, you are also a priest with a philosophy of life. I am sure that you will be quite able to sustain this disappointment without any bitterness. Above all I would suggest to you that you not indulge in any self recrimination. I cannot imagine what you should have done, that you have not done. You are

clearly the most knowledgeable man on Separate School questions in the area, and only the impenetrable mind of electors could explain your defeat.

Not being a member of the School Board is not exactly the end of the earth either. You will have many more opportunities to serve as you have served in the past. I for one offer my sincere gratitude for what you have already achieved for Catholic Education and for what the future holds.

Please count on my support and friendship.[42]

****

The archbishop's letter presented a mixture of high praise, sound advice and hope for Father Matthews' future in Catholic education. In the meantime, he needed a job, as he told Father William Ryan, S.J., his provincial; preferably one in the area in which he had lived for the past eleven years. On his return from a week's holiday in Clearwater, Florida, Matthews told Ryan that he was interested in an offer from Father Basil Courtemanche to become the associate pastor at the parish of Our Lady of Perpetual Help, which is located at St. Clair Avenue and Mount Pleasant Road, beginning in January 1979. Instead, Father Matthews landed at the Jesuit-run parish of Our Lady of Lourdes, on Sherbourne Street, south of Bloor Street. He had to leave Bellarmine Hall and move out of Ward 9.

Father Matthews would be stationed full-time at Our Lady of Lourdes from 1979 to 1989. It would be the longest stretch of time he would spend in any parish until his posting to St. John the Evangelist parish in Waubaushene in mid-May 1994. Many friends of Father Matthews would recognize him more as a priest in a parish than as a separate school lobbyist, a high profile trustee or later as a newspaper editor. He always loved celebrating Sunday Masses and preaching to the faithful, every weekend if possible; it sustained and defined him in all his other work.

Prior to his arrival at Our Lady of Lourdes, he was a regular weekend priest at St. Monica's in north Toronto (1968-1972), St. Norbert's in North York (1972-1975) and Holy Spirit in north Scarborough (1975-1978). After he left Our Lady of Lourdes, he was acting pastor at Good Shepherd in Thornhill (1989-1990) and then served part-time at Our Lady of Perpetual Help in central Toronto (1990-1992) and St. Michael's Cathedral (1992-1993). He served full time at the cathedral from October 1993 to May 1994.

He was also on the summer staff at the Martyrs' Shrine in Midland in 1989 and 1993. While he was editor of the *Catholic Register*, he drove from Toronto to the Shrine every third weekend during the summer months (May to September) and preached without notes at the five Sunday Masses.

An extra ministry at Lourdes was the chaplaincy at nearby Wellesley Hospital. Starting on 16 January 1979, Father Matthews spent about twenty hours a week at the hospital. He anointed patients with the Sacrament of the Sick, and every second day, he distributed Holy Communion and made time for private prayer with them. On average, he visited from fifty to sixty patients a week, on floors 4, 5 and 7 of the hospital. Wednesday at Lourdes was a day off, which Father Matthews usually spent at the Ontario Legislature, when it was in session, visiting the library, talking to politicians and watching the debates from the Speaker's Gallery, his old haunt from the 1960s.

****

Priestly ministry at Our Lady of Lourdes parish and Wellesley Hospital, plus regular visits to the Legislature, made for a busy and fulfilling life during Father Carl Matthews' unexpected two-year interregnum as an MSSB trustee. He was at home wherever he went, always smiling, always willing to listen, never without his Roman collar. But it was impossible for him to remain aloof from the matter dearest to his heart – separate schools. Although he was no longer a trustee, he remained a director of OSSTA until April 1979 and a director of CCSTA until June 1979, when his respective terms of office were officially over. More importantly, he was active on many other fronts. Father Matthews wrote articles on the Jackson commission on declining school enrolment in both systems and on trends in separate school enrolment; he gave an address at the blessing of St. Paul's School in Newmarket, on 22 April 1979, which was published in *Catholic Trustee* under the title "Catholic Schools in Ontario's Future"; on 12 June 1979, in Vancouver, he was the moderator of a forum on the development of Catholic elementary and secondary education; in the first months of 1980 he completed an article on the early history of the Canadian Catholic School Trustees' Association, which he wrote without fee; and on 19 April 1980, he participated on a panel at an OECTA province-wide Conference on Unjust Financing of Catholic High Schools.[43]

All of this activity was laudable, but Father Matthews' most important work at this time was a background paper on the financing of Grades 9 and 10 in separate schools. He thought that there was a good case to be made for more adequate funding of these two grades. Commissioned by OECTA, this report was completed by November 1979. The subject was the byzantine but vital business of legislative grants. Aside from the civil servants who tabulated and distributed the grants, very few people understood the nature and complexity of these grants. Father Matthews was one of a handful in the separate school camp who did, and he was not shy about sharing his considerable knowledge on grants or, when necessary, correcting people on their mistaken notions about them.[44] In his OECTA report he used ministry figures to show that the per-pupil grant for elementary separate schools (JK to 10) was substantially larger than that for public elementary grades (JK to 8) and that the per-pupil grant for separate school Grades 9 and 10 was larger than that for the same grades in public high schools. But grants were not the same as total revenue. To achieve funding parity in terms of total revenue for separate school Grades 9 and 10 (which had never received any support from local taxes), the difference in grants between the two systems had to continue to increase; this could be achieved by the use of weighting factors (grant plus a percentage of the grant.). The weighting factor in 1978 was 12.5 per cent, the result of lengthy negotiations with the education ministry. According to Father Matthews the goal had to be regular increases in the weighting factor for Grades 9 and 10.[45]

This was not an arcane matter. In lieu of full funding for the separate school system, which was not on the political horizon in 1979, effective and consistent bargaining on the weighting factor was absolutely crucial to the financial viability of Grades 9 and 10, on which completion of the last sixth of the system could be built at some future date. There was no room for timidity on the part of OSSTA, which dealt directly with the ministry of education on grants and weighting factors. For about twenty years, Dr. Joe Fyfe, a Sudbury physician and school trustee, had provided leadership on all issues of legislative grants. He was a hero to Father Matthews.

****

As the 10 November 1980 municipal election approached, Father Carl Matthews decided to run as a candidate in Wards 6 and 7, which covered an area south of Bloor Street and Danforth Avenue, from Palmerston Avenue in the west to Logan Avenue in the east, down to Lake Ontario. There were twelve schools. Our Lady of Lourdes rectory, where he lived, was situated in the combined wards. Charles Arseneault, the owner of Champlain Books and the incumbent, had decided not to seek re-election and actively encouraged

Father Matthews to place his name on the ballot. Matthews did and won the election. He was acclaimed in the 1982 election, for a three-year term, and was elected to what later turned out to be a final three-year term in 1985.

Father Matthews' second turn as a separate school trustee was far more eventful than his first. In the midst of board meetings, committee work and public relations, there were controversies, moments of high drama and even public recognition of his work. There was also a secret satisfaction in the knowledge that one of his anonymous writings helped to change Premier Davis's mind on completion. During these eight years, Father Matthews was his usual frenetic self. He resigned from the OSSTA executive, in January 1982 (he would return to the board of directors in 1984 and to the executive in 1985, when he became MSSB chairman); he wrote editorials on education for the *Catholic Register*, from 1983 to 1985; he was invited by Premier Davis to witness his announcement on completion in June 1984; he strenuously opposed any amendments to Bill 30 that might weaken the Catholic identity of separate schools; he was chairman of MSSB, from December 1985 to December 1986, fulfilling a long-held goal; and he strenuously opposed homogenous French-language school boards (Catholic and non-Catholic trustees on the same board), much to the chagrin of several French bishops in Ontario. In all that he said or wrote, in every debate, public or private, he always kept his eyes on the prize – separate school completion.

****

Father Carl Matthews resigned from OSSTA's board of directors on 14 January 1982. He did not go quietly. The issues at stake and the events leading up to his resignation explain why there was so little public noise surrounding his departure. The Secondary Education Review Project (SERP), in its Report of 31 October 1981, recommended that Grade 9 and 10 separate school students be recognized as secondary students and that these grades be funded accordingly. This was known as Recommendation 89. If the government did a volte-face and accepted this recommendation, it would put an end to the legal fiction that Grade 9 and 10 separate school students were elementary students and had to be funded accordingly. "This change," according to historian Robert T. Dixon, "would not only have closed the gap between per pupil weighting factor grants and high school grants but recognized a separate school as both an elementary and a secondary school."[46] In fact, the change, if adopted, would be nothing short of historic and set a precedent to be referred to in any future call for separate school completion.

OSSTA's response to the SERP *Report* was a position paper, "The Status of Secondary Education Under Separate School Jurisdiction." The earliest draft was dated 12 November 1981. A shorter version, bearing the date 4 December 1981, was sent to officials in the ministry of education. The paper made eight recommendations and two proposals. Three of those recommendations are worth noting:

> Recommendation (1): We recommend that a county and district Roman Catholic Separate School Board which passes a resolution to maintain or establish a secondary programme for pupils in Grades 9 and 10 be immediately deemed to be a Roman Catholic Board of Education with an elementary and secondary panel, each panel having the same trustee membership.

> Recommendation (7): We recommend that the usual weighting factors for secondary purposes be applied to the secondary panel of the Roman Catholic Board of Education.

> Recommendation (8): We recommend that, for the present school year [1981], the Grade 9 and 10 weighting factor be applied to grants receivable for approved extraordinary expenditures for Grade 9 and 10 purposes, as well as ordinary expenditures, and that it be raised to at least .20 [grant plus 20 percent].[47]

OSSTA's first proposal called for a subsidy – in effect, partial funding – for separate school grades beyond Grade 10 (the SERP *Report* suggested the abolition of Grade 13). Its second proposal asked the government to provide partial funding for all private religious schools.[48]

Interestingly, the final version of OSSTA's position paper carried only a brief mention of separate school extension. At a meeting on 12 January 1982, between Cardinal G. Emmett Carter and Chris Asseff, OSSTA's executive director, and Father Raymond Durocher, the author of the position paper, the cardinal insisted that extension appear in the paper.[49] Asseff and Durocher agreed. Later that same day, the OSSTA board of directors met to confirm the paper. Dissenting was Father Matthews. The debate was so heated that the president had to call a recess. Matthews thought that the proposal for partial funding betrayed the association's 1969 Equality Brief and that Recommendation 8 (referred to as paragraph 75), in the wake of the SERP *Report*, undermined the association's stated efforts to achieve financial parity for Grades 9 and 10. He placed his resignation on the table, and nothing said after the recess convinced him to remove it. The president was furious.

Father Matthews made his resignation official in a letter to Chris Asseff of 14 January 1982. He gave one reason only for resigning from the board. It was not OSSTA's proposal for partial funding, as one might suspect, but its request for a .20 weighting grant:

> With this letter I am tendering to the Board of Directors my resignation as a Director of the Ontario Separate School Trustees' Association.
>
> With much regret, I am taking this action solely because it seems the right thing to do before informing the Government of Ontario that in my opinion, in this year of the SERP Report, our 35,000 students in Grades 9 and 10 deserve much better in next month's grants regulations than our Association is seeking for them in the position paper sent to the Premier last November. The difference involves several million dollars.
>
> I have the highest regard for you, the officers and staff of our Catholic Trustees' Association, and pray that God will bless you in your apostolic work for all our school children in the Province.[50]

Having resigned, Father Matthews was free to pursue his own agenda. He made good on his promise to inform the government of his opposition to OSSTA's position paper, writing directly to Premier Davis on 15 January 1982. In a tightly argued two-page letter, he asked his friend to ignore paragraph 75. For effect, Matthews quoted part of it for him: "'We recommend that for the present year, the Grade 9 and 10 weighting factor ... be raised to at least .20.'"[51] He then continued: "Just to bring us up to the grantable ceiling for ordinary expenditures would have required in 1981 a weighting factor of .389."[52] And he further demonstrated to the premier the correct arithmetical calculation that led to the .389 factor. Not once did Father Matthews refer to the partial funding proposal or the Equality Brief. However, fearing that the matter might die on the premier's desk, he sent copies of his letter to many people, including the members of every separate school board with Grades 9 and 10.

Now it was Chris Asseff's turn to be furious. "In your own cunning way," he wrote to Father Matthews on 27 January 1982, "you did not even quote the whole paragraph 75 to explain the complete recommendation. If you are going to spill the beans, why not spill the whole pot rather than deceive people with excerpts out of context?"[53] Next he had his say in a *Toronto Star* story. Asseff claimed that Father Matthews' letter to Premier Davis did not give the whole story: "He has left out key parts of our recommendation to the premier. We have always asked for and continue to ask for parity in funding with the public schools."[54]

Matthews replied to Asseff in a letter of 8 February 1982. He told him that to ask for a weighting factor of .20 was not to seek parity in ordinary funding with the public schools, when according to the 1981 grant regulations the factor would be .389. OSSTA had asked for scarcely half of what it should have demanded. Moreover, "If the writer of that major position paper thinks that 'weighting factors' have anything to do with 'extraordinary expenditure' grants (for transportation, debt charges and capital from revenue), then manifestly he does not know a basic aspect of how the grants formula works."[55] This was a jibe at Father Durocher. OSSTA was embarrassing itself and, more seriously, shortchanging Catholic students in Grades 9 and 10 by failing to distinguish the rather elementary difference between ordinary and extraordinary grants. Father Matthews also criticized OSSTA for asking the ministry of education for a statistical comparison between the separate and public schools in costs to educate Grade 9 and 10 students, and he rebuked OSSTA for repudiating its own 1969 Equality Brief. Those were strong words. Now that they were part of the written record, they were bound to antagonize just about everyone at OSSTA.

The immediate upshot of this controversy was that OSSTA presented its position paper as a brief to Premier Bill Davis, on 8 February 1982, and awaited his answer. Except for the Cardinal Carter amendment on extension, it was the same as the draft of 12 November 1981. Meanwhile, acceptance of Father Matthews' resignation generated more controversy than the OSSTA executive thought that the matter deserved. What began as an in-house debate ended up as a public relations fiasco. George Saranchuk, president of OECTA, and Robert Hall, chairman of the Dufferin-Peel Roman Catholic Separate School Board, wrote lengthy letters of protest.[56] Ed Nelligan, MSSB director of education, submitted a nine-page reply to OSSTA's position paper. In summation, Nelligan wrote: "this Board does not believe that a two panel Roman Catholic Board of Education or a subsidy to support private Catholic high schools is an appropriate solution to the problems faced by this Board and the private Catholic secondary schools. This Board continues to support the completion of the Catholic school system to Grade 13 with provincial funding for the Catholic secondary schools at a level similar to public secondary schools."[57] He chastised OSSTA for not inviting school boards to review the position paper prior to its submission to the government, and he strongly suggested that OSSTA not pursue its recommendations.

For its part, the Conservative government decided not to implement Recommendation 89 of the SERP *Report*. Grades 9 and 10 in separate schools would not be considered secondary grades and would not receive secondary funding. It was all very disappointing and deflating for the Catholic side. As for OSSTA, it did not budge from its partial funding proposal. Indeed, on 30 April 1984, more than two years after the submission of the OSSTA's position paper, the Catholic bishops of Ontario endorsed OSSTA's stand on partial funding, unaware that just six weeks later full funding would be promised.[58] Premier Bill Davis was about to turn the world of school politics upside down.

****

In March 1983, Larry Henderson, editor and general manager of the *Catholic Register*, phoned Father Matthews at the rectory of Our Lady of Lourdes and invited him to join a new editorial team at the *Register*. The invitation came as a complete surprise, but Father Matthews quickly accepted.[59] In addition to Henderson and Matthews, there were three more members: Alfred De Manche, a thirty-year veteran of Catholic journalism, Stanley P. Koma, associate editor of the *Register*, and Dr. Suzanne Scorsone, the director of the Office of Catholic Family Life for the Archdiocese of Toronto.[60] Together they formed a solid line-up of knowledgeable, experienced and orthodox Catholic thinkers and writers. Henderson assigned Father Matthews to write every fifth editorial, dedicated to the topic of Catholic education. The stipend was a nominal seventy-five dollars per editorial, but it was a dream assignment.

Father Matthews would write twenty-seven editorials and hand deliver each one to the premier and to both opposition leaders. He always felt that his editorials for the *Register* were far more effective than anything else he had done on behalf of Catholic education, including his extensive private and public lobbying of politicians. His first editorial appeared on 16 April 1983, and his last was published on 14 December 1985. By law, he had to relinquish his position at the *Register* when he had become MSSB chairman. Father Matthews editorialized on a variety of topics: separate school completion (three times); the teaching of religious knowledge and the Canadian catechism; the pooling of corporate taxes; Catholic identity, Catholic heritage and Catholic teachers; the retention of religious schools in Quebec; and separate school trustees. He also paid handsome and well-deserved salutes to B.E. Nelligan, Bishop Joseph F. Ryan of Hamilton, Roland Bériault, Monsignor Percy Johnson, Bishop Paul Reding of Hamilton and Bill Davis on his retirement from politics. Father Matthews celebrated in glorious style Premier Davis's announcement on completion, in his editorial of 23 June 1984, but he settled back down to earth in his editorial of 25 August 1984, when he asked with unease and anxiety, "Will schools stay Catholic?" Such a question prompted other editorials concerning Bill 30, the legislation that completed the separate school system: "Strength and weaknesses in school bill"; "No time for a weak stand"; and "Keep our schools Catholic in law."

---

[1] Matthews Papers, Box 4, File 19, CJM to William G. Davis, 13 December 1972.

[2] Ibid., CJM to Vincent Pellettier, 6 November 1972.

[3] Ibid., CJM to Norman Kelly, 15 November 1972.

[4] Ibid., William A. Allen to CJM, 5 December 1972.

[5] Ibid., William G. Davis to CJM, 22 December 1972.

[6] Box 5, File 1, "Statement of Trustee Father Carl J. Matthews, S.J.," 3 January 1973.

[7] CJM, telephone interview by the author, 11 March 2004; Box 5, File 17, CJM to Berchmans Kipp, 12 December 1985.

[8] CJM, "Ontario Catholic nursing schools are to cease," *Catholic Register*, 10 February 1973. 17.

[9] M. Josephine Flaherty, "Nurse-educator answers Fr. Matthews," *Catholic Register*, 3 March 1973.

[10] *Catholic Register*, 17 March 1973, 4.

[11] Box 5, File 1, William G. Davis to CJM, 21 February 1973.

[12] Ibid., CJM to William G. Davis, 19 March 1973.

[13] Ibid., CJM to His fellow trustees of Ontario Separate Schools, 20 March 1973.

[14] Ibid., J. Pace, Lambton County Roman Catholic Separate School Board, to CJM, 22 March 1973; Raymond J. Doyle, Frontenac-Lennox and Addington County Roman Catholic Separate School Board, 28 March 1973.

[15] "Disposition of Resolutions Presented at 1973 Annual Convention," *Catholic Trustee* (June 1973), 41-42.

[16] Box 5, File 1, CJM to His fellow trustees of Ontario Separate Schools, 3 May 1973.

[17] Ibid., CJM to Task Force on Consolidation of the School Acts, 12 April 1973.

[18] Box 5, File 2, "Consolidation of the Education Acts," 30 November 1973.

[19] *Catholic Register*, 9 February 1974, 4.

20 Box 5, File 3, CJM to William G. Davis, 5 March 1974.

21 Ibid., William G. Davis to CJM, 12 March 1974.

22 Ibid., CJM to William G. Davis, 22 March 1974.

23 Ibid., William G. Davis to CJM, 6 May 1974.

24 Ibid., J. Sweeney to CJM, 28 February 1974; "Trustees hear both sides of school Consolidation," *Catholic Register*, 23 March 1974.

25 CJM, "A Role for the Catholic Educator in Ontario," OECTA *Review* (April 1974), 7.

26 CJM, "The Separate Schools Act: keeping the faith," *Globe and Mail*, 1 April 1974, 7.

27 "Trustees divided on Consolidation Act," *Catholic Register*, 20 April 1974, 11.

28 Box 5, File 5, CJM to Thomas L. Wells, 21 January 1975; Thomas L. Wells to CJM, 24 January 1975.

29 *Statutes of Ontario* 1974, 23-24 Elizabeth II, c. 109, "The Education Act, 1974." CJM, telephone interview by author, 9 March 2004.

30 Box 5, File 5, CJM to Peter F. Bargen, executive director of the Ontario School Trustees' Council, 14 February 1975; Box 5, File 6, Peter F. Bargen to CJM, 5 February 1976.

31 Ibid., CJM to Peter F. Bargen, 8 December 1976.

32 Box 5, File 7, CJM to Chris Asseff, 21 August 1976; Box 5, File 8, Chris Asseff to All Separate School Boards, 18 October 1976.

33 Box 5, File 8, CJM to Very Rev. T.G. Walsh, S.J., 20 April 1977.

34 Box 5, File 9, Rev. P.H. Fogarty, C.S.C. to CJM, 22 August 1977.

35 Ibid., "A Submission to the Task Force on National Unity," 28 November 1972. There were nine constituent members of the Federation of Catholic Education Associations of Ontario. OSSTA was one of them.

36 Ibid., CJM to Jean-Luc Pepin, 29 November 1977; Jean-Luc Pepin to CJM, 16 December 1977; CJM to Gerard LaForest, 1 December 1977; CCSTA, *News Bulletin* (April 1978), "Canada's Constitution."

37 Ibid., CJM to Frank Carter, 1 December 1977.

38 Ibid., "Self memo to the chairman of the CCSTA committee on the BNA Act," 12 December 1977.

39 Box 5, File 9a, a collection of reviews, news stories and letters concerning the publication of *Catholic Schools in Canada*.

40 Box 5, File 9, Thomas L. Wells to Clifford Pitt, 1 November 1977; CJM to The Committee to Review the Proposed Governing Structure of the Ontario Institute for Studies in Education, 19 December 1977.

41 Box 5, File 10, Mother to CJM, 14 November 1978.

42 Ibid., Archbishop G. Emmett Carter to CJM, 14 November 1978.

43 CJM, "Study urges equitable school tax," *Catholic Register,* 3 March 1979, 11; "Trends in separate school enrolment," OECTA *Review* (June 1979), 14; "Catholic Schools in Ontario's Future," *Catholic Trustee* (September 1979), 20-21; "Canadian Catholic School Trustees' Association: Its Beginning"; and Box 5, File 11, CJM to Molly Boucher, 16 November 1979.

44 Box 5, File 1, CJM to John J. Andrachuk, 26 January 1973.

45 Box 5, File 11, CJM, "Financing Separate Schools at Grades 9-10: Background Paper," November 1979.

46 Robert T. Dixon, *Catholic Education and Politics in Ontario, 1964-2001* (Toronto: Catholic Education Foundation of Ontario, 2003), 230-31.

47 OSSTA, "The Status of Secondary Education Under Separate School Jurisdiction: A Position Paper," 12 November 1981, 18, 21.

48 Ibid., 24.

49 Dixon, *Catholic Education and Politics in Ontario, 1964-2001,* 231.

50 Box 5, File 13, CJM to Chris Asseff, 14 January 1982.

51 Ibid., CJM to William G. Davis, 15 January 1982.

52 Ibid., 2.

53 Ibid., as quoted in CJM to Chris Asseff, 8 February 1982.

54 "Catholic trustee resigns over provincial grants," *Toronto Star,* 5 February 1982, 7.

55 Box 5, File 13, CJM to Chris Asseff, 8 February 1982.

56 Ibid., George Saranchuk to Mary O'Connor, 25 January 1982; R.F. Hall to Chris Asseff, 21 February 1982.

57 Ibid., "A Response from the Metropolitan Separate School Board to the OSSTA Position Paper on 'The Status of Secondary Education Under Separate School Jurisdiction,' " May 1982.

58 Franklin A. Walker, *Catholic Education and Politics in Ontario,* vol. 3 (Toronto: Catholic Education Foundation, 1986), 375.

59 Box 5, File 14, Larry Henderson to CJM, 17 March 1983; information supplied by CJM, 30 November 2003.

60 "Editorial Notice," *Catholic Register,* 26 March 1983, 4.

CHAPTER SIX

COMPLETION AT LAST! ALLELUIA!

This brings us to Father Matthews' involvement in the process whereby Bill 30 finally became law and was upheld, as amended, by the Supreme Court of Canada. To establish his involvement, it is necessary to parse events as they unfolded:

12 June 1984: Premier Davis's announcement on completion and the establishment of three commissions: Planning and Implementation, School Finances and Independent Schools

October 1984: Premier Davis retires but stays on until February 1985, when his successor is chosen

2 May 1985: Provincial election, Conservative minority

18 June 1985: Liberal and NDP accord for two years

4 July 1985: Sean Conway, minister of education, introduces Bill 30

11 July 1985: Second Reading of Bill 30 passes, 117-1, and is sent to the Social Development Committee

September 1985: Social Development Committee hearings begin; Bill 30 sent to the Ontario Court of Appeal

18 February 1986: Ontario Court of Appeal upholds constitutionality of Bill 30

22 April 1986: Bill 30 re-introduced with four amendments; First and Second Reading

23 June 1986: Third Reading

24 June 1986: Royal Assent for "An Act to amend the Education Act"

25 June 1987: Supreme Court of Canada upholds constitutionality of "An Act to amend the Education Act"

****

On the morning of 12 June 1984, Miss Anderson, Premier Bill Davis's secretary, phoned Father Matthews at Our Lady of Lourdes rectory and asked him to be present in the Legislative Gallery at 2 pm. He sat in the front row of the side Gallery, facing the premier. As usual on a school day in June, the five galleries were filled that afternoon, but there was only one other Catholic educator in attendance. He was Kevin Kennedy, the president of OECTA, who came to hear an announcement on Grades 9 and 10! The members of the Legislative Assembly had taken their seats. The atmosphere was such that everyone expected a major announcement. Even the opposition leaders thought that the premier might announce secondary grants for Grades 9 and 10. However, as the premier began to speak, he quickly made it clear that he was reversing his 1971 decision on separate schools and authorizing the completion of Ontario's Catholic system to the end of Grade 13.

Premier Davis spoke for thirty minutes to a silent legislature and gallery. When he finished, he received a standing ovation from both sides of the house. The last to rise was Robert Nixon, the former leader of the Liberal Party. He was still nursing the wounds of Davis's 1971 "No" to completion that did so much to defeat the Liberals in that year's election. On a point of order from Bob Rae, the NDP leader, the leaders of the opposition parties spoke to the premier's historic statement. David Peterson, the Liberal leader, delivered a gracious speech. He was followed by Bob Rae, who was not only gracious but also eloquent.[1] As soon as he was done, he crossed the floor of the house and congratulated the premier. There was another robust round of applause from the members. Father Matthews was so caught up in the moment that he stood up and began to applaud, which was strictly forbidden for those sitting in the gallery. A security guard came over and told him to stop or he would be thrown out.[2]

As the excitement died down, Father Matthews ran to a pay phone in the lobby and called Chris Asseff at OSSTA. Then he made his way to Cardinal Carter's home in Rosedale to report on the speeches. That night he stayed up to four in the morning to write his "Completion at last! Alleluia!" editorial for the *Catholic Register* and a letter of profound thanks to Premier Davis.

About midmorning that day, Father Matthews drove over to St. Joseph's College on Wellesley Street West, parked his car and walked the two long blocks to the premier's office at Queen's Park. He handed his letter to the premier's receptionist and left to return to his car, walking at a brisk pace. Just before he reached the parking lot at St. Joseph's, he heard someone in the distance shouting, "Father! Father!" Turning around, he began to retrace his steps, and after several minutes he met a middle-aged man who was out of breath and had to pause between every word. He asked, "Are you Father Matthews? I am the deputy minister of transportation, and the premier sent me to bring you back." Father Matthews answered, "Yes" and returned to Queen's Park with a flush-faced deputy minister, who was not used to chasing after people. Premier Davis was at a meeting on the revitalization of the Toronto waterfront. When he heard that Father Matthews was waiting for him, he came out of the meeting and said, with a big smile, "I hope that you are satisfied now, Carl."

****

Father Carl Matthews was definitely satisfied. His satisfaction was deep and personal, for he felt that something that he had written almost five years previous to 12 June 1984 might have provided Premier Davis with the final, the clinching, argument in favour of completion. Every October, the priests of the archdiocese of Toronto gathered for a three-day session to discuss sacramental life in the parishes. Dress was casual; so was the atmosphere. October 1979 was no different. That year, the meeting took place at the Toronto Airport Holiday Inn. Significantly, Father Matthews was not a trustee at the time. When, club bag in hand, he walked through the front door of the hotel, several priests rushed forward and exclaimed, "The Cardinal wants to see you, Carl, right now in his room." Cardinal Carter had received the red hat the previous June.

Sensing that the cardinal would be dressed in clericals, Father Matthews was embarrassed to appear before him in sports clothes, but the cardinal was most welcoming and offered him a glass of orange juice. Right away Cardinal Carter told Father Matthews that he wanted to present a compelling case to Premier Davis for completion of the separate school system. Now that he was a cardinal, he felt that completion was a matter of public importance that he could influence. He was ready to play his hand.

Cardinal Carter and Premier Davis were good friends. They knew and respected each other. They were consummate actors on the public stage, who were also aware of the power of private persuasion. In between the two stood Father Carl Matthews, so to speak. He was a solid supporter of Cardinal Carter, having worked with him on different school matters since the 1960s, and he was on a first-name basis with Premier Davis.

Cardinal Carter wanted to know what compromises did Father Matthews think would be impossible for separate school supporters to make, and what compromises might one propose in a brief to the premier. Without hesitation, Father Matthews replied that Grades 11, 12 and 13 should be phased in, one year at a time, and that such a phase-in could be accomplished without recourse to the public board's realty tax base. The solution was the principle of the 1964 Foundation Tax Plan. On hearing that, the cardinal laughed and remarked that Father Matthews' 1969 memorandum (regarding no local taxes initially to fund extension) had changed *his* mind on *that* subject.[3] Left unsaid was a fond hope that Matthews, writing under the cardinal's name, might be able to convince *the premier* on the *whole works*.

After a long pause, the cardinal asked Matthews to write him a brief on completion for the premier. He wanted it on his desk in three weeks, but he did not bother to explain the need for all the rush, and he demanded that nothing be said about the brief to anyone as long as he was alive. Matthews agreed to write the brief and remain mum about it, but he told the cardinal that he would have to ask his superior at Our Lady of Lourdes, Father Joe Johnson, S.J., for time off from some of his parish duties during the next three weeks. "Fine," said the cardinal, and Matthews left the room.

Father Matthews met the deadline. He wrote a twelve-page brief with five appendices. The cover sheet simply said "To Premier Davis From Cardinal Carter" and was dated October 1979. He handed it to the cardinal's secretary, and the cardinal phoned to express his pleasure at receiving the document. That was the last that Matthews heard about the brief until the autumn of 1983, when the cardinal's secretary rang him to say that Premier Davis's office had phoned. The premier had mislaid his copy of the October 1979 brief. Would the cardinal be so kind as to send another copy to the premier's office by taxi? Well, Cardinal Carter could not find his copy either! The cardinal's office asked Matthews if he had a copy. He answered, "Yes." In fact, he made two more copies and delivered them in person to the chancery on Church Street the same day. A phone call expressed appreciation and informed Father Matthews that a copy of the brief was back in the hands of the premier.

When Father Matthews arrived at Cardinal Carter's home, on 12 June 1984, to tell him about Davis's historic announcement in the legislature, the cardinal greeted him with a big embrace. Father Matthews remarked, "A scarlet robe opens more doors than a black suit." They smiled, knowingly, without having to say a word about the secret brief of October 1979.[4]

****

After the euphoria of 12 June 1984 had worn off, and the Alleluias had subsided to a collective sigh of relief, separate school supporters of all brands needed to remind themselves that Premier Davis's announcement was only the beginning of what would be a lengthy and potentially divisive process. Time and politics, not intentions, would determine the final shape of any legislation. This was no time to make compromises that in the long run would undermine, perhaps even destroy, the Catholic identity and raison d'etre of the very school system that countless Catholics over the decades had struggled to preserve, strengthen and complete.

As a school trustee, editorial writer and long-time public defender of separate schools, Father Matthews from the outset adopted an attitude of active vigilance and timely intervention in the ensuing debate. He wrote a strong rebuttal of a Kingston *Whig-Standard* editorial of 21 June 1984 that had argued against full funding of Catholic high schools because it would be unfair to other religious sects.[5] Betty Kennedy of CFRB radio in Toronto interviewed him on 18 July 1984. The subject was the conditions for completion. Father Matthews acquitted himself well.[6] He contributed an article to *Orbit 73*, a publication of the Ontario Institute for Studies in Education. It appeared under the banner "Responses to the Separate School Funding Initiative." Arguing against him in the same issue was Marilyn Rowe, the president of the Public School Trustees' Association.[7] On 28 March 1985, Father Matthews and Patrick Brennan, Hamilton's director, debated Malcolm Buchanan, president of the Ontario Secondary School Teachers' Federation, and Ernie Checkeris, president of Northern Ontario Trustees, for ninety minutes on the TV Ontario program "Speaking Out." The topic was "How Catholic Should the Completed Separate High Schools Be?" The response to the show was nothing short of overwhelming.[8] Again, Father Matthews held his ground, but the ground had been shifting under his feet for several months.

The shift began with the Ontario Catholic bishops' statement of 3 October 1984. It contained this sentence: "We wish to assure our people that the arrangements required with reference to the employment of non-Catholic secondary school teachers or the admission of non-Catholic pupils can be made without endangering the Catholic character of our schools."[9] The background to this startling claim was straightforward. Several days prior to 12 June 1984, the premier's office and the Bishops' Commission for Education came to an understanding that separate school boards would employ any non-Catholic secondary school teachers deemed redundant due to the transfer of Catholic students from the public to the separate system, as the result of completion.[10] Armed with this understanding, Davis then proposed in his announcement on completion a ten-year hiring period, after which Catholic boards would no longer be required to offer contracts to non-Catholic teachers from the public boards. (Bette Stephenson, the minister of education, subsequently modified this understanding, when she told the *London Free Press* in September 1984 that Mr. Davis's real intention on this matter was for Catholic boards to hire non-Catholic teachers only if there were not enough Catholic teachers on hand to deliver a board's programs.) However, Mr. Davis was not categorical on the issue regarding the admission of non-Catholic students to Catholic schools. He hoped only that Catholic boards would consider their admission. (Stephenson would confuse everyone on this issue when she threatened to force Catholic boards to endorse universal admission.)

The bishops were prompted to make a commitment to the admission of non-Catholic students due to an intervention by Bishop Jacques Landriault of Timmins. He pointed out that the French-language public secondary school in Timmins had 650 Catholics and fifty non-Catholics. Surely the separate school board would not bar the non-Catholic teachers and students when it took over the school, he told his brother bishops at their annual autumn meeting. In a letter to Father Angus J. Macdougall, S.J., general secretary of the Ontario Conference of Catholic Bishops, Father Matthews was sympathetic to Bishop Landriault's Timmins solution, but he also argued that it could not be applied to Toronto, Hamilton, Windsor or any place in Ontario where conditions were different from those in francophone communities. It was incumbent upon the bishops, Matthews continued to Macdougall, to publish a second statement that contained a qualification to this effect.[11]

The day after the appearance of the bishops' statement, Father Matthews publicly disagreed with the bishops. He told Robert Matas of the *Globe and Mail* that he wanted MSSB to hire only Catholic teachers and admit only Catholic students.[12] It was a matter of Catholic identity, he later wrote in a letter to the *Globe*. To make his point, he quoted Penny Moss, the vice-chair of the Metro Toronto Public Board of Education. She said, "I don't understand how you can have a separate system open to everyone. One of the rationales for Roman Catholic schools is that religious teachings must infuse the entire program, and that's also a rationale for discriminating about who teaches in it and who studies in it."[13] Father Matthews would quote these same words in a *Register* editorial of 31 August 1985 and in his testimony to the legislature's Standing Committee on Social Development.

In December 1984, the Bishops' Commission for Education issued a pastoral guideline that urged separate school trustees to ensure that Catholic teachers formed at least ninety percent of each board's staff. The commission felt that this ceiling was needed to maintain the Catholic nature of separate schools. Cardinal Carter disagreed. He said that the bishops had no business making specific proposals. "I think it is silly to postulate that if there are 11 percent non-Catholic teachers in your school, it's going to be a failure; if 90 percent [Catholic], then the school is fine. That's ridiculous ... the spirit of the school is what is going to matter and you could have a very wide range of Catholic and non-Catholic teachers in a school and still have a Catholic school. I don't think that you can tie that down to a number."[14] Things were becoming rather odd. It appeared that Penny Moss, who probably wished that separate schools had never existed, had a better grasp of their true nature than did Cardinal Carter, who had done so much to persuade Premier Davis to embrace completion.

The irony was not lost on Father Matthews. As Bill 30 snaked its way from the Ontario Legislature, with its minority government, to the Court of Appeal and back to the legislature, a process that began with first reading on 4 July 1985 and ended with royal assent on 24 June 1986, Father Matthews fought against the inclusion of any amendments that favoured non-discriminatory hiring of teachers, universal access for non-Catholic students and automatic exemption for them from religious studies.[15] He made his case in person to the Standing Committee on Social Development on 26 September 1985.[16] However, the version of Bill 30 that was presented at second reading on 11 July 1984 was not the same as the version of Bill 30 that became law on 24 June 1986. When Bill 30 was returned to the legislature, on 22 April 1986, having survived the court challenge on its constitutionality, the bill received four amendments. One was inconsequential, but three of them would directly affect the identity of Catholic schools. One amendment declared that after ten years, Catholic boards would no longer hold the right to discriminatory hiring of teachers (this was a bombshell); the second abolished any conditions on non-Catholic student access to separate schools; and the third effectively exempted non-Catholic students from compulsory religious education.

Father Matthews never quit. He appeared for a second time before the Standing Committee on Social Development, in May 1986, this time in his capacity as MSSB chairman.[17] He spoke for the entire board. It was a gallant but futile effort. All the amendments passed and Bill 30 was returned to the legislature.

Third reading took place on 23 June 1986. In the gallery was Father Matthews. Robert Nixon, Liberal deputy premier and minister of finance, rose from his seat and paid tribute to Archbishop Philip Pocock and Father Carl Matthews:

> Probably my greatest recognition must go to the late Archbishop Pocock who, in his senior position in those days, undertook to assist politicians of all parties to review the past and consider reasonable alternatives. I will never forget his ability in a reasonable and moderate way to persuade politicians such as myself, representatives of the Progressive Conservative Party and the New Democratic Party, to come to a meeting of minds. He, probably more than anyone else, made it possible for me to support this policy. I am very grateful to have known such a great man.
>
> I would also like to recognize the role played by Carl Matthews, S.J., the present chairman of the separate school board of Metropolitan Toronto who has attended many sessions of this Legislature and is in the gallery now. For many years, he saw that all sides of the Legislature were adequately and fully informed of the statistical situation associated with the funding of separate schools, particularly compared with the then public system. I appreciated his tenacity, his ability to set the facts forward fairly and his continuing friendship.[18]

When Robert Nixon's marked his twenty-fifth anniversary as a member of the Legislative Assembly, in January 1987, Father Matthews thanked him for his "gracious words in the House last June 23rd," telling him that "were it not for your courageous stand from 1969 to 1975 on the need to complete the last sixth of the Separate School system, nothing that has happened in the House in the last three years would have been possible."[19] Immediately after the passage of Bill 30, Father Matthews praised Sean Conway for the leadership that he had shown on a truly historic matter.[20] But he reserved his most heartfelt praise for his friend of twenty years, Bill Davis. "Countless young people in Ontario now and for generations to come will be the beneficiaries of your 'Yes.'"[21]

****

Father Matthews became chairman of the Metropolitan Separate School Board on 2 December 1985.[22] Although it was a one-year term of office, it was customary for the chairman to serve an additional year. But Father Matthews chose not to seek a second term. To take on the chairmanship for just one year meant that he had to give up any involvement in parish meetings at Our Lady of Lourdes, his hospital ministry and his turn on the twenty-four-hour on-call system at the parish. The compromise was a one-year chairmanship. In any event, this allowed Father Matthews to nominate his successor for 1986-87, Caroline DiGiovanni, who became MSSB's first woman chair.[23]

It was an extraordinarily busy year for Father Matthews. He had more than 300 engagements: board meetings, committee meetings, conferences, interviews, graduation addresses, the legislature, school visitations, special correspondence and meetings with the minister of education.[24] Of particular importance were the meetings, every second or third Wednesday of each month, of COSS (Completion, Ontario Separate Schools). They were chaired by Tom Reilly, director of the Dufferin-Peel board. Lasting the entire morning, they were absolutely vital to a successful transition to full funding. In the midst of all this productive activity, there took place the first-ever teachers' strike in MSSB's history. Parity with public school salaries and smaller class sizes were the main points of contention between the board and OECTA. The strike by 5,800 teachers commenced 7 April 1986 and affected 99,000 students. It ended a week later, to everyone's relief.[25] Father Matthews did not participate in negotiations, but he was busy at the microphone, representing the board to the media.

Beginning in 1986, MSSB faced an unprecedented $13.4 million deficit, due to inadequate grants and unfair taxation policies. The board had a reserve of $7.25 million, but that still left a shortfall of more than $6 million, another first in the board's history.[26] After warning his fellow board members about the looming financial crisis, in his inaugural speech as chairman, Father Matthews decided to take matters into his own hands. Every year, the board's director of education prepared for the Advisory Committee (composed of the board chairman and the chairmen of all the committees) a brief on behalf of the board in advance of the April Grants Regulations. Because MSSB was facing a huge deficit in 1986, Father Matthews, as he had done so often since 1962, wrote the brief himself. It was dated 13 January 1986. He did so without informing the other trustees on the Advisory Committee. That was his first mistake, several trustees pointed out loudly.

His second was to write to Sean Conway, the minister of education, and ask for a meeting. MSSB chairmen never discussed official business with the minister without being in the company of the director of education. Father Matthews, however, chose to go it alone. Conway's office replied to his letter by inviting him to a breakfast meeting at the restaurant of the Bradgate Arms Hotel. It took place on 16 January 1986. Only Matthews and Conway were present. During the course of their conversation, Matthews explained MSSB's deficit, and Conway asked Matthews if he had anything in writing. Matthews did. It was a copy of the brief that had yet to be approved by the Advisory Committee and submitted to a vote of the entire board. Conway took it and thanked Matthews. At the heart of the brief were two indisputable facts: one, total income for Grades 9, 10 and 11 in the separate school system was $3,441 per pupil but operating costs were $4,791 per pupil, for a difference of $1,350; and two, Catholic elementary schools received $890 per pupil less than public elementary schools.[27]

Later that same day, the Advisory Committee met. Father Matthews' brief was on the agenda. Someone wondered aloud why the chairman was writing briefs. Then someone else asked, "Does the minister know about your brief?" Father Matthews replied, "Yes." That seemed to stun everyone in the room. "How dare you submit something to the minister without the board's approval!" When things calmed down, the committee examined the brief, saw no need to change it and voted to accept it.[28] The entire board also gave its approval. Conway took the brief seriously and made improvements in the grant regulations, so that MSSB received substantially more money for operating expenditures (but not enough to eliminate the entire deficit). This money was separate from the $5.5 million that MSSB received in February 1986 to purchase property and improve Grade 9 and 10 classrooms, a fact that Father Matthews had to clarify in a letter to the *Catholic Register*.[29] Although two mistakes of judgment were instrumental in producing a beneficial outcome for Catholic students in Toronto, never again did Father Matthews play the lone wolf, in his capacity as board chairman.

****

Father Matthews never stopped working during his final two years as a school trustee. He was the MSSB representative on the City of Toronto Assessment Reform Working Group, supporting the pooling of corporation taxes for school purposes as recommended by the Ian Macdonald Commission; he attended the Supreme Court of Canada hearing on the constitutionality of Bill 30, in early 1987, as the guest of Attorney General Ian Scott; he remained on the OSSTA executive until April 1987; he explained to the press the board's decision to admit only Roman Catholic children to its 191 elementary schools; he published an article, "Teachers touch the future," in *Canadian Messenger of the Sacred Heart*; he participated in the early stages of the legal action against Section 136la of "An Act to amend the Education Act" (this was Bill 30's requirement for the non-discriminatory hiring of teachers by separate school boards, after a ten-year grace period, which the Ontario Court of Appeal overturned in 1997); and he conducted a spirited campaign against Bill 109, which became the Ottawa-Carleton French-Language School Board Act of 1988.[30]

Father Matthews' last hurrah as a trustee was his attempt to derail the government's plan to form what was essentially a homogenous (or umbrella) French-language school board in Ottawa-Carleton that would have a public section and a Catholic section. He had always been a strong advocate of French-language education under the constitutional jurisdiction of Catholic schools boards. Starting in January 1981, Father Matthews had moved a total of seven motions at MSSB meetings to establish a Catholic French-language high school in Toronto.[31] As chairman of the board's Five Year Guidelines Study Committee, he made sure that the committee's final published report included a recommendation on the need for a French-language school.[32] His persistence paid off when École Secondaire Mgr. de Charbonnel opened its doors in 1985.

Father Matthews, however, had always opposed the establishment of homogenous French boards because they would deprive the rights of some Catholics in the province to their own Roman Catholic separate school boards, as guaranteed by Section 93 of the BNA Act. On this issue he aroused the ire of Bishop Eugene LaRoque of Cornwall-Alexandria, as early as 1978, and of Archbishop Joseph-Aurèle Plourde of Ottawa, in 1987, during the debate on Bill 109.[33] Both prelates believed that French-speaking Catholics had little to fear from school boards that were not distinctly and independently Catholic but instead made sufficient accommodation for Catholic trustees. Father Matthews thought otherwise. Bill 109 asked French-speaking Catholics to choose language over religion, when, in fact and in law, there was no reason not to have a Catholic board that would provide both. He took his opposition to Bill 109 to Sean Conway, to Chris Ward, his successor as minister of education, to the bishops of Ontario, to the *Globe and Mail*, to the Carleton Separate School Board and to the legislature's Standing Committee on Social Development.

Father Matthews appeared before the committee on 31 May 1988. The question under consideration was "Are Roman Catholic Separate School supporters in Ontario entitled to school boards or simply to sections of school boards?" For Father Matthews the answer was straightforward. The province's Roman Catholics were entitled to their own school boards. The constitution said so, and the continuous existence of separate school boards for nearly 150 years said so. "I respectfully submit that the only defensible position for the Legislature of Ontario to take on this matter," he told the committee, "is to provide for a wholly autonomous Roman Catholic francophone school board in Ottawa-Carleton and a wholly autonomous francophone public school board in Ottawa-Carleton."[34]

Time would vindicate Father Matthews. Bill 109 received royal assent on 29 June 1988 and took effect on 1 January 1989. The Ottawa-Carleton board was plagued by endless bickering and squabbling between the two sections and lasted a mere five years. On 1 July 1994, the NDP government under Premier Bob Rae created two French-language school boards, one Catholic and one secular, in its place.[35] And to Father Matthews' great satisfaction, the Progressive Conservative government of Premier Mike Harris extended that provision right across Ontario in 1999.

****

Father Matthews had every intention to seek re-election as a separate school trustee in 1988. But Father Bill Addley, S.J., his provincial, had other plans. "Carl, do something else with your life now that you are fifty-six," he told Matthews on 14 July 1988. "Apply your experiences to something other than the school board."[36] Father Addley's words hurt, but Father Matthews was too loyal a Jesuit to let them sting for long. In his final trustee report for Ward 6, he listed four challenges that lay ahead for the Metropolitan Separate School Board and its supporters. The board needed to keep its elementary and secondary schools thoroughly Catholic; it needed to maintain its autonomy and work with other separate school boards to maintain theirs; it would have to secure more equitable funding for Catholic schools; and it needed to open up its thirty-four secondary schools for evening courses for adults.[37]

During his time as an MSSB trustee, Father Matthews had worked with many outstanding people. Among them were Ed Brisbois, Monsignor Percy Johnson, Dr. John Andrachuck, Bruno Suppa, Paul Duggan, Father (later Monsignor) Ed Boehler, Ed McMahon, Caroline DiGiovanni and Don Clune. Each one gave excellent leadership as MSSB chair. He also greatly admired three directors of education – Ed Nelligan (1965-1983), who became a dear and lasting friend, Berchmans Kipp (1983-1988) and Anthony Barone (1988-1995) – as well as Leo Dupuis, deputy director.

To this list of honourable mentions must be added the names of the most influential people in separate school matters, at a provincial level, with whom Father Matthews had shared many a struggle on the road to equality and completion, starting in 1962. They were Archbishop Philip Pocock and his successor, G. Emmett Cardinal Carter, of Toronto; Bishop Joseph F. Ryan of Hamilton; Chris Asseff, Father Raymond Durocher, O.M.I., Albert Klein and Dr. Joe Fyfe (OSSTA); Peter Lauwers, solicitor for OSSTA; Father Frank Kavanagh, O.M.I., Sister Anna Clare, G.S.I.C., George Saranchuk, Peter Gazzola and Mary Babcock (OECTA); Father Patrick Fogarty, C.S.C. and Michael Carty (ECEAO); Tom Reilly of the Completion Office; Father Thomas Mohan, C.S.B. (CCSTA); Monsignor Dennis Murphy; Frank Clifford; Monsignor Ken Robitaille (OCCB); and for a second time, Ed Brisbois (ECEAO) and Ed Nelligan (MSSB). The giants were Dr. Fyfe at the elementary level and Bishop Ryan and Ed Nelligan at the secondary level. The latter two had grown up in downtown Hamilton, a generation apart.

However, the struggles of all these fine people would have been for nothing if Catholic teenagers had not chosen to attend Catholic high schools. Writing in 2002, Father Matthews paid tribute to them:

> The Grade 8 students were voting with their feet as they trudged across town, year after year, to the Catholic school. In fact, between 1971 and 1983, enrolment from Grade 9 to Grade 13 more than doubled to 72,000. The 46 Catholic high schools by then in the archdiocese of Toronto were packed all day like the subway trains at rush hour. The story was the same right across the province. And Bill 82 stipulated that these schools were obliged to educate every Catholic student who applied, and not just university-bound scholars.

All of the then teenagers referred to in the last paragraph made the "completion" announcement possible for Premier Davis on June 12, 1984. These adults today, fathers and mothers of families, are heroic profiles in courage for what they did daily during their teenage years.[38]

****

As Father Matthews looked back on the past sixteen years, he realized that many worlds, many people, had passed on. His father, C.P. Matthews, had died in Kingston on 12 February 1978. If Catholic education was in Father Matthews' bones, it was due to his father. "Truth to tell," he told Cardinal Carter, "my father, the Catholic school inspector, put it in my marrow when he took me, a four- and five-year-old, to visit lots of schools. Then every year as a teenager I got to sit beside him at the Easter Convention and watch Father [Vincent] Priester introduce Cardinal McGuigan, who in turn would introduce Premier Frost."[39] Father Matthews' mother, Florence, followed her husband on 2 March 1981. With her death, the familial ties to his hometown of Kingston began to weaken and become more a matter of happy memories than a living connection.

There were other deaths. Ed Brisbois passed away in December 1976. Father Matthews was the homilist at his funeral Mass, which was attended by 700 people. Father Patrick Fogarty, C.S.C. died on 18 January 1985. They had been friends and colleagues since July 1966. Next to be called were two Jesuit confreres who had a profound influence on Father Matthews' life. They were Father Clement Crusoe, S.J., who died in May 1987, and Father Alfred J. Colliard, S.J., who died less than a year later, in March 1988. Father Matthews preached at Father Crusoe's funeral Mass, and he wrote a wonderful piece on Father Colliard for the September 1988 issue of the *Newsletter* of the Upper Canada Jesuit Province. Then there were the politicians: Premier George Drew and Premier Leslie Frost, both of whom died in 1973. Father Matthews was the only Catholic priest and separate school trustee to attend Drew's funeral, and he praised Frost as a friend of Catholic schools, in a front-page article for the *Catholic Register*.[40]

Also to come to an end were the "Dear Carl" and "Dear Bill" letters. On the verge of retirement as premier, Bill Davis wrote a last letter to Father Carl Matthews, dated 1 February 1985: "Our exchange of correspondence over the years has meant a great deal to me, Carl. While we may not always have been in complete agreement, I believe we have always respected each other's integrity. At the moment I do not know what the future holds in store for me;

however, I do hope that our undertakings will continue to create opportunities for our paths to cross."[41] Three years later, at the end of 1988, Father Carl Matthews was wondering about his own future. Yes, many worlds had come to an end, and a life of "feverish activity" on behalf of separate schools was over, but more worlds would open up for him.[42]

---

[1] Ontario, Legislature of Ontario, *Debates*, 12 June 1984, 2414-18.

[2] Cy Jamison, "Just a quiet afternoon, on the road from Queen's Park to Damascus," OECTA *Reporter*, 15 June 1984, 1.

[3] Matthews Papers, Box 3, File 13, Bishop G. Emmett Carter to A.E. Klein, 19 September 1969. See Chapter Two.

[4] Information supplied by CJM, 30 November 2003. Of course, the October 1979 brief from Carter to Davis should not be understood as the whole story of Davis's "conversion" to completion. That story should be read within a greater context, as outlined in Robert Dixon, "William Davis and the Road to Completion in Ontario's Catholic High Schools, 1971-1985," Canadian Catholic Historical Association, *Historical Studies* 69 (2003): 7-33.

[5] CJM, "BNA Act guarantees support for separate Catholic schools," Kingston *Whig-Standard*. 7 July 1984, 8.

[6] Box 5, File 15, "Betty Kennedy interviews Fr. Carl Matthews, S.J."; an abbreviated version of this interview appeared as "School funding concerns discussed," *Catholic Register*, 25 August 1984.

[7] CJM, "Completion of the Seventh of a School System," *Orbit 73* (February 1985), 14, 16.

[8] Box 5, File 16, Birchmans Kipp to All Trustees, 25 March 1985; Moira Potter to CJM, 9 April 1985.

[9] Quoted in Dixon, *Catholic Education and Politics in Ontario, 1964-2001*, 249.

[10] "Davis received assurances on teachers, Carter says," *Globe and Mail*, 21 February 1985.

[11] Box 5, File 15, CJM to Rev. Angus J. Macdougall, S.J., 12 November 1984.

[12] "Government financing divides Catholic clergy," *Globe and Mail*, 4 October 1984.

[13] CJM, "Catholic identity," *Globe and Mail*, 30 October 1984; published earlier in *London Free Press*, 22 October 1984 and the *Catholic Register*, 20 October 1984. Moss's words originally appeared in the *Globe and Mail*, 13 September 1984.

[14] "Davis received assurances on teachers, Carter says," *Globe and Mail*, 21 February 1985.

[15] Box 5, File 17, CJM to Fellow Separate School Trustees, 20 October 1985.

16 Ontario, Legislature of Ontario, *Debates*, Standing Committee on Social Development, 26 September 1985, S-1520-26.

17 Box 5, File 18, CJM to Richard Johnson, MPP, 24 May 1986; CJM to Dear Parents, 14 May 1986; MSSB, "Submission to the Social Development Committee of the Legislature of Ontario in Response to the Proposed Amendments to Bill 30," May 1986.

18 Ontario, Legislature of Ontario, *Debates*, 23 June 1986, 1847.

19 Box 5, File 20, CJM to Robert Nixon, 9 January 1987.

20 Box 5, File 18, CJM to Sean Conway, 2 July 1986.

21 Ibid., CJM to William G. Davis, 24 July 1986.

22 Box 5, File 17, CJM to "Dear Colleagues," 17 November 1985; "Jesuit priest to head Metro separate school board," *Toronto Star*, 27 November 1985; "Father Carl Matthews elected chairman of MSSB," *Catholic Register*, 21-28 December 1985, 22.

23 "Catholic board picks female head for first time," *Toronto Star*, 25 November 1986, 7.

24 Box 5, File 18, CJM to "All Trustees," 18 November 1986.

25 Box 5, File 17, CJM to "All Metropolitan Separate School Board Teachers," 2 April 1986; "Strike ends in RC schools after 1 week," *Globe and Mail*, 14 April 1986, 1; "Money, class size triggered teachers' strike," *Catholic Register*, 19 April 1986, 3.

26 "Separate school board anticipates deficit," *Globe and Mail*, 4 December 1985.

27 Box 5, File 18, "Brief to the Ontario Minister of Education, The Honourable Sean Conway. Re: Metropolitan Separate School Board - Finances," 13 January 1986; "Conway to look into $7 million debt as enrolment rises at Catholic board," *Toronto Star*, 20 January 1986.

28 CJM, interview by author, 10 December 2003.

29 "MSSB receives $5.5 million," *Catholic Register*, 15 February 1986; CJM, "Pool corporate taxes for schools," *Catholic Register*, 1 March 1986.

30 Box 5, File 21, CJM to Advisory Committee of MSSB, "Corporation Assessment," 9 November 1987; Box 5, File 18, CJM to Ian Scott, 29 December 1986 and Ian Scott to CJM, 27 January 1987; CJM to Directors of the Ontario Separate School Trustees' Association, 18 April 1987; CJM, "Why Catholic Board closed the door," *Toronto Star*, 6 June 1988, A14; CJM, "Story behind school board action," *Catholic Register*, 11 June 1988; CJM, "Teachers touch the future," *Canadian Messenger of the Sacred Heart* (October 1988), 4-5; Box 5, File 19, all documents relate to Section 136la.

31 Box 5, File 12a, "Notice of Motion at the Board Meeting of December 18, 1980 for consideration at the Meeting of January 22, 1981"; CJM, "French Catholic high school for Toronto?" *Catholic Register*, 29 August 1981, E3.

32 Box 5, File 14, CJM to Chris Asseff, 3 January 1983; Box 5, File 13, MSSB, "Five Year Guidelines Study 1983-87: A Position Paper on Catholic Secondary Education," 1982.

33 Box 5, File 14, CJM to Chris Asseff, 3 January 1983; Box 5, File 20, CJM to Joseph-Aurèle Plourde, 4 January 1987.

34 Ontario, Legislature of Ontario, *Debates*, Standing Committee on Social Development, 31 May 1988, S-10.

35 Dixon, *Catholic Education and Politics in Ontario, 1964-2001*, 170-73.

36 Information supplied by CJM, 30 November 2003.

37 CJM, "Your Trustee's Report," (June 1988).

38 Ibid., "Profiles in Courage in Ontario Catholic Education," *Catholic Register*, 3 March 2002, 24.

39 Box 5, File 22, CJM to Cardinal G. Emmett Carter, 17 July 1988.

40 Box 5, File 1, CJM to William G. Davis, 8 January 1973; CJM, "Premier Frost: A friend of Catholic schools," *Catholic Register*, 19 May 1973, 1.

41 Box 5, File 16, William G. Davis to CJM, 1 February 1985.

42 "'Feverish activity' was an apt description for the doings of Matthews himself." See Walker, *Catholic Education and Politics in Ontario*, vol. 3, 290. Father Matthews loaned his own papers to Walker, when he was researching volume 3. See Box 5, File 10, Franklin A. Walker to CJM, 5 April 1985.

Father Matthews holding a framed copy of the front page of the 100th anniversary issue of the Catholic Register, 20 February 1993. It was signed by his staff

CHAPTER SEVEN

HIGHS AND LOWS OF A PUBLISHER AND EDITOR

Father Carl Matthews' life was in a state of flux for more than sixteen months after he left the Metropolitan Separate School Board. During that time, his long-term future was on hold. The first thing that he did was to accept a half sabbatical. On 8 January 1989, he flew to Rome, with Father Terry Walsh, S.J., for the Twelfth Ignatian Course (in English). It was a well-earned break after fourteen years of intense school board work. From Rome he paid a brief visit to northern Italy and then to the Marian shrine at Medjugorje, Yugoslavia. On 20 February, he left for the Holy Land, where he spent the next eight days completing the course in the Spiritual Exercises.[1]

While Father Matthews was away in Europe, the Catholic High School Commission of the Archdiocese of Toronto, on the recommendation of Cardinal Carter, chose him as the 1989 recipient of its Award of Merit, *honoris causa*.[2] The dinner and ceremony took place at St. Michael's College on 4 February 1989. Monsignor Clement Schwalm, the commission chairman, made the presentation, and Father Patrick Boyle, S.J., assistant to the Jesuit Provincial, received the award on behalf of Father Matthews. Many members of the Matthews family were in attendance and thought that the evening was a grand affair, despite the oddity of Father Carl's absence overseas. Among the many congratulatory letters that Father Matthews received on this occasion was one from Archbishop Aloysius Ambrozic, at that time coadjutor archbishop of Toronto. The archbishop wrote that the commendation stood for "a tremendous amount of intelligent and steadfast work done for our schools. Your effort is impossible to measure because it went on day by day and year by year, and will continue echoing in time and eternity. It is so pleasant to know of your dedication and utter fidelity to the faith."[3]

This was not the first or the last award given to Father Matthews for his separate school work. He had already received the Monsignor Harrigan Award from the Federation of Catholic Parent-Teacher Associations of Ontario, on 24 October 1987. The ceremony was held in St. Catharines.[4] On 21 October 1989, at the Bristol Place Hotel, in Toronto, the Catholic Education Foundation of Ontario gave him its Medal of Honour. It was the unanimous decision of the executive and the board of directors, wrote Ed Nelligan, his old friend and fellow warhorse. He continued: "The selection was based upon your life-long commitment to Catholic Education in Ontario and your selfless single-minded efforts to achieve justice and equity for the children attending Catholic Schools in the Province."[5] On 2 December 1991, the Metropolitan Separate School Board recognized Father Matthews with its own Award of Merit. Part of the citation read: "All his adult life he has been tireless in working toward a three-fold educational goal: completion of the Catholic system to Grade 13/OAC; financial parity from kindergarten upwards; and strengthening the Catholicity in all our schools."[6]

Returning to Our Lady of Lourdes parish in early March 1989, Father Matthews took the next two months to prepare a series of lectures for a course on the History of Catholic Education in Ontario. It was for separate school teachers and was offered at the MSSB headquarters, through the extension department of St. Augustine's Seminary. Father Matthews met his first class in the autumn of 1989. He taught the course five times over ten years. He was a popular instructor who knew his subject intimately and made his students feel directly involved in the historic struggles of Ontario's separate schools. For many, the course was a revelation that prompted dozens of them to write the program director most flattering letters of recommendation.

In addition to his course preparation, Father Matthews accepted the March 1989 offer from the Canadian Catholic School Trustees' Association to update his 1977 book, *Catholic Schools in Canada*. He took no payment and no royalties, but he insisted on complete editorial control and proper payment for his typist.[7] The result was *Catholic School Systems Across Canada*, which was published a year later in 1990. Except for Father Matthews, who wrote the chapter on Ontario, and T.A. Weninger, who wrote the one on the Yukon, there were eight new contributors. Father Matthews also accepted a $1,000 award from the Ontario Separate School Trustees' Association, in November 1989, to write an article on the following topic: "In Adversity, Progress. How the negative bombshell of the Hope Commission report in 1950 turned the Ontario Separate School system from loser to winner."[8] He worked on it, off and on, during the first half of 1990, producing a twenty-two-page article on the official Catholic reaction to the final report of the Hope Commission. He focused on the persons of Cardinal James C. McGuigan of Toronto, Bishop J.F. Ryan of Hamilton and Archbishop J.A. O'Sullivan of Kingston and of the commission's four Catholic representatives. They were Arthur Kelly, Joseph Piggott, Henri St. Jacques and E.F. Henderson. When Father Matthews wanted to have his article published, so that it would have an audience, OSSTA refused him permission, pointing out that the material belonged to them by virtue of the award. On the advice of Father Angus Macdougall, S.J., his house superior, Father Matthews returned the $1,000 and printed the article in the 19 January 1991 issue of the *Catholic Register*, under the title "Catholic leaders of steel and of vision."[9] It sold more than 40,000 copies, mainly to school boards. As a result, OSSTA rethought its position and graciously returned the $1,000 to his religious order.[10]

Father Matthews was rarely absent from the pages of the *Catholic Register*. In 1989, as he waited for a permanent posting and was busy with his projects, he contributed at least four items to the newspaper. In June, he cautioned the paper for claiming that the government's intention to pool corporate assessment for both school boards would achieve financial equity for separate schools and complete full funding. Not so, claimed Father Matthews. Although separate schools would be receiving more money, the revenue gap between the two systems would persist because the government intended to give back to the public boards what they would lose in the proposed division of corporate taxes.[11] For the 26 August education issue, he wrote the editorial, "Separate system: schools with a difference" and an article, "Legislation could erase Catholic identity," on the need to repeal Section 136.1.a of the Education Act.[12] In December, he waded into the highly emotional and divisive debate on Bill C-43, the bizarre and hypocritical attempt by the Conservative government of Brian Mulroney to return abortion to the Criminal Code but without any restrictions. Father Matthews' letter to the editor appeared alongside a special guest editorial by Cardinal Carter, on the same topic. They held different views on the Bill, a fact that did not reveal itself until publication. Father Matthews wrote:

> Every day for 10 years, the pro-abortion leaders across Canada shouted their slogan: "Let the decision be made by a woman and her physician." Every day, the pro-life leaders had replied: "That is abortion on demand. There is absolutely no protection for the human life growing inside the mother's body."

Now what happens? The Government of Canada has introduced legislation providing for a decision on abortion to be made solely by a woman and her physician. They call it a compromise. To throw off the pro-life forces (including some pro-life MPs), the pro-abortion forces (including all the secular media) scream that this bill is outrageous. The militantly pro-choice Minister of Justice tells them that she will close the loopholes in committee after second reading of the bill.

Am I living in a dream world? Let's call a spade, a spade, or even as an Englishman would say, a bloody shovel. A Catholic Prime Minister has laid down the law to his cabinet and intimidated his caucus to support abortion on demand....[13]

Within six months, and under different circumstances, Father Matthews would revisit this contentious topic.

****

Father Matthews spent the first two weeks of May 1989 in Auriesville, New York, where he had spent his Tertianship in 1969. He used the time to make his annual retreat. At the end of May, he left Our Lady of Lourdes parish and moved back to the Jesuit residence at 2 Dale Avenue. From 1 June to 9 October 1989, he was on the staff at the Martyrs' Shrine in Midland. In the autumn, he began to teach the history course, still not knowing where he would be assigned.

All that changed on 1 December 1989, when Cardinal Carter appointed Father Matthews acting pastor of Good Shepherd parish in the Steeles Avenue and Don Mills Road area of Thornhill. He replaced Father Neil Varley, who was on extended sick leave. The parish was fifteen years old and had about 525 families, most of whom were young. On his first weekend, Father Matthews celebrated four Masses and preached at each one, heard confessions between Masses and interviewed nine couples about baptisms and marriages. He loved every minute of it. Although there was a rectory, he continued to live mostly at 2 Dale, so that he could work on his second book. His Wednesday Masses were mainly for the benefit of the children in parish schools. His regular visits to the school children and his assistance in the preparation of the Grade 8 students for Confirmation were greatly appreciated by parents and teachers.[14] He was very impressed by the many lay volunteers in the parish.

Father Matthews was delighted finally to be in charge of something in the Church. However, the novelty would not last for long. He was scheduled to leave for Martyrs' Shrine on 15 May 1990, and his future beyond that summer appointment had yet to be decided. In a letter of 11 March 1990 to Father Bill Addley, S.J., his provincial, he examined his prospects. The Shrine directorship was out of the question. Father Jim Farrell, S.J., despite his seventy-two years, was firmly in charge. Also impossible was the position of pastor of Our Lady of Lourdes. Father Pat Byrne, S.J., the current pastor, was doing a fine job. What was left? "There is the possible ideal combination of Publisher of the *Catholic Register* and pastor of Good Shepherd," Father Matthews suggested to Father Addley. "For both of those positions the Cardinal would have to approach you. Well, I can dream, can't I? The acting publisher since Fr. Sean O'Sullivan's death, Richard Alway, leaves on July 1st to become President of SMC [St. Michael's College]."[15] In his reply, Father Addley was anxious that they "keep looking for opportunities which might allow you to be in charge of something in the Church and to utilize your talents and leadership to the fullest. I would certainly be open to looking at the *Catholic Register* possibility if it ever presented itself...."[16]

The possibility presented itself within several weeks. Archbishop Aloysius Ambrozic became the new archbishop of Toronto on 17 March 1990. After conferring with Father Addley in early April, he summoned Father Matthews and invited him to become both the publisher and editor of the *Catholic Register*, which was owned by the archdiocese. Father Matthews was momentarily stunned by the offer. It was a complete surprise. This was what he wanted and now it was his to have. He said, "Yes." The appointment was effective 23 April 1990, and formal responsibility for the paper began with the 5 May edition.[17] As a priest and religious, Father Matthews did not sign a contract but worked at the pleasure of the archbishop.

Father Matthews remained at the helm of the *Register* until 28 February 1993. His career at Canada's largest-circulation English-language Catholic newspaper was all too brief – lasting not even three full years – but it was productive and provocative in ways that Father Matthews himself did not imagine when he accepted the archbishop's offer. Although he had written dozens and dozens of articles, he was not a professional journalist, let alone a trained newspaper editor, but being a greenhorn at anything new had never bothered him. He had nerve in abundance and took to the job as if he had been in the newspaper business all his life.

Father Matthews addressed his first letter in his capacity as publisher and editor to Monsignor J.G. Hanley of Kingston. Monsignor Hanley had been at St. Mary's Cathedral when Father Matthews had been an altar boy there, and he had been an editor of the *Register* when it was printed in Kingston and known as the *Canadian Register*. Monsignor Hanley was a role model and a source of inspiration for Matthews, who told his old parish priest, "The Church in English-speaking Canada will always be indebted to you for spreading the good news of the Lord to countless people over several decades."[18] Father Matthews, orthodox to his fingertips, intended to do the same. He wrote John Paul II, telling him that he was putting the *Catholic Register* at the service of the Pope, the Vicar of Christ, and he instructed his staff always to the refer to the newspaper as *The Catholic Register*, instead of the *Register*.[19]

The best barometer of Father Matthews' opinion on the role of the *Catholic Register*, as a distinctly Catholic newspaper in a world increasingly hostile to Catholic voices in the public square, can be found in the editorial of 12 May 1990. He wrote it and signed it as a testament to his own commitment to the Church and the paper. Simply called "Our mandate," it was unabashedly and unapologetically Catholic from the first to the last word, dividing reality into the sacred and the secular and professing allegiance, not to the world, but to Christ and to the Pope:

> *The Catholic Register*, a weekly newspaper, has served the Church for almost 100 years. In some respects, it has been a changeless Church, for doctrine is ageless. In other respects, it has been a changing Church, for practice is contemporary.
>
> Over the decades, this paper has not only recorded the stable and evolving features of the Church in Canada, but it has influenced actions through its editorial stand.
>
> Recording and influencing: such are the roles of any newspaper. The challenge is to do so with distinction.
>
> Editorials in the giant metropolitan dailies, especially at election time, are tub thumpers for a political party and its leader. At other times, they thump the tub for secular causes like easier abortion. Week in and week out, *The Catholic Register* is a tub thumper for Christ, the King of kings and the Servant of all. He never said it would be easy to follow Him, the Way, the Truth and the Life.

The death of an innocent man on a cross was the ultimate sign of contradiction to the standards of the secular world, and so we humbly yet proudly work under the banner of that Cross.

We take our lead from the Vicar of Christ on earth, Pope John Paul II. His standards are our standards. His causes are our causes.

Justice and peace, prayer and worship, caring and serving, loyalty and faithfulness – these are our hallmarks.

Just as a bishop is leader of the diocese, a teacher is instructor in the classroom, a parent is role model in the family, a pastor is servant of the parish, so too an editor in the Catholic press has a teaching and preaching mission in the Church. That mission we intend to carry out in the name of the Father and the Son and the Holy Spirit.

The teacher needs students. The writer in the newsroom needs readers. These readers are the modern-day disciples of the Lord. They share the Good News with others. Like St. Paul, they write us about what is on their minds – though more briefly, please.

They grow in wisdom and in grace from reading the Catholic press and then sharing the fruit at home and in the workplace. They seek out new subscribers who become new readers who build up the body of Christ in their parish.

As *The Catholic Register* approaches its centennial in 1993, it continues to welcome the challenge to record and influence.[20]

There is no doubt that the *Catholic Register* under Father Matthews lived up to "Our mandate." Even the most cursory examination of the 136 issues that he edited provides ample evidence in support of this claim. Therefore, any catalogue of the Catholic character of the newspaper, from April 1990 to February 1993, would be unnecessary. What interests us, however, is the fact that Father Matthews, by dint of hard work and the force of his own personality, stopped the paper's slide towards extinction and stabilized its circulation at 30,000 copies. (It had been losing 4,000 readers a year since Larry Henderson left the editorship in 1986.) His most important move was to restore to the paper an identity more in keeping with its traditional Catholic persona and its professed loyalty to the Magisterium of the Church. The move worked, for the most part quite wonderfully, despite the paper being unfairly labeled right wing and reactionary by its liberal critics.[21] The label may have stuck, as such politically motivated labels usually do, especially after Father Matthews refused to run an advertisement for *In the Eye of the Catholic Storm: The Church Since Vatican II*. But the label made no sense to Father Matthews or to the paper's readers, and it certainly did not harm the paper's ability to survive and even flourish during the economic recession of the early 1990s, when many Canadian newspapers and magazines lost money and had to fire staff to stay afloat.[22]

Father Matthews led by example, spending an average of sixty hours per week editing forty-seven issues per year (beginning in 1991). A hands-on editor, he wrote half the editorials, farming out the other half mainly to Alan Atkins of Barrie, and Father Gregory Smith of Vancouver, and he also wrote a column composed of news excerpts from the pages of the *Register* fifteen and thirty years ago.[23] During his tenure, he cultivated a wide range of freelance writers. Father Matthews was responsible for the "Come Home to the Catholic Register" campaign, an attempt to win back some of the 20,000 subscribers who abandoned the paper. The first advertisement in the campaign appeared in the *Catholic Register* on 20 November 1990. He took seriously the results of an October 1992 survey of readers and responded to a number of suggestions. Many found the paper interesting and orthodox. Of particular interest to Father Matthews were the once-a-year special issues. These could run from one-and-a-half to more than three times the usual length of twenty pages. The 7 December 1991 special issue marked the 150th anniversary of the Archdiocese of Toronto. (On 24 August 1991, the paper published a twenty-page special supplement on the sesquicentennial of Ontario's separate schools.) On 30 May 1992, the paper featured the Catholic shrines of Canada. The 20 February 1993 issue, which took Father Matthews and his staff many months to assemble, celebrated the centennial of the *Catholic Register*.

Concerning his twelve loyal and talented co-workers, Father Matthews showered many compliments on their work and rewarded them with regular pay raises. Every September, following the summer break, the staff gathered together as a community for a meeting, Mass and dinner. Father Matthews had nothing but the highest praise for the contributions of Rosemary McCracken, Cathy Paul, Mike Mastromatteo, Elizabeth Wilson, Steve Tyson, Gwen Gruenwald and Patty Rivera, to name some of the people who worked for him. He hired Sherrilynn Colley-Vegh as the *Catholic Register*'s first youth columnist and promoted her weekly column, which began on 22 September 1990, in a letter to each Catholic high school principal in Ontario.[24]

When Father Matthews left the paper in February 1993, he wrote a personal letter of genuine thanks to each staff member.[25]

The rent for office space at 67 Bond Street was always paid on time (in 1991, it was nearly $30,000), debts were liquidated and desktop publishing was introduced in 1993, which saved considerable money on production costs. The *Catholic Register* supported itself and stayed out of a deficit. Except for a loan for new computers, it never asked for a cent in subsidies from the archdiocese of Toronto.

Father Matthews was a fine administrator, a good writer, an excellent manager of people and an editor with a nose for news. He had no problem staying loyal to the Magisterium – that was the easiest part of his job – but he had to walk a tightrope between editorial independence and the possibility, however remote it might be, of an archdiocesan hammer, even if he were loathe to admit the need for such a balancing act. Archbishop Ambrozic never tried to influence editorial opinion, the selection of news items or the hiring of staff. He had no desire to run a weekly newspaper. Neither did he relish the prospect of being embarrassed in any way by the editor of what was essentially his newspaper. Father Matthews, who was a natural political hound unafraid of courting controversy in the search for the truth, worked for the archbishop at his discretion. He understood and accepted this reality and knew that if there ever arose a conflict between the expression of his political instincts on the pages of the *Catholic Register* and the reaction of the archbishop to them, his position might be untenable.

****

As Bill C-43 wound its way through parliament, in April and May 1990, Father Matthews revisited the topic, this time not as a letter-writer but as editor of the *Catholic Register*. Two events prompted his wading into the politically charged abortion debate. The first was Bishop Robert Lebel's response of 5 April 1990 to government opposition to all amendments to the bill. Bishop Lebel, of Valleyfield, Québec and president of the Canadian Conference of Catholic Bishops (CCCB), told members of the House of Commons, "If the bill remains as is, it cannot have our approval."[26] On 1 May, he reminded the members that they had "the awesome responsibility to shape and enact a law that will respect human life from its very beginning."[27] Father Matthews was gratified by Bishop Lebel's public stand. It was unequivocally pro-life, an editorial noted. The second event was a statement of Justice Minister Kim Campbell, the sponsor of the legislation, to CBC Radio.

Campbell said that Bill C-43 would legalize a "woman's entitlement to access to abortion."[28] This was unequivocally pro-choice. She assured her listeners that no woman seeking an abortion and no doctor performing one would be made criminals under Bill C-43. If, in the opinion of a doctor, the continuation of a pregnancy would harm in any way the physical, mental or psychological health of the woman, an abortion was perfectly legal and no prosecution would take place.

Father Matthews saw this for what it was, in an editorial titled "A dreadful abortion bill." It was "abortion on demand, protected by the law of the land." In language uncommonly blunt for any kind of Canadian newspaper, he continued:

> Yet abortions are not therapeutic – they treat no disease, remove no pathological tissue, cure no symptom. In fact, they result in a mortality rate of 100 per cent for one of the two patients. Each year in Canada, about 80,000 pre-born babies are killed in the most gruesome manner. That means that 240 lives will be snuffed out in the next 24 hours. Bill C-43 will do nothing to cut down on the slaughter of the innocents.
>
> On the contrary, it will, in effect, legalize that slaughter, in aborturies that will receive protection of the law from coast to coast in our nation.
>
> The issue is not about a weed that has invaded a woman's body, and must be rooted out. No. Ultrasound pictures clearly show a baby with eyes, ears, nose, mouth, fingers, toes. If left alone for nine months, to grow in the mother's womb, a beautiful child will be born. That's how every man and woman on the face of the earth began the journey of life.
>
> Bill C-43 is not pro-life. It is pro-death.
>
> What is the alternative? If the bill is defeated in the Commons, no other will be introduced by this government. But after the next general election, the MPs will know that they must deal with the issue, for there will be no law on the books.
>
> Some Members of Parliament will be new then, elected by the people of all Faiths who are determined to give pre-born babies the same opportunity to live and contribute to the community as they themselves were once given.[29]

Father Matthews' next editorial on Bill C-43 appeared on 3 November 1990. By that time, the bill had passed the House of Commons and was in the hands of the Senate. The parliamentary battleground had changed, but the war was the same. Unfortunately, for Catholic pro-lifers, the same Bishop Lebel who had denounced Bill C-43 on 1 May seemed to backtrack four weeks later, on 29 May. Father Matthews raised high the pro-life banner in "Save the baby," saving his most scathing remarks for Bishop Lebel:

> The choice facing honorable senators this fall as they debate Bill C-43 is simple: either save the bill and kill the baby or save the baby and kill the bill.
>
> Once conception takes place – see the dramatic photos in the August, 1990 issue of *Life* magazine – life begins, and in just a few months we hear a baby cry and then a baby laugh.
>
> All of us (parliamentarians and judges included) are here today because we were given the opportunity to live when life's journey began for us in our mother's body and we were defenceless against mortal attack. Bill C-43 gives the seal of approval to that mortal attack.
>
> In one of the great ironies of life, the pro-abortion forces in the daily press don't like the bill because it "re-criminalizes abortion." None other than the senior law enforcement officer in the land, the Minister of Justice, disagrees with them. The Honorable Kim Campbell says over and over again: "It is thoughtless and misleading to say that Bill C-43 is making criminals out of women and doctors. The personal aspirations of the woman ... as well as social factors, could be taken into account in assessing the individual's ... health."
>
> What about the personal aspirations of the baby who has started life's journey? What about that individual's health when he or she is facing a sentence of death?
>
> Bill C-43 provides as much protection for the pre-born baby as a screen door on a submarine. It provides for abortion on demand. The Minister proudly says so.
>
> What is incomprehensible to many readers of *The Catholic Register* is the present stand of Bishop Robert Lebel, president of the Canadian Conference of Catholic Bishops. On May 29, he informed members of the House of Commons that Bill C-43 is "better than the legislative vacuum which existed for the past two years." When

Catholics complain about this stunning endorsement, the bishop reminds them of his earlier (April 5) statement: "If the bill remains as is, it cannot have our approval."

Well, the bishops' president cannot have it both ways. He either endorses the stand of the Minister of Justice or he opposes it. He is for the bill or he is against it.

What this country needs badly today are bishops who are men of steel, men of vision.

If the senators vote according to their conscience, the bill will be defeated. The legislative vacuum will be filled after the next general election, which will likely see a record number of new MPs elected. Hopefully, a majority of them will stand up in the Commons and defend defenceless babies.[30]

Father Matthews correctly predicted the bill's demise in the Senate. In a free vote taken on 31 January 1991, the Senate voted 43-43, with the Speaker, Rhèal Belisle, refusing to cast the tiebreaker, although he later said that he would have voted against the bill. Under Senate rules, a tie vote defeats a bill. Father Matthews was also correct in his prediction that the next federal election (1993) would usher in many new faces in the House of Commons, but he was uncharacteristically naïve to believe that MPs would enact pro-life legislation. No such thing happened under the succeeding Liberal governments led by Jean Chrétien, who was avowedly pro-abortion and never allowed the matter to be taken up by the Commons. A legislative vacuum exists to this day.

Predictions about the Senate vote and the next election, however, were the least of Father Matthews' worries following the November publication of the editorial. By criticizing Bishop Lebel and by calling for bishops "who are men of steel, men of vision," Father Matthews had crossed a line. It was one thing to point out the hypocrisy of politicians, but it was quite another to call into question a bishop and by implication the entire hierarchy. The archdiocese of Toronto immediately distanced itself from the editorial, and through the chancery expressed its complete support of Bishop Lebel's stand. As for Bishop LeBel, he said, "This bill is bad but it would be worse if there was nothing. It does save some babies but not enough. Having no law would be worse."[31] The *Toronto Star* quoted these words of the bishop in a story under the headline, "Editorial on abortion divides Catholics."

Archbishop Ambrozic was in Rome attending the Synod of Bishops when the *Register* editorial of 3 November 1990 appeared, but he knew about it because Father Matthews had faxed him a copy. On the archbishop's return to Toronto, at the beginning of November, Father Matthews sent him a letter, in which he went to some length to explain his opposition to Bill C-43.[32] He then wrote a second letter, inviting the archbishop to write a signed editorial on his views and the views of the CCCB on the legislation.[33] Archbishop Ambrozic gently declined and asked Father Matthews that if he had to run letters to the editor on the editorial that he limit their publication to two or three issues.[34] Father Matthews complied. He ran a total of eleven letters over three issues (17 November, 24 November and 1 December 1990). Nine of them favoured the editorial. The two dissenting letters advocated the advantages of having a law on abortion on which pro-lifers could build in the future. The *Catholic Register* remained quiet on abortion until the defeat of the legislation. It covered the story with two front-page articles and an editorial by Father Matthews, in the 16 February 1991 issue.[35]

****

The national referendum on the Charlottetown Accord, scheduled for 26 October 1992, was the occasion for Father Matthews' undoing. Up until several days prior to the publication of the last pre-referendum issue of the *Catholic Register*, on 24 October 1992 (but printed nine days before that date), he had decided to keep the paper out of the debate and to vote "No" to the proposed changes to the constitution.[36] He was following the recommendation of Pierre Trudeau, the architect of the 1981 constitution and one of the leaders of the "No" forces, and of Father Alphonse de Valk, CSB, the editor of the pro-life monthly *The Interim* and a staunch critic of Trudeau because he had legalized abortion. Father Matthews admired Trudeau for having inserted Section 29 on denominational schools (Section 93 of the BNA Act) in the constitution.[37] The old and popular cliché about politics making for strange bedfellows was never truer than it was at the time of the 1992 referendum.

If Father Matthews had followed his initial political instincts and left well enough alone, his position at the *Catholic Register* would have been safe, but for most of his life he preferred to be a player rather than an onlooker, to be active rather than passive. It worked for him in separate school politics; why would it not work for him on the bigger stage of national politics. A question came to mind: Did the Charlottetown Accord repeal Section 29? Having asked the question, it immediately became a frantic concern. Father Matthews rang several newspaper experts on the Accord. Each one replied that no one had asked that question before he did. He would have to call a second time for an answer. From each expert came the same reply: Section 29 would remain in the constitution. Tom Wappel, a Liberal MP, confirmed that opinion.

It was at this juncture that Father Matthews should have stayed silent on the issue, according to his own logic. The Charlottetown Accord included Section 29; therefore, if one were to judge the Accord simply on Section 29, it did not matter if the voters accepted or rejected it. In either case, it would continue to be a part of Canada's constitution. Acceptance would mean that it was in Mulroney's version of the constitution; rejection would mean that it would remain in Trudeau's constitution.

That would have been the end of the conundrum for most people but not for Father Matthews. In a memorandum addressed to the bishops of Ontario, dated a year *after* the referendum, Father Matthews revealed his reasons for his switch to the "Yes" side and his decision to write a front-page editorial that urged the readers of the *Catholic Register* to vote "Yes." The core of his argument, *as presented to the bishops*, was the need for Catholic school supporters to prepare themselves for any future political attempt to delete Section 29 from the constitution:

> There was now a lot at stake for me and for Catholic school supporters across the province. But it was now Monday [13 October] and I had only one day to compose an editorial. It would acknowledge that the Accord was going down to defeat because all the polls showed that Westerners felt that it gave too much to Quebec (the Trudeau case), and most Quebecers felt that it did not give them nearly enough....
>
> Polls that day showed Ontario going either way. My immediate goal was to put this province in the YES column, to retain some respectability for the Charlottetown Accord, so that the next time that the Prime Minister and 10 Premiers re-opened the Pandora's box they would have some ammunition to withstand the Public School leaders' demands to drop Section 29.[38]

This reasoning was based on several large assumptions: Section 29 was in jeopardy; another round of constitutional talks would take place in five or ten years; at that time, public school supporters would demand the removal of Section 29 from the constitution. It is a pity that Father Matthews did not run this by someone before he wrote his editorial on 13 and 14 October 1992. He might have saved himself a great deal of grief.

In the editorial that he finally wrote, "Why Vote No?" Father Matthews appealed to Canadian unity and the tradition of political compromise that founded and had defined Canada since Confederation. That tradition lived on in the Accord, which was supported by all three federal parties, the ten premiers, the Territories and aboriginal leaders and by business and labour. He also warned that the triumph of a "No" vote would cause lasting bitterness across the country and might propel the nation to break up, as Yugoslavia had.

The mention of Yugoslavia was a blunder. Many people, including Catholic bishops, supported the right of Slovenes, Croats and Bosnians to leave Serb-dominated Yugoslavia. Aside from that, the content of the editorial was hardly controversial. Appeals to Canadian unity and warnings about the dire consequences of any break-up were a staple of Canadian politics. It was rather tame stuff. But to have given the entire first page to the editorial, with a red Maple Leaf stuck in the centre, and to end it by pleading with Canadians to vote "Yes" was bound to disturb that old hornets' nest of the separation of church and state in Canada. With that in mind, Archbishop Ambrozic issued a statement on 16 October 1992:

> The editorial is the opinion of the publisher/editor, which he has a right to express. I wish to make it clear that the Archdiocese is not giving direction to anyone on how to vote in the referendum.
>
> The Archdiocese's position is that of the Ontario bishops, which encourages Canadians to vote, and in preparation for voting to examine the Charlottetown Accord, to determine if it honours the values we all share, particularly our commitment to social justice and devotion to the common good.[39]

The archbishop's statement was straightforward and fair enough. It supported the right of Father Matthews to write editorials for the *Catholic Register*, and it made clear that the Church had no intention of meddling in referendum politics. Any tempest aroused by the editorial would simply play itself out, and once the referendum was over, public memory of the editorial would quickly fade.

Not so. On 22 October, six days after the release of his statement, Archbishop Ambrozic called Father Matthews into his office and quietly asked for his resignation. Father Matthews was shocked. According to his recollection of events, the archbishop told him that the editorial would anger the separatist bishops in Quebec. On hearing that, the shock deepened. He asked himself, When was the last time a Quebec bishop had read the *Catholic*

Register? However, Father Matthews kept the question to himself. He decided not to explain his editorial stand and to accept the archbishop's demand to leave by 31 January 1993, acquiescence to the decisions of a superior being the Ignatian way. Father Matthews did offer to show the archbishop any future editorials, but he correctly and politely declined. Both men knew that that was no way to run a newspaper.

Crestfallen, Father Matthews returned to his office and wrote his letter of resignation. It was thoroughly gracious.

> As you requested in your office today, I hereby submit my resignation as Editor and Publisher of *The Catholic Register* because of the poor judgment I showed in writing and publishing the editorial in the current paper (Oct. 27), urging our readers to vote "Yes" in the national referendum next week.
>
> I am grateful for the privilege that has been mine to work with a fine team since late April 1990. *The Catholic Register* begins its second century in early February and I have been spending Saturdays in the office working on that anniversary issue, commissioning articles, etc. Last fall when we did the 64-page issue on the Archdiocese, I discovered that it took 60-hour weeks for six months. It turned out fine.
>
> In my old age I'll look back on these as the golden years, rather than my 26 years around Queen's Park. In closing, I apologize profusely for embarrassing Your Grace with this week's editorial. I thank you for your kindnesses over the years.[40]

The next thing Father Matthews did that day was to represent the paper at the annual Archbishop's Dinner, at the Metro Toronto Convention Centre. He was embarrassed to be there. Then an unusual thing happened. As the dignitaries for the head table marched by, his old friend, Bill Davis, bolted from the long line to grab his hand. Davis was the chairman of the Ontario "Yes Committee" for the referendum and said, "Well done, Carl!" Father Matthews was in a fog for the rest of the dinner. Not even when Premier Bob Rae urged the 2,000 Catholics at the dinner to vote "Yes" did it lift. As Rae spoke, the Toronto Blue Jays were preparing to win their first-ever World Series, at the Skydome next door.

There was no immediate fallout from the resignation. Archbishop Ambrozic instructed Father Matthews not to say or write anything about it until a formal announcement in January 1993. He could not even tell his staff. In accepting Father Matthews' resignation the archbishop extended his tenure as publisher/editor to 28 February 1993, so that he could complete the 100th anniversary issue of the *Catholic Register*. In the meantime, the "No" forces won the referendum, but Ontario narrowly went "Yes," as Father Matthews hoped that the province would. In letters to the *Catholic Register*, the majority of writers thanked Father Matthews for his referendum editorial. Among them were Joseph Ghiz, Liberal premier of Prince Edward Island, Bob Rae, NDP premier of Ontario, and Joe Clark, the Conservative minister responsible for constitutional affairs.[41] Bittersweet were the words of thanks and praise from these non-partisan signers of the Charlottetown Accord.

Father Matthews' resignation was finally made public on the front page of the 30 January 1993 issue (once again, printed nine days earlier). It included excerpts from his letter of 22 October 1992 to Archbishop Ambrozic and mention of the archbishop's response of 5 November 1992. As well, in the middle of the announcement was a photograph of Archbishop Ambrozic and Father Matthews, standing side by side, giving the story an odd and unsettling look. What made the whole story even stranger was the fact that at a Cathedral Mass of thanksgiving two weeks earlier, on 14 January, Archbishop Ambrozic had bestowed the archdiocesan medal on Father Matthews for his fine work at the *Catholic Register*. Father Matthews accepted the medal and immediately gave it to his staff for the paper's offices.

The archdiocese of Toronto reacted to the announcement's publication with a second press release, dated 22 January. Archbishop Ambrozic said that he requested Father Carl Matthews' resignation because he was convinced that "the Church has no right to dictate, or seem to dictate, on matters which are of a purely political matter." The October referendum was one such matter, and he did not want the *Register* "to convey the impression that episcopal authority is being used to promote purely political options."[42]

Many readers were sorry to see Father Matthews leave the *Catholic Register*, and many of them were perplexed. Jim Hughes, president of Campaign Life Coalition, said, "I thought the paper had found a new focus and was doing a wonderful job on life issues under his direction."[43] The conservative *Catholic Insight* was unconvinced by the reason for the abrupt resignation, coming as it did on the heels of the 16 October 1992 press release, in which Father Matthews' editorial freedom was defended. The magazine called it a firing and speculated that Father Matthews had been a "marked man" for defying the bishops on Bill C-43, Mulroney's abortion legislation.⁴⁴ The liberal *Catholic New Times* devoted a whole editorial by Janet Somerville to the episode, arguing that it was not wrong for Father Matthews as the editor of a Catholic newspaper to take a stand on a national issue. Referring to the archbishop's statement of 22 January 1993, the paper also claimed that episcopal authority was not at stake in the referendum editorial because Father Matthews had never quoted any bishop in support of his opinion.⁴⁵

Bob Bettson, the president of the Canadian Church Press, wrote a strong letter of protest to Archbishop Ambrozic: "We recognize the right of church publishers to make personnel decisions. However, the firing of Fr. Matthews for writing an editorial in favor of the "Yes" side in the recent referendum is a blow to editorial freedom."⁴⁶ Father Matthews appreciated the support, but he asked Bettson, Larry Henderson, a former editor of the paper, and Carolyn Purden, editor of the *Anglican Journal* (which took the same stand on the referendum), not to make an issue of his departure in the daily press.⁴⁷ He reminded them that as a cleric he gladly served at the pleasure of the archbishop. It would have been different if he had been a layperson.

Father Matthews was deeply hurt by the whole affair, but he accepted his fate, willingly and without rancour. As a priest and as a Jesuit, he hoped that the future would bring him another meaningful apostolate. He had no stomach to wage a backroom campaign against Archbishop Ambrozic or to leave the archdiocese of Toronto, his home for many years. Father Matthews would always support and work with Archbishop Ambrozic, and he did not have to wait long to come to the archbishop's defense. In a letter to the *Catholic Register* of 19 June 1993, he castigated Judy Steed and Lois Sweet of the *Toronto Star* for their vicious attacks on the Catholic Church. Their feature stories appeared on 5 May. "The excuse for writing their articles was two inappropriate words by Archbishop Ambrozic. But he had already apologized for using them, and in a civil society apologies are accepted."⁴⁸ The archbishop thanked Father Matthews in a handwritten note.⁴⁹

In his farewell editorial, Father Matthews quoted from the *Catholic Register*'s inaugural editorial of 5 January 1893, written by the paper's first editor, Father John Teefy, C.S.B.: "The fact that we are a Catholic journal will not by any means lessen the interest we take in the institutions, the growth and prosperity of our country."⁵⁰ These words had been a guiding inspiration for Father Matthews during his tenure as publisher and editor. He signed off with these words: "As a supporter of a great Pope, I'm grateful for the privilege of serving here for almost three years. From May until September I'll be working at the Martyrs' Shrine in Midland, praying for all of you, new friends through *The Catholic Register*."[51] His final gift to the paper's loyal readers was the splendid centennial issue of the *Register*. No better editor could have been on hand to close out the paper's first 100 years.

---

[1] Matthews Papers, Box 5, File 22, CJM to Father James Farrell, S.J., 19 August 1988; Our Lady of Lourdes, *Parish Newsletter* (Spring 1989), 2.

[2] Box 5, File 23, L.J. Dupuis to CJM, 9 January 1989.

[3] Ibid., Archbishop Aloysius M. Ambrozic to CJM, 7 February 1989.

[4] "Education awards for priest, layman," *Catholic Register*, 7-13 November 1987, 21.

[5] Box 5, File 23, B.E. Nelligan to CJM, 25 April 1989.

[6] Box 5, File 27, "Metropolitan Separate School Board Award of Merit, 1991."

[7] Box 5, File 23, CJM to B.E. Nelligan, 15 March 1989.

[8] Ibid., Caroline F. Di Giovanni, Director of Research, OSSTA, to CJM, 28 November 1989.

[9] CJM, "Catholic leaders of steel and vision," *Catholic Register*, 19 January 1991, 9.

[10] CJM, telephone interview by author, 6 May 2004.

[11] CJM, "Read between the lines," *Catholic Register*, 24 June 1989, 4.

[12] CJM, "Separate system: schools with a difference" and "Legislation could erase Catholic identity," *Catholic Register*, 26 August 1989, 4 and ES2.

[13] CJM, "Who hears their muffled cries?" *Catholic Register*, 2 December 1989, 4.

[14] Box 5, File 23, CJM, Circular Letter, December 1989; Box 5, File 24, CJM to Father William Addley, S.J., 11 March 1990; Ibid., Toni McDermott to CJM, 25 February 1990.

[15] Box 5, File 24, CJM to Father William Addley, S.J., 11 March 1990.

[16] Ibid., Father William Addley, S.J. to CJM, 16 March 1990.

[17] Ibid., Archdiocese of Toronto. News Release, 6 April 1990; information supplied by CJM, 30 November 2003.

[18] Ibid., CJM to Monsignor J.G. Hanley, 24 April 1990.

[19] Ibid., CJM to Pope John Paul II, 31 May 1990; CJM, Memo to Staff, 15 June 1990.

[20] CJM, "Our mandate," *Catholic Register*, 12 May 1990, 4.

21 "The rival Catholic voices," *Toronto Star*, 8 December 1990, G9.

22 News item, *Globe and Mail*, 24 January 1992.

23 CJM, "The production of this newspaper," *Catholic Register*, 2-9 January 1993, 7.

24 Box 5, File 24, CJM to Principals of our Catholic High Schools in Ontario, 14 September 1990.

25 Box 5, File 25, a collection of letters from CJM to the staff, each one dated 25 February 1993.

26 As quoted in CJM, "A dreadful abortion bill," *Catholic Register*, 26 May 1990, 4.

27 Ibid.

28 Ibid.

29 Ibid.

30 CJM, "Save the baby," *Catholic Register*, 3 November 1990, 4.

31 "Editorial on abortion divides Catholics," *Toronto Star*, 2 November 1990.

32 Box 5, File 26, CJM to Archbishop Aloysius Ambrozic, 3 November 1990.

33 Ibid., CJM to Archbishop Aloysius Ambrozic, 7 November 1990.

34 Ibid., Archbishop Aloysius Ambrozic to CJM, 9 November 1990.

35 CJM, "Abortion bill," *Catholic Register*, 16 February 1991, 4.

36 Box 5, File 28, CJM to the Bishops in Ontario, 22 October 1993.

37 Box 2, File 14, CJM to Pierre Elliott Trudeau, 12 December 1982.

38 Box 5, File 29, CJM to the Bishops of Ontario, 22 October 1993.

39 Box 5, File 28, Archdiocese of Toronto, "Statement re The Catholic Register Editorial on Referendum," 16 October 1992.

40 Ibid., CJM to Archbishop Aloysius Ambrozic, 22 October 1992.

41 For a range of letters, see *Catholic Register*, 7 November 1992, 4; 14 November 1992, 4; 28 November 1992, 4; 2-9 January 1993, 4.

42 As quoted in "Between bishop and editor: a precious space," *Catholic New Times*, 21 February 1993, 5.

43 "Register chief will step down," *The Interim*, February 1993, 13.

44 "Archbishop fires editor," *Catholic Insight*, March 1993, 10.

45 "Between bishop and editor: a precious space," *Catholic New Times*, 21 February 1993, 5.

46 Box 5, File 29, Bob Bettson to Archbishop Aloysius Ambrozic, 25 February 1993.

47 Ibid., CJM to Carolyn Purden, 27 February 1993.
48 CJM, "Heaped With Abuse," *Catholic Register*, 19 June 1993, 4.
49 Box 5, File 29, Archbishop Aloysius Ambrozic to CJM, 6 June 1993.
50 CJM, "Farewell, readers, *Catholic Register*, 6 March 1993, 4.
51 Ibid.

St. John's Church, Waubaushene, Ontario

St. Francis Xavier Mission Church, Christian Island, Ontario. It was built in 1999

CHAPTER EIGHT

JESUIT PASTOR AND BUILDER

*W*hen Father Carl Matthews left the *Catholic Register*, he had just turned sixty-one years of age and found himself discerning once again where he might go next in his life as a Jesuit. Always resilient, he made sure that his departure from the weekly paper was as graceful as possible, and he wisely chose not to dwell too long on his misfortune. Instead of working sixty-hour weeks, he had time on his hands, an odd experience. So, he became chaplain to a group of twenty-one people who were going on a ten-day pilgrimage to major shrines in Mexico, beginning 16 April 1993. It was the perfect tonic for the jobless Jesuit. He was doing something useful and spiritual. Since Mexican law still forbade priests and religious from wearing clerical garb in public, he wore a suit and tie for the first and only time since high school.

Next was Father Matthews' posting to Martyrs' Shrine near Midland. His appointment ran from 15 May to 15 October 1993, and he would remain a member of the 2 Dale Avenue community. He had always enjoyed working at the Shrine, a place he had first visited with his family in 1949 and where he had spent three weeks as a novice. He also agreed to edit the semi-annual *Martyrs' Shrine Message*. His first issue was devoted to the 400th anniversary of the birth of St. Jean de Brébeuf.

When the Shrine closed right after Thanksgiving, Father Matthews returned to Toronto, as planned. During the last year and a half at the *Catholic Register*, he had preached every other weekend at the four Masses at Our Lady of Perpetual Help parish. That was part-time work. He needed a full-time assignment, and he landed one, at St. Michael's Cathedral. Monsignor Kenneth Robitaille, the rector, was happy to have him on staff as an associate pastor and not have to feed and lodge him! By agreement, Father Matthews continued to live at 2 Dale Avenue, but he did spend his on-call days at the cathedral rectory. This wonderful assignment, which had been agreed to as early as August, began on 15 October 1993 and would end on 15 May 1994, at which time, Father Matthews assumed, he would start another season at the Shrine, continuing his peripatetic ministry.

Circumstances changed things. Father Francis Micallef, S.J., pastor of the Jesuit-run parish of St. John the Evangelist in Waubaushene, since 1987, had a stroke in November 1993 and had to be relieved of his duties and transferred to the Jesuit infirmary in Pickering. At the urging of Bishop Robert B. Clune, the auxiliary bishop in charge of the Northern Pastoral Region, Father Eric Maclean, S.J., the provincial, asked Father Matthews to become the next pastor. Father Maclean said, "It's yours, Carl, if you want to move there."[1] Although Father Matthews had always liked the idea of being a parish priest, he had never been at the helm of a parish, except at Good Shepherd in Thornhill, for seven months prior to his appointment to the *Catholic Register*. Moreover, Waubaushene was almost two hours from Toronto, his home for thirty-plus years. He must have asked himself, "Could a big city priest survive year-round in a hamlet on the northern edge of the archdiocese?" Father Matthews hesitated. His provincial gave him a week to consider. At the end of the week, Father Matthews said that he would accept. He moved into the parish with his books and his six-foot, six-inch bed on 12 May 1994 and has been there ever since.[2] (He is a member of the La Storta Jesuit community in Pickering.) As he told a reporter from the *Midland Free Press*, he felt right at home in Huronia.[3]

Father Matthews is the fourteenth pastor of St. John's in Waubaushene, which is roughly midway between Midland and Orillia and a fifteen-minute car ride from Martyrs' Shrine. It began as a mission of St Ann's in Penetanguishene and then of St. Margaret's in Midland before Archbishop Denis O'Connor, C.S.B. of Toronto made St. John's a parish in its own right in July 1906 and immediately entrusted it to the Jesuit Fathers. He did so because within the parish's territory, about three kilometres west of Waubaushene, is St. Ignace, where St. Jean de Brébeuf and St. Gabriel Lalemant were martyred in 1649.

In addition to Waubaushene itself, the parish serves Catholics in Coldwater, Moonstone, Fesserton and many homes in between. There are even some Catholics from Port Severn, in the diocese of Peterborough, who consider St. John's their parish church. In 1994, there were about 250 souls in the parish, a far cry from St. Michael's Cathedral, where Father Matthews had preached his unscripted sermons to 2,500 people every second Sunday. To this day, the congregation of St. John's has remained quite stable. On average, 250 people, mostly "young" retirees, attend Mass every Sunday. There are 125 envelope users.

Outside the identified boundaries but also included in the parochial territory are Christian Island, Hope Island and Beckwith Island. Christian Island, which is about fifty-two kilometres from Waubaushene (48 kilometres to the dock at Cedar Point and another four kilometres across Georgian Bay), is the home of the Beausoleil First Nation. On the island is St. Francis Xavier Mission, which is attached to St. John's and is served by its parish priest. It has approximately 200 parishioners.

The first St. John's church was a small frame structure that was located several blocks from Pine Street, the site of the second and then third church. In the early hours of 14 November 1914, fire destroyed the second church and the rectory, killing a workman and the first pastor, Father Jean-Baptiste Nolin, S.J., who had tried to rescue the Blessed Sacrament from a chapel in the rectory. He died two days later. Father Stanislaus Bouvrette, S.J. built the present church, which included a basement hall, in 1916. The Georgian Bay Lumber Company, Waubaushene's most prominent employer at the time, provided a great deal of the lumber free of charge. The first Mass was celebrated on Christmas Day 1916. Simple and traditional in style, and built of brick with a prominent steeple, St. John's church radiates its own quiet beauty and sense of permanence.

Father Matthews threw himself into the work of St. John's parish and St. Francis Xavier Mission with all the enthusiasm of a newly ordained priest, and that enthusiasm, evident to all who work with him, has never faded. On his first weekend in Waubaushene, St. John's was about half full at the Saturday evening Mass and Sunday morning Mass. At the noon Mass at St. Francis Xavier, sixty people packed the tiny and tottering mission church. Afterwards, there was a banquet to mark his arrival, at the Christian Island community centre. Later in the week, the Native people erected a white fence around the church property. It was a good beginning, a harbinger of more good things to come. Father Matthews wrote Archbishop Ambrozic that he was initially surprised at the number of business decisions that he had to make concerning the church, mission and St. John's cemetery.[4] Having to make some of those decisions on behalf of a parish (plus a mission) was a first for him.

At St. John's, Father Matthews took it upon himself to give Holy Communion to the parish's shut-ins, who were happy to see their priest on Sundays and First Fridays; he reconstituted the finance committee in

September 1994, which had not functioned since 1991; and he gave a short course in the new *Catechism of the Catholic Church* during the autumn months. Eighty-four families actually purchased a copy of the *Catechism*.[5] This was a good sign of the peoples' commitment to the faith and their enthusiasm to learn more about their Catholicism. Most people in the parish live on very modest incomes, but, as Father Matthews quickly learned, they never complain and are generous to a fault with their time and their money. Father Matthews inherited a debt-free parish and mission and was happy to report in 2004 that St. John's has $58,000 in the bank and that St. Francis Xavier has about half that total. The parish and mission have separate accounts, both of which have doubled in a decade.[6] With prudent management, he and his finance council built up healthy bank balances and gently coaxed parishioners to make generous contributions to the annual Sharelife campaign.

St. John's survival depends on volunteers. There is no caretaker, housekeeper or a secretary. Instead, parishioners cut the grass, plant the flowers, plough the snow, wash the sacristy linen, clean the church and hall every two weeks, type the Sunday bulletin and do the bookkeeping. One volunteer, Mrs. Teresa Elliott, has faithfully done the bookkeeping for the past twenty-six years. Parishioners also organize the annual bazaar and dinner at the end of each June. It attracts 450 people to the dinner alone. Next to the Sunday Offertory, the bazaar generates the largest figure in the revenue column of the annual financial report.

Over the years, priest and people have worked together to improve the fabric of the church. They replaced the roof, repaired the spire and built a ramp for handicap access. Each project was paid for on completion. As necessary as these repairs and alterations were, however, the most significant change to the church was the installation of nine stained glass windows, beginning in 2000: eight in the nave at $10,000 each and one in the narthex over the front door of the church at $15,000. Luxfor Studios of Concord designed, executed and installed the windows, which are coloured leaded glass, with staining applied only to the flesh and small details.[7] Completely stained glass windows would have been prohibitively expensive. The windows in the nave are as follows: The Birth of Jesus Our Saviour (Luke 2: 15-16); Joseph Teaches Carpentry to the Boy Jesus (Luke 2: 39-40); Jesus and the Children (Luke 18: 16-17); Jesus Heals the Sick (Mark 1: 32-34); Jesus Raises the Daughter of Jairus (Luke 8: 53-55); The Sermon on the Mount (Matthew 5: 1-10); Jesus Meets His Mother on the Road to Calvary (John 19:

26-27); After Resurrection from the Dead, Jesus Meets His Mother (tradition; no scriptural reference). The window over the front door, the last to be installed, features the five Jesuit Martyrs who died in Canada: St. Jean de Brébeuf, St. Gabriel Lalemant, St. Antoine Daniel, St. Charles Garnier and St. Nöel Chabanel.

****

Christian Island holds a unique status as the only Native mission in the Archdiocese of Toronto. In the winter of 1649-50, when it was known as Ile St-Joseph, it was home to seventeen Jesuits and hundreds of Hurons at Ste-Marie II. They had fled to the island after they had destroyed the original Ste-Marie and other Huron villages to save them from falling into the hands of the Iroquois. After a difficult winter that killed many people, the Jesuits and the Hurons departed the island for what is now Quebec City, arriving on 28 July 1650. The Hurons established a community in Loretteville, a suburb of the city. Christian Island remained deserted for the next 190 years. In 1856, as a result of pressure from the white settlement, the Ojibway of Coldwater, near Orillia, settled the island. Bishop John Joseph Lynch of Toronto ordered that a chapel be erected for the island's Catholics. In 1862, a small stone church was opened and named in honour of St. Francis Xavier, the Jesuit patron of all Catholic missions around the world. Bishop Lynch himself dedicated the church on 1 September 1864. To reach Christian Island, he traveled from Collingwood by Indian canoe. Father Joseph Cadot, S.J. added a brick exterior to the church, a cornerstone and interior walls in 1904.

Christian Island was a mission of Wikwemikong on Manitoulin Island, from 1862 to 1904, and a mission of Cape Croker in the Bruce Peninsula, from 1904 to 1943, when it became a mission of St. John's in Waubaushene. It has always existed under Jesuit administration. By the time that Father Matthews had arrived in 1994, the Band's engineer had already condemned the church as an unsafe structure. It may have been built of stone and brick, but the wood was rotting, the gallery was too unstable to be used and every time people walked up to communion, the floor would shift up and down.[8] Without blinking, Father Matthews promised to build a bigger church. The proof of his promise was his faithfulness in serving the people of Christian Island. Only winter whiteouts on the mainland road to Cedar Point have occasionally kept him from saying Sunday Mass. Not even winter ice in the channel between Cedar Point and the island can defeat him. Bundled in three layers of winter clothes, he hops on a snowmobile or accepts a ride in a car over the ice. When he is away from the parish for an extended period of time, it is imperative that his replacement celebrates Sunday Mass at St. Francis Xavier. (Father Matthews takes three weeks of vacation. One week is spent in St. Petersburg, Florida, and the other two are devoted to acting as a chaplain on pilgrimages to Catholic shrines. He has taken pilgrims to Europe, the Balkans, Israel and Central America.)

The first and biggest hurdle was finding $225,000, the cost of a circle-shaped church large enough to hold 130 people. It took four years to develop a funding solution. Cardinal Ambrozic gave $75,000 in the name of the archdiocese of Toronto. This was not a loan but a one-time gift. The Beausoleil First Nation offered to donate $75,000 worth of labour costs, through a special employment program sponsored by the federal Department of Indian Affairs. The department agreed to pay the salaries of four labourers for four months. In effect, the Band Council under the leadership of Chief Paul Sandy became the general contractor. The Band Council also donated the land and promised to demolish the old church and clean up the property. The site for the new church has a frontage of 200 feet and a depth of 190 feet and is situated adjacent to the location of the first church and directly across the road from historic Ste-Marie II. Father Matthews said that he would raise the final $75,000, which would be spent on materials, furnishings and skilled tradesmen.

He sent a circular letter of 1 April 1998 to seventy relatives and friends across Canada, and he acknowledged in writing each donation regardless of its size.[9] An article in the *Catholic Register*, 20 April 1998, prompted thirty people to give an average of twenty-five dollars each. As a result of an advertisement in the May 1998 issue of *Catholic Insight*, twenty-two people, many of them total strangers to Father Matthews, gave an average of $1,100 each. Within a month of his own personal fundraising, he had already added $31,000 to the bank account of St. Francis Xavier mission.[10] He was well on the way to reaching his share of the costs.

Ground was broken for the new church on Pentecost Sunday, 31 May 1998. The architect was Robert Mitchell of Barrie. His plans called for an eight-sided church that resembles a circle, which is a sacred symbol of unity to First Nation Peoples. Joanne Sandy was the project coordinator; Carl Monague was site superintendent; Henry Jackson was liaison with the Band Council; Anthony Jemec of Lafontaine designed the stained glass windows on the left-hand side of the church and on the front door, and he redesigned a single vertical window, the gift of Ste-Croix parish in Lafontaine, into four separate windows on the right-hand side of the church; Bill Monague created the dream catcher, which is four feet in diameter; and he painted the Miracle of the Loaves and Fishes, employing a Native motif. The many volunteers included Mike Sandy, contractor, who cleared the land, dug the foundation, put in the septic tanks and water pipes and leveled the old church site; Cecchetto Contractors, who built the concrete steps; and Wilson and Somerville Contractors, who transported and leveled twenty loads of soil.

Some items from the old church were incorporated into the new one. They were the statues, bell, Stations of the Cross, the main crucifix and several windows. The decorative back wall in the sanctuary is made of bricks from the first church. Additional furnishings came from a number of churches and convents and were refurbished by people from the parish and the mission. Annunciation parish in Toronto is the source of the matching oak pews that had to be cut to fit the octagonal shape of the church.

The first Mass took place on Palm Sunday, 28 March 1999. At the Easter Mass, eleven children received baptism in a font carved from a tree stump in the Philippines. In the presence of nine priests and two deacons, and a full church of Native worshippers, Cardinal Ambrozic formally blessed the new mission Church on 17 June 1999. Carl Monague greeted him at the door with these words:

> Your Eminence, the People of God at St. Francis Xavier Mission on the Beausoleil First Nation welcome you with great joy. We believe that God has inspired us to build this house to be a temple of prayer and praise.
>
> Our architect, Mr. Robert Mitchell, presents to you his blueprints. As a parishioner and as the general contractor, I present to you this symbolic key.
>
> We ask you to dedicate this Church, the work of our hearts and hands, and to set it aside for Catholic worship of God the Father, Son and Holy Spirit.[11]

Cardinal Ambrozic was very impressed by the church. When he walked through the front door for the first time, he exclaimed, "What a beautiful little church!"[12] On the following Sundays, Bishop Anthony Meagher and Bishop Robert B. Clune celebrated Mass. On 1 August, Archbishop Terence Prendergast, S.J. of Halifax presided over the Sunday liturgy and blessed a stone cairn and plaque erected at the site of the first church.

Two years before the opening of what many people now realize is a gem of a church on Georgian Bay, Chief Paul Sandy and Remi Sylvester, elders of the Beausoleil First Nation, bestowed upon Father Matthews a Native name. The naming ceremony took place in January 1997 at a banquet on Christian Island attended by several hundred people. His Ojibway name is *Wau-Goosh* and means "Wise as a Fox." As the guiding hand behind the construction of the present St. Francis Xavier mission church, Father Matthews certainly lived up to his Native appellation.

****

As if taking care of St. John's parish and St. Francis Xavier mission was not enough work for Father Matthews, he has kept busy on other fronts during his days in Waubaushene. He continued to edit the *Martyrs' Shrine Message* until 2001 and to preach at all five Masses on three Sundays at the Shrine, until three years ago when that number was reduced to one Sunday a season. He taught his course on Catholic Education in Ontario, for the fifth and last time in Toronto, in 1995, and then to twenty-eight vice-principals in the Simcoe County Separate School Board, in 1996. He supported the construction of a new elementary school for the Catholic families of Tay Township, to replace St. John's in Waubaushene and St. Mary's in Victoria Harbour. Called St. Antoine Daniel, in remembrance of the Jesuit martyr who died at Mount St. Louis in 1648, it is located in Victoria Harbour and has 310 students. Lastly, Father Matthews solicited Canadian funds for the Jesuit-run Gregorian University in Rome. In 1994, he and Brother Alexandre Dion, S.J. of Quebec raised $86,500, and in 1995, the two men sent nearly $140,000 to the university. Father Matthews relinquished this responsibility in 1999. When he was in his late sixties, he celebrated four Masses on Vision TV's national special.

One interest that has never left Father Matthews is Catholic education. It has been a constant in his life and the inspiration for this biography. Serving as a parish priest in Waubaushene, living in contented obscurity, has not silenced his pen nor dulled his opinions. If anything, he has returned to the independent action that he enjoyed and used so fruitfully when he began his career as a player in the School Question. That Question took on many different faces over the years, but the core essentials remain the same: the fully funded Catholic school system in Ontario, with its hundreds of thousands of students, "will not survive if it does not return to its strong Catholic roots, in unwavering support of the Pope's teachings,"[13] and that the governance of Ontario's Catholic schools "solely by Catholic trustees must continue in provincial law."[14]

In letters to the editor and in articles, Father Matthews argued against umbrella boards, the amalgamation of public and separate school boards, open student admission to Catholic schools, non-Catholics on Catholic school parent councils and the absorption of Catholic principals and vice-principals into a single provincial council dominated by non-Catholics.[15] He carried on a vigorous campaign to preserve denominational schools in Newfoundland and Quebec, correctly pointing out that neither a government on its own legislative initiative nor a province-wide referendum, addressed to all the voters, could overturn constitutionally guaranteed rights to a minority. Only the minority who enjoyed these rights could put an end to them.[16] It was a losing cause – with the key support of Prime Minister Chrétien, both provinces abolished denominational education, Quebec in the name of language and Newfoundland by means of two referenda – but Father Matthews went down fighting the good fight. "Suppression in Newfoundland" is a superb analysis of the murky political process that led to the abolition by popular vote of Catholic and Pentecostal schools in that province.[17] For the 3 March 2002 issue of the *Catholic Register*, Father Matthews wrote a 6,200-word article entitled, "Profiles in Courage in Ontario Catholic education during the past 200 years." In his introduction, "Unmasking the strangers in our faith community," Joseph Sinasac, the editor, remarked that Father Matthews' article was written with style and passion.

Arguably Father Matthews' most significant writing on Catholic education, during the past ten years, has been "Will Ontario's Catholic Schools Survive the Next 25 Years?"[18] He devoted the first half of the article explaining and defending two pieces of legislation passed by the Conservative government of Premier Mike Harris. Bill 104 amalgamated school boards, public with public and separate with separate, greatly reducing their number and turning them into district boards, and it created a new French Catholic school system. Bill 160 ("Education Quality Improvement Act," 1997) was far more contentious and divisive. In order to close the revenue gap between assessment-rich boards and assessment-poor boards, and to do the same between public and separate schools boards, across the province, the Conservative government removed the traditional right of local school boards to levy property taxes as well as their access to commercial and industrial taxes, which had always been a source of wealth to large urban public school boards. In the new funding formula, the public boards in Toronto, Ottawa and

Hamilton would be the big losers. Father Matthews supported Bill 160 because it was the only realistic way to finally achieve equal funding for separate school children. Agreeing with Father Matthews were the Ontario Separate School Trustees' Association and, quietly, the Ontario Catholic bishops. The Ontario English Catholic Teachers' Association did not support the legislation and staged a two-week strike when Bill 160 was tabled in the legislature in the autumn of 1997. Father Matthews next took aim at Mr. Justice Peter Cumming when he ruled that Bill 160 could not tamper with the right of separate school trustees to tax Catholic ratepayers.[19] (He was happy that a higher court subsequently reversed Justice Cumming's ruling.)

The second half of the article spelled out what Father Matthews called "Dark clouds on the horizon." There were five of them. Number one dealt with Bill 160. Catholic educators, English and French, had to support Bill 160 and remind the minister of education that the wealth sharing needed to achieve equal per-pupil funding had to begin immediately. Number two: membership on parent councils. Number three: the council of Catholic principals. Number four: umbrella boards. He had already treated each of these topics, although separately, in previous published letters and articles. They were now presented together. Number five had the heading "Preparation for first Sacraments." This was his most urgent concern:

> What a heading for my fifth dark cloud on the horizon! Let me hasten to affirm that children must be well prepared to receive in Grade 2 the Sacraments of Reconciliation and Eucharist for the first time, and in Grade 8 the Sacrament of Confirmation. Traditionally, in Ontario at least, this preparation was done largely by the teachers in our Catholic schools. The new emphasis is on parish preparation, either by priests or lay people. If this approach is taken to an extreme, and dedicated teachers in our schools are made to feel incompetent to do what they have done for years and years, then someone at Queen's Park is going to start asking, "Why have Catholic schools? Why not let the Church do its thing in church, and be rid of a publicly funded Catholic school system?"
>
> In 32 years as a priest, I have watched dozens of Grade 2 and Grade 8 teachers with their pupils. A more committed body of lay men and women I can't imagine. I'm talking about a commitment to their Catholic Faith, and a real desire to pass on the practice of Faith to children entrusted to their care. It seems to me that Sacramental preparation must involve a cooperative partnership of home, church

and school. If, in that preparation, parishes cut out teachers in the Catholic school, I submit they are putting at risk our Catholic school system in Ontario with its 640,000 students.[20]

****

As a boy, Father Matthews was an avid ball player. He slept with his baseball glove and never forgot the experience of viewing Babe Ruth in his coffin at Yankee Stadium. He remains a devoted baseball fan. He sees about ten Toronto Blue Jay games a year, on his day off. When the Blue Jays played at Exhibition Stadium, he sat either along the third base line or in the two-dollar Dominion Store grandstand seats. At the Skydome, he sits on the fifth level, directly behind home plate. He loudly cheers on the Blue Jays and silently calls the balls and strikes. His European-born friends think that he is crazy.

****

On 15 August 2001, the Feast of the Assumption of Our Lady, Father Carl Matthews celebrated the fiftieth anniversary of his entry into the Jesuit community, with an evening Mass at Our Lady of Lourdes in Toronto. In attendance were many members of his family and hundreds of friends and colleagues. After the Mass, but before the final hymn, five people spoke about him. They were Michael Matthews, his brother; Ed Nelligan, the long-time director of the Metropolitan Separate School Board; Patty Rivera, the former news editor of the *Catholic Register*; Graham Webb, a member of St. John's parish in Waubaushene; and Bishop Robert B. Clune, who represented the archdiocese of Toronto. They covered all the bases of his life, each giving unvarnished praise to a remarkable priest.

Also that night plaques were presented to Father Matthews by Guy Giorno, the chief of staff to Premier Mike Harris, on behalf of the government of Ontario, and by Michael Del Grande, chairman of the Toronto Catholic District School Board. A week earlier, at St. John's in Waubaushene, there was a reception at which plaques to Father Matthews came from the parishioners, the Township of Tay and the Simcoe-Muskoka Catholic District School Board. There were also tributes from the Beausoleil First Nation, in a reception on Christian Island.

Father Matthews continues to live his life *Ad Majorem Dei Gloriam*. And there is more to come, beginning with the 100th anniversary of St. John's parish in Waubaushene, in 2006...

1. CJM to author, 31 May 2004.

2. Matthews Papers, Box 5, File 31, Father Eric Maclean, S.J. to "Dear Brothers in Christ," 11 March 1994; CJM to "Dear family and friends, old and new," 14 March 1994; Box 5, File 39, Bishop Robert B. Clune to CJM, 13 May 2004.

3. "New pastor feels at home in Huronia," *Midland Free Press*, 8 July 1994, 6a.

4. Box 5, File 31, CJM to Archbishop Ambrozic et al., 19 May 1994.

5. Ibid., CJM to Tonia Desiato, 7 September 1994.

6. Ibid., CJM to Archbishop Ambrozic et al., 12 May 1995.

7. "Great enthusiasm greets Waubaushene church project: Scenes from the life of Christ adorn St. John's windows," *Catholic Register*, 28 May 2001.

8. "Native parish seeks help to rebuild its chapel," *Catholic Register*, 20 April 1998, 10.

9. Box 5, File 35, CJM to _____, 1 April 1998.

10. Ibid., CJM to William F. Broadhurst, 4 May 1998.

11. St. Francis Xavier Mission, Program of Dedication, 17 June 1999.

12. "Native mission church blessed," *Catholic Register*, 5 July 1999.

13. CJM, "Keep councils Catholic," *Catholic Register*, 7 October 1996, 4, in response to David M. Brown, "Is Ontario next in line for school reform," *Catholic Register*, 16 September 1996, 5.

14. CJM, "Managing educational bureaucracies," *Globe and Mail*, 12 May 1993.

15. Umbrella boards: CJM, "Far too risky," *Catholic Register*, 8 January 2001, 4; Amalgamation and Replacement: CJM, "Managing educational bureaucracies," *Globe and Mail*, 12 May 1993; Open Admission: Box, File 38, CJM to Johanne Stewart, 11 April 2001 and Box 5, File 40, CJM to Premier Dalton McGuinty, 12 January 2004; Parent Councils: CJM, manuscript letter to the *Midland Free Press*, 25 April 1996, in response to an editorial, 24 April 1996; Catholic principals and vice-principals: CJM, "Will Ontario's Catholic Schools Survive the Next 25 Years?" *Catholic Insight* (March 1998), 9.

16. CJM, "Denominational schools a constitutional right," *Catholic Register*, 24 June 1995; "Newfoundland's 'useless vote,'" *Globe and Mail*, 30 August 1995; "Be consistent," *Catholic Register*, 12 February 1996, 4; Box 5, File 33, CJM to Prime Minister Jean Chrétien, 17 May 1996; Box 5, File 34, CJM to Prime Minister Jean Chrétien, 25 January 1997.

17. CJM, "Suppression in Newfoundland," *Catholic Insight* (January/February 1998), 25-28.

18. CJM, "Will Ontario's Catholic Schools Survive the Next 25 Years?" *Catholic Insight* (March 1998), 8-10.

[19] CJM, "Ruling harms Catholic education," *Catholic Register*, 24-31 August 1998, 5.
[20] CJM, "Will Ontario's Catholic Schools Survive the Next 25 Years?", 10.

BIBLIOGRAPHY

Primary Sources

Reverend Carl J. Matthews, S.J. Personal Papers.

Printed Primary Sources

Ontario. Legislature of Ontario. Debates.

_____. Statutes of Ontario.

Secondary Sources

Dixon, Robert. T. *Catholic Education and Politics in Ontario*, 1964-2001. Vol. IV. Toronto: Catholic Education Foundation of Ontario, 2003.

_____. "William Davis and the Road to Completion in Ontario's Catholic High Schools, 1971-1985," Canadian Catholic Historical Association, *Historical Studies* 69 (2003): 7-33.

Flynn, L.J. *At School in Kingston 1850-1973: The Story of Catholic Education in Kingston and District*. Kingston: The Frontenac, Lennox and Addington County Roman Catholic Separate School Board, 1973.

Power, Michael. *A Promise Fulfilled: Highlights in the Political History of Catholic Separate Schools in Ontario*. Toronto: Ontario Catholic School Trustees' Association, 2002.

Walker, Franklin A. *Catholic Education and Politics in Ontario*. Vol. III. Toronto: Catholic Education Foundation of Ontario, 1986.

Publications of Father Carl J. Matthews, S.J.

NOTE: CPTA = Catholic Parent-Teacher Association

ECEAO = English Catholic Education Association of Ontario

OECTA = Ontario English Catholic Teachers' Association

Books

Catholic Schools in Canada. Toronto: Canadian Catholic School Trustees' Association, 1977.

Catholic School Systems Across Canada. Toronto: Canadian Catholic School Trustees' Association, 1990.

Articles

"Annual Saving to the Ontario Taxpayer." ECEAO, *The Spotlight: News & Views on Catholic Education* (October 1968).

"Catholic High Schools — Our Right, Our Heritage." OECTA *Review* (April 1967): 8-11, 62.

"Catholic Leaders of steel and vision," *Catholic Register*, 19 January 1991, 9-12.

"Catholic Schools in Ontario's Future." *Catholic Trustee* (September 1979): 20-21.

"The Close of a Chapter at '403.'" *The Canadian Scholastic* (May 1958): 1-4. Different versions of this article appeared in *Toronto Telegram*, 2 November 1963, 29, and the *Globe and Mail*, 12 February 1974, 5.

"Closing the Gap." CPTA, *Echo* (February 1971): 6.

"Completion of the Seventh of a School System." *Orbit 73* (February 1985): 14, 16.

"Eighty-Five Years Ago." CPTA, *Echo* (February 1972): 6-9.

"English Catholic High Schools in Ontario 1968-1969." OECTA *Review* (December 1968): 52-54.

"Funding Catholic Schools: A Canadian Way." *America* (September 1969): 231-32.

"The Hows and Whys of School Grants." OECTA *Review* (March 1971): 38-40.

"How We Have Grown." ECEAO, *The Spotlight: News & Views on Catholic Education* (Autumn 1967): [2]-[3].

"Legislation could erase Catholic identity," *Catholic Register*, 26 August 1989, ES2.

"Let's Finish the Job." OECTA Review (October 1968): 25-28. This was also published in *Catholic Trustee* (November 1968): 15-19.

"1971 Budgets of Ontario School Boards." OECTA *Review* (December 1971): 22.

"Ontario Catholic nursing schools are to cease," *Catholic Register*, 10 February 1973, 17.

"Premier Frost: A friend of Catholic schools," *Catholic Register*, 19 May 1973, 1.

"The production of this newspaper," *Catholic Register*, 29 January 1993, 7.

"Profiles in Courage in Ontario Catholic education during the last 200 years," *Catholic Register*, 3 March 2002, 3-11.

"Report on 1966-67 Questionnaire to Catholic High School Principals." OECTA *Review* (April 1967): 45-46.

"Richard W. Scott: Architect of the Catholic School System in Ontario." OECTA *Review* (October 1969): 5-8.

"A Role for the Catholic Educator in Ontario." OECTA *Review* (April 1974): 7.

"The Separate Schools Act: keeping the faith," *Globe and Mail*, 1 April 1974, 7.

"Some Facts and Figures on the English Catholic High Schools in Ontario, 1968-1969." *Catholic Trustee* (March 1969): 11-14.

"Study urges equitable school tax," *Catholic Register*, 3 March 1979, 11.

"Suppression in Newfoundland," *Catholic Insight* (January/February 1998): 25-28.

"Teachers Touch the Future." *Canadian Messenger of the Sacred Heart* (October 1988): 4-5.

"Trends in Ontario Separate School Finance." *Catholic Trustee* (February 1962): 4. And various issues thereafter.

"We Want a Vigorous System." *OECTA Review* (December 1970): 40-41.

"Will Ontario's Catholic Schools Survive the Next 25 Years?" *Catholic Insight* (March 1998): 8-10.

INDEX

Note: CJM = Carl Joseph Matthews

abortion, 141-42, 147-52
ACEBO (l'Association des commissions des écoles bilingues d'Ontario), 26, 29
ACHSBO (Association of Catholic High School Boards of Ontario), 23, 40, 41-42, 54, 56; *Completing Their Schooling*, 59-60; Equality Brief, 58; Study Congress (1966), 42-43, (1967), 52-53
Addley, Bill, 132, 143
Allen, William A., 95
Alway, Richard, 143
amalgamation of school boards. *See* larger units of administration
Ambrozic, Aloysius, 139, 143, 151, 163, 167; CJM's resignation from *Catholic Register*, 153-56
Anderson, Helen, 122
Andrachuck, John, 49-50, 133
Anna Clare, Sister, 133
"A Reasonable Solution to the Problem Facing Catholic Public Schools in Ontario" (Arthur Maloney speech), 52-53
Arseneault, Charles, 112-13
Asseff, Chris, 30, 40, 57, 65, 70-71, 115-16, 122, 133
Asselin, David, 9
L'Association des commissions des écoles bilingues d'Ontario. *See* ACEBO
L'Association des écoles secondaires privées Catholiques Franco-Ontariennes, 43
Association Catholic High School Boards of Ontario. *See* ACHSBO
Atkins, Alan, 146

Babcock, Mary, 64, 133
Barone, Anthony, 133
Beausoleil First Nation, 163, 166
Belanger, Gerard, 8
Bennett, John, 53, 56
Bériault, Roland, 29, 117
Bettson, Bob, 156
Bill 30 (An Act to amend the Education Act), vii, 121; amendments, 127-28
Bill 53 (Saskatchewan), 44
Bill 104, 169

Bill 109, 131-32
Bill 140, 44
Bill 160, 169-70
Bill 168, 57
Bill 255 (Education Act), 101-5
Bill C-43. *See* abortion
Boehler, Edward, 133
Bouvrette, Stanislaus, 163
Boyle, Patrick, 139
Brébeuf High School, 50
Brennan, Patrick, 125
Brisbois, Ed, 49, 51, 55, 58, 60, 133; death, 134
Brunelle, René, 83
Buchanan, Malcolm, 125
Burge, Des, 64
Burns, Kenneth, 41
Byrne, Pat, 143

Cadot, Joseph, 165
Callaghan, Morley, 94
Campbell, Kim, 147-48, 149
Canadian Catholic School Trustees' Association. *See* CCSTA
Carter, Francis G., 25, 26, 28, 29, 56
Carter, Frank, 107-8
Carter, G. Emmett, 31, 32, 40, 43, 49, 108, 109-110, 133; completion of the separate school system, 122, 123-24; High School Crisis, 46; local taxes, 66-67, London Separate School Board, 53-56
Carty, Joseph, 7
Carty, Michael, 7, 9, 17, 68, 133
Casey, Florence Mary (CJM's mother). *See* Matthews, Florence Mary
Catholic bishops of Ontario, 28, 31, 40, 67, 117, 125-26
"Catholic High Schools – Our Right, Our Heritage," 50-51
Catholic identity of Catholic secondary schools, 125-27
"Catholic leaders of steel and vision," 141

Catholic Register: circulation under CJM, 145; CJM as publisher and editor, 139-57; CJM's editorials (1983-85), 117; mandate under CJM, 144-45
Catholic Schools in Canada, 108
Catholic School Systems Across Canada, 140
CCSTA (Canadian Catholic School Trustees' Association), 107-8, 111
Charlottetown Accord, 151-53
Cheal, John E., 15
Checkeris, Ernie, 125
Chrétien, Jean, 150, 169
Christian Island, 165-68
Clark, Joe, 155
Clarke, Bill, 17
Clifford, Frank, 133
Cloran, Brendan, 10-11
Clune, Donald, 96, 133, 171
Clune, Robert, 162, 167
Colley-Vegh, Sherrilynn, 146
Colliard, Alfred, 8, 10, 17; death, 134
Collins, Jerry, 71
Completing Their Schooling (ACHSBO's Equality Brief), 59-60
Completion, Ontario Separate Schools (COSS), 129
completion of the separate school system, 35, 58, 121-35; Bill Davis, 61, 122, 123-24; campaign, 61-72; CJM, 121-35; G. Emmett Carter, 122, 123-24
Conway, J. Harold, 54
Conway, Sean, vii, 128-29, 130, 132
Copps, Bill, 102
Copps, Vic, 23
Corporation Tax Adjustment, 35, 48, 60
Côté, Raymond, 30
Courtemanche, Basil, 110
Crusoe, Clement J., 8, 17; death, 134
Culnan, James, 109
Cumming, Peter, 170

Danson, Barnett "Barney," 51, 70
Davis, Bill, vii, 27, 28, 32, 38, 40, 50, 68, 117-18, 154; Bill 255 (Education Act), 102-3; CJM's resignation from OSSTA's board of directors, 115; completion of the separate school system, 61, 122, 123-24;

friendship with CJM, 28, 81-90, 123, 129, 134-35; G. Emmett Carter, 123-24; High School Crisis, 46-47; nursing schools, 98-99; response to Equality Brief, 72
Dehler, David, 101
Del Grande, Michael, 171
De Manche, Alfred, 117
Dennis, Lloyd, 51
DePoe, Norman, 94
Desjarlais, Laurent, 44, 45
Deslauriers, Omer, 43
de Valk, Alphonse, 151
Dewey, Martin, 95
DiGiovanni, Caroline, 129, 133
Dixon, Robert T., 105, 113
Doolan Almon F., 6, 7, 95
Downey, Bill, 17
Doyle, Michael, 48
Drew, George, 134
Driscoll, Joe, 9
Duffin, Gordon, 52
Duggan, Paul, 133
Dupuis, Leo, 133
Durocher, Raymond, 44, 56, 60, 63-64, 116, 133; Bill 255 (Education Act), 102, 104; Implementation Brief, 68; local taxes, 67

ECEAO (English Catholic Education Association of Ontario), 24, 25, 30, 53
Education Act. *See* Bill 255
Elliott, Teresa, 164
English Catholic Education Association of Ontario. *See* ECEAO
Equality Brief, 58-61
"Equal Opportunity for Continuous Education in Separate Schools in Ontario," 61

Farrell, Jim, 143
FCPTAO (Federation of Catholic Parent-Teacher Associations of Ontario), 24, 53, 68
Federation of Catholic Parent-Teacher Associations of Ontario. *See* FCPTAO
financial parity. *See* Foundation Tax Plan
Finn, Joseph P., 15, 26
Flaherty, M. Josephine, 98

Flanagan, Michael, 109
Flynn, Fred, 7
Fogarty, Patrick, 42, 51, 58, 60, 63, 107, 133; death, 134; London Separate School Board, 53, 54, 55
Foundation Tax Plan, 21, 24-33, 60
French-language school boards, 131-32
Frost, Leslie, 87, 89, 103, 134
Fryer, Ken, 6
Fullerton, Joseph, 86
Fulton, Thomas B., 68
Fyfe, Joseph, 35, 40, 45, 56, 68, 112, 133

Gaudet, Bob, 17
Gazzola, Peter, 133
Ghiz, Joseph, 155
George, Gordon, 14, 39
Gilhooly, Frank, 105, 107
Giorno, Guy, 171
Good Shepherd parish, 142
Greer, Harold, 95
Gruenwald, Gwen, 146
Guindon, Fern, 83

Hale, Jack, 96
Hall, Emmett, 44, 45, 49, 52
Hall, Robert, 116
Hall-Dennis Committee, 44-45
Hanley, J.G., 144
Hansen, Wendy, 70
Harris, Mike, 132, 169
Henderson, E.F., 141
Henderson, Larry, 117, 145, 156
High School Crisis, 46-56
Hope Commission (1950), 140-41
Hughes, Jim, 155

Implementation Brief, 23, 65, 67-68

Jackson, Henry, 166
Jackson, R.W.B., 25
Jemec, Anthony, 166
Jerome, James, 9
Jesuit Seminary (403 Wellington Street West), 11-13
Johnson, Joe, 124

Johnson, Percy, 50, 117, 133

Kavanagh, Frank, 68, 133
Keddy, J. Arthur, 38
Kelly, Arthur, 141
Kelly, Norman, 95
Kennedy, Betty, 125
Kennedy, Kevin, 122
Kipp, Berchmans, 133
Klein, A.E., "Ab," 40, 55, 56, 57, 58, 66, 68, 133; Equality Brief, 60, 61
Klein, Francis, 49
Koma, Stanley P., 117
Kovacs, Frank, 58, 59, 60

LaForest, Gerald, 107
Laidlaw, Robert, 25, 26, 28, 32, 33
Landriault, Jacques, 126
larger units of administration, 56-57
LaRoque, Eugene, 131
Lauwers, Peter, 133
Lebel, Robert, 147, 149, 150
Leddy, J. Francis, 44
legislative grants, 112
LeSarge, John, 17
"Let's Finish the Job," 58
Liberal Party of Ontario: completion of the separate school system, 69-70
Living and Learning, 45, 56
local taxes, 65-67
London Separate School Board, 53-56
Lord, Daniel, 6
Lottridge, Hank, 56
Lundy, Bill, 9
Lynch, John Joseph, 165

MacDonald, Donald C., vii, 27, 40, 51, 69, 72, 95
Macdougall, Angus, 39, 50, 52, 56, 62, 126, 141
Maclean, Eric, 162
MacNamara, Francis J., 59-60
Maloney, Arthur, 52-53
Mancini, Nick, 58, 60, 61, 68, 105
Manese, Grayce, 60
Maple Leaf Gardens Rally, 71
Marrese, Joe, 102

Marrocco, Francis A., 17, 31
Marson, Peter, 7
Martel, Elie, 62
Martin, G.T., 2
Martyrs' Shrine Message, 12, 161, 168
Martyrs' Shrine (Midland), 142, 157, 161
Mastromatteo, Mike, 146
Matas, Robert, 126
Matthews, C.P. (CJM's father), 1, 5; career as a teacher and school inspector, 3-4; death, 134
Matthews, Carl Joseph (CJM): ACHSBO, 42, 71; Aloysius Ambrozic, 139, 143, 151, 153-56; Arthur Maloney, 52-53; awards, 139-40; Bill Davis, 81-90, 98-99, 123-24, 129, 134-35; Bill 30 (An Act to amend the Education Act), 127-28; Bill 109, 131-32; Bill 255 (Education Act), 101-5; birth, 1; Brébeuf High School, 50; "Catholic High Schools – Our Right, Our Heritage," 50-51; Catholic identity of Catholic secondary schools, 125-27; "Catholic leaders of steel and vision," 141; *Catholic Register*, 117, 139-57; *Catholic School Systems Across Canada*, 140; CCSTA, 107-8, 111; *Completing Their Schooling*, 59-60; completion of the separate school system, 121-35; doctoral dissertation, 14, 15-16; elementary school, 6-7; Emmett Hall, 45; employment opportunities, 63; Equality Brief, 60-61; family history, 1-2; family life, 4-6; final vows, 18; first Mass, 17; first vows, 11; Foundation Tax Plan, 21, 24-33; High School Crisis, 46-56; Jesuit Seminary (403 Wellington Street West), 11-13; Juniorate, 11; larger units of administration, 57; lecturer, 140; legislative grants, 112; "Let's Finish the Job," 58; local taxes, 65-66; Metropolitan Separate School Board (MSSB), 93-117, 129-32; "Mr. Klein's Position Paper," 54-55; novitiate, 10-11; OECTA, 41, 64-69, 71-72; Ontario College of Education, 13; ordination, 16, 17; OSSTA, 40, 64-69, 106-8, 113-15; Our Lady of Lourdes parish, 110, 111; paradox, 22-23; parents, 1-2; parish work, 110-11, 142; "Profiles in Courage in Ontario Catholic education during the past 200 years," 169; publications, 12-13, 15, 26, 30, 39, 42, 50-51, 58, 71-72, 104-5, 175-77; public speaker, 46, 58;

Regency, 13-14; Regiopolis College, 8-10, 13, 18; St. Francis Xavier Mission (Christian Island), 165-68; St. John the Evangelist parish (Waubaushene), 162-65; siblings, 5; statistics, 25, 35-39; "Suppression in Newfoundland," 169; Tertianship, 18, 62, 142; theology, 16, 39; "Trends in Ontario Separate School Finance," 26, 30, 35-39; umbrella boards, 67-71; University of Toronto, 14-15; "Will Ontario's Catholic Schools Survive the Next 25 Years?" 169

Matthews, Florence Mary (CJM's mother), 1-2, 5; death, 134
Matthews, Michael, 5, 171
Matthews, Paul, 5
Matthews, Theresa, 5
Matthews, Theresa (sister to C.P. Matthews), 2
Matthews, Ursula, 5
Mathews, Victor, 5
Mattson, Joe, 7, 9
McCarthy, J.R., 50
McCracken, Rosemary, 146
McDonald, Donald, 107
McKenna, J. Kevin, 13-14
McKenna, T.J. "Ted," 17, 30-31, 41, 42, 43, 49, 55
McMahon, Ed, 133
McMaster, John, 13
McNie, John, 99
Meagher, Anthony, 167
Meagher, Robert, 50
Metropolitan Separate School Board (MSSB), 46-51; CJM as trustee and chairman, 93-117, 129-31
Micallef, Francis, 162
Milne, Edmund, 17
Mitchell, Robert, 166
Mohan, Thomas, 133
Moher, John, 60
Monague, Bill, 166-67
Monague, Carl, 166
Moss, Penny, 126-27
Mulroney, Brian, 141
Murphy, Dennis, 133
Murphy, James, 96

NDP: completion of the separate school system, 69
Nelligan, Ed, 49, 50, 56, 59, 60, 61, 65, 68, 102, 116, 117, 133, 171
New Democratic Party. *See* NDP
Newman, Bernard, 36
Nixon, Robert, vii, 40, 51-52, 61, 70, 72, 95, 122; CJM, 128; completion of the separate school system, 61
Nolin, Jean-Baptiste, 163
nursing schools, 98

OECTA (Ontario English Catholic Teachers' Association) 24, 41; CJM, 40, 41, 64, 71-72, 112
OISE (Ontario Institute for Studies in Education), 108
O'Neill, C.P., 57, 60
Ontario Catholic Education Council, 40, 44, 55
Ontario Catholic Student Federation, 24, 71
Ontario elections: (1963), 31-32, (1971), 72
Ontario English Catholic Teachers' Association. *See* OECTA
Ontario Federation of School Athletic Associations, 100
Ontario Institute for Studies in Education. *See* OISE
Ontario School Trustees' Council, 106, 108
Ontario Separate School Trustees' Association. *See* OSSTA
OSSTA (Ontario Separate School Trustees' Association), 23, 28; Bill 255 (Education Act), 102, 104; CJM, 40, 64-69, 106-8; Equality Brief, 60-62; Foundation Tax Plan, 30; Implementation Brief, 23, 65, 67-68; larger units of administration, 56-57; local taxes, 67; "Mr. Klein's Position Paper," 54-55; Secondary Education Review Project (SERP), 113-15, 117
O'Sullivan, J.A., 8, 10, 141
O'Sullivan, Sean, 143
Our Lady of Lourdes parish, 110, 111

Paul, Cathy, 146
Pearson, Lester, 43
Pelletier, Leon, 17
Pellettier, Vince, 94, 95
Pepin, Jean-Luc, 107

Peterson, David, 122
Phillips, Charles E., 14
Piggott, Joseph, 141
Pitman, Walter, 58
Plourde, Joseph-Aurèle, 131
Pluard, Wilfred, 8
Pocock, Philip, 23, 32, 38, 40, 42, 51, 52, 64, 128, 133; High School Crisis, 46, 47-48; London Separate School Board, 55, 56
Power, Kevin, 23
Prendergast, Terrence, 167
Priester, Vincent, 25, 26, 30, 31, 34
"Profiles in Courage in Ontario Catholic education during the past 200 years," 169
Provincial Committee on the Aims and Objectives of Education in the Schools of Ontario. *See* Hall-Dennis Committee
Purden, Carolyn, 156

Quinn, Martin, 31

Rae, Bob, vii, 122, 132, 155
Reding, Paul, 117
Regiopolis College, 8-10, 13, 18
Reilly, Tom, 129, 133
Rideout, Brock, 24, 25, 26, 54
Rivera, Patty, 146, 171
Robarts, John, vii, 25, 27, 30, 31, 35, 87, 89, 107; completion of the separate school system, 61, 64-65; French-language schools, 43
Robertson, Gordon, 108
Robida, Mary E., 68
Robitaille, Kenneth, 161
Rodriguez, José, 17
Rowe, Marilyn, 125
Rudden, Mary L., 60
Ryan, Joseph F., 16, 22, 23, 40, 41, 42, 64, 117, 133, 141; CJM, 24; *Completing Their Schooling*, 59; Equality Brief, 58; High School Crisis, 46; London Separate School Board, 54, 55; umbrella boards, 68
Ryan, William, 110

St. Francis Xavier Mission (Christian Island), 163, 165-68
St. Jacques, Henri, 141
St. John, J. Bascom, 63

St. John the Evangelist parish (Waubaushene), 162-65
St. Stanislaus Novitiate, 10-11
Sandy, Joanne, 166
Sandy, Mike, 167
Sandy, Paul, 166, 168
Saranchuk, George, 116, 133
Schneider, George, 49
Schwalm, Clement, 139
Scorsone, Suzanne, 117
Scott, Ian, 131
Secondary Education Review Project (SERP), 113-15, 117
Separate Schools Act, 101-5
sharing school facilities, 99-101
Sheridan, Edward, 23
Sinasac, Joe, 169
Smith, Gregory, 146
Somerville, Janet, 156
Spry, G.D., 38
Stanford, Lionel, 51
Stanley, David, 17
Steed, Judy, 156
Stephenson, Bette, 126
Stewart, E.E., 38
Suppa, Bruno, 133
"Suppression in Newfoundland," 169
Swain, John, 11
Sweeney, John, 104, 105
Sweet, Lois, 156
Sylvester, Remi, 168

Task Force on Canadian Unity, 107
Teefy, John, 156
Thorson, Donald, 108
Tiny Township Case, 61
Trainor, Edgar, 3
Trainor, John, 17
Traynor, John J., 2-3
Traynor, Tom B., 3
"Trends in Ontario Separate School Finance," 26, 30, 35-39
Trudeau, Pierre, 107, 108, 151
Tyson, Steve, 146

umbrella boards, 67-71, 83-84, 131-32

Walker, Franklin, viii, 15, 22
Walsh, Bernard J., 17
Walsh, T.G., 95, 139
Wappel, Tom, 152
Ward, Chris, 132
Webb, Graham, 171
Webster, Benjamin I., 17
Wedlock, Matthew J., 2
Welch, Robert, 38, 88
Wells, Thomas, 36, 102, 105
Welsh, Art, 3
Weninger, T.A., 140
"Will Ontario's Catholic Schools Survive the Next 25 Years?" 169
Wilson, Bob, 36
Wilson, Elizabeth, 146
Wintermeyer, John, 27, 33, 52, 94

Zaritsky, John, 87, 88